Psychosocial and Relationship-based Practice

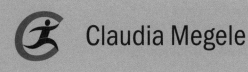

Claudia Megele

Other books you may be interested in:

Anti-racism in Social Work Practice
Edited by Angie Bartoli
ISBN 978-1-909330-13-9

Evidencing CPD – A Guide to Building Your Social Work Portfolio
By Daisy Bogg and Maggie Challis
ISBN 978-1-909330-25-2

Modern Mental Health: Critical Perspectives on Psychiatric Practice
Edited by Steven Walker
ISBN 978-1-909330-53-5

Personal Safety for Social Workers and Health Professionals
By Brian Atkins
ISBN 978-1-909330-33-7

Positive Social Work: The Essential Toolkit for NQSWs
By Julie Adams and Angie Sheard
ISBN 978-1-909330-05-4

Practice Education in Social Work: Achieving Professional Standards
By Pam Field, Cathie Jasper & Lesley Littler
ISBN 978-1-909330-17-7

Social Media and Social Work Education
Edited by Joanne Westwood
ISBN 978-1-909682-57-3

Starting Social Work: Reflections of a Newly Qualified Social Worker
By Rebecca Joy Novell
ISBN 978-1-909682-09-2

The Critical Years: Child Development from Conception to Five
By Tim Gully
ISBN 978-1-909330-73-3

Understanding Substance Use: Policy and Practice
By Elaine Arnull
ISBN 978-1-909330-93-1

What's Your Problem? Making Sense of Social Policy and the Policy Process
By Stuart Connor
ISBN 978-1-909330-49-8

Titles are also available in a range of electronic formats. To order please go to our website www.criticalpublishing.com or contact our distributor NBN International, 10 Thornbury Road, Plymouth PL6 7PP, telephone 01752 202301 or email orders@nbninternational.com

Psychosocial and Relationship-based Practice

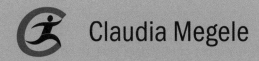 Claudia Megele

First published in 2015 by Critical Publishing Ltd.

All rights reserved. No part of this publication may be reproduced, stored in a retrieval system, or transmitted in any form or by any means, electronic, mechanical, photocopying, recording or otherwise, without prior permission in writing from the publisher.

Copyright © Claudia Megele

British Library Cataloguing in Publication Data
A CIP record for this book is available from the British Library

ISBN: 978-1-909682-97-9

This book is also available in the following e-book formats:

MOBI ISBN: 978-1-909682-98-6
EPUB ISBN: 978-1-909682-99-3
Adobe e-book ISBN: 978-1-910391-00-6

The rights of Claudia Megele to be identified as the Author of this work have been asserted by her in accordance with the Copyright, Design and Patents Act 1988.

Cover design by Greensplash Limited
Project Management by Out of House Publishing
Typeset by Newgen Knowledge Works
Printed and bound in Great Britain by Bell & Bain, Glasgow

Critical Publishing
152 Chester Road
Northwich
CW8 4AL

www.criticalpublishing.com

FSC
www.fsc.org

MIX
Paper from responsible sources
FSC® C007785

Contents

Meet the author

Claudia Megele is a Senior Lecturer and PQ/CPD Programme Leader and Digital Lead at Middlesex University, and she is also the Head of Practice Learning at Enfield Council. Claudia's psychosocial and inter-disciplinary approach is shaped by her studies which include psychology, sociology, social work and psychotherapy, and her professional experience which ranges from play therapy with terminally ill children at Red Cross Children's Hospital to psychotherapy with adults at the NHS, and from front-line social work with children and families to research on identity, mentalisation, empathy and relationships.

Claudia has also served in a number of public and third-sector posts and organisations including: Member of the advisory board of the National Children's Bureau (NCB), Trustee at Mind, and the Chair and Vice-Chair of Tower Hamlets Police and Community Safety Board.

Foreword

If you really render social work to its basics then there isn't much left other than the relationship between worker and client, practitioner and service user. Of course, social workers have statutory duties and powers, can access and organise resources, and do employ a variety of theoretically based techniques and interventions. But each of these only takes place in the medium of the worker–client relationship. The quality and character of the relationship therefore matters; it matters a great deal.

I began my career in social work more years ago than I care to remember. Two of the key texts that I valued reading during my first days as a childcare officer (we're talking pre-Seebohm, pre-1971 here) were Margaret Ferard and Noel Hunnybun's (1962) *The Caseworker's Use of Relationships* (with a foreword by John Bowlby, no less) and Isca Saltzberger-Wittenberg's (1970) *Psycho-analytic Insight and Relationships: A Kleinian Approach.* Since those days, the importance of the relationship in social work has had something of a roller-coaster career. At the moment, relationship-based practice is enjoying a slight renaissance. In part, this is a reaction to the many years of political and bureaucratic enthusiasm for measuring, checking and assessing everything that could be measured, checked and assessed. A measure is a dangerous tool, said the economist Robert Skidelesky, for it tends to take the place of whatever it purports to measure. And because the humanity of relationships is not easily captured by these measuring instruments, the fundamental importance of the relationship lost its status under performance-minded regimes. Its value was diminished. Losing sight of the relationship was always bound to end with social work losing its heart and with it, irony of ironies, losing its efficacy and social credibility.

The relationship between one human being and another has long fascinated social scientists, philosophers and the helping professions. It is, after all, where so much of our life takes place, as people, parents, partners, professionals and service users. But it is a complicated, often tricky place, subject to the turbulence of our own and other people's thoughts, feelings and behaviour. And it gets more complicated and even trickier when feelings are running high. Anxiety, anger, fear, shame, sadness – they can all confuse and confound the normal give-and-take of social behaviour. And stress, of course, is one of the main culprits when it comes to upsetting and derailing relationships. Under stress, our anxieties rise, our reflective capacities are thrown. Past experiences distort the way we see and feel about present events. Reason is lost and our defences distort, disfigure and disturb. The world of stress and anxiety, fear and anger, worry and loss, hope and despair, heartache and joy is the world in which social workers find themselves on a daily basis. Therefore, if they don't give thought to matters of feeling – their own, as well as those of their clients and colleagues – then their practice will, at best, be in danger of being at sea and at worst, be insensitive and brutal.

Claudia Megele has written a book in which the *emotional labour* of being a social worker is beautifully and fully explored. She brings conviction as well as scholarship to the task of describing and defining a relationship-based practice. We are introduced to many of the great figures who have devoted their lives to thinking about human relationships and what is involved when we seek to help a fellow human being. Freud, Adler, Bion, Klein, Bowlby, Ainsworth, Fairbairn, Winnicott, Fonagy and Berne are all discussed. Their ideas for relationship-based theories, practices and understandings are explained and evocatively applied to a number of rich, detailed, unflinching case examples. The cases are the heart of the book. They capture the everyday reality of social work, making the idea of a well-thought-through psychosocial, relationship-based practice all the more compelling.

Each chapter explores a number of key relationship ideas and applies them to a case, in place and over time. We are helped to think about and feel things from both the worker's and client's point of view. Cases begin to make sense as, step by step, we are shown how to humanise our practice by applying the insights of psychoanalytic thinking, object relations theory, narrative therapy, attachment theory, transactional analysis, family therapy and motivational interviewing. The part that defence mechanisms, transference and counter-transference play in relationships under stress, including worker–client relationships, is threaded throughout the pages. The effects of early life experiences, trauma and loss are recognised. And the value of reflecting, mentalising and helping people mend their broken, incomplete stories is described and explained.

Claudia has woven the raw realities of front-line social work with current thinking about how our psychological development and emotional make-up influence the way we engage with relate to clients and colleagues. When we recognise ourselves and others as complex, often flawed but ever-hopeful, then we can edge our way towards being more understanding, empathic, patient and tolerant. Our relationships might then be helpful; our practices supportive and therapeutic. Claudia Megele's excellent book, *Psychosocial and Relationship-based Practice*, is for all those who would like their social work to be inspired by the best in evidence-based thinking and relationship-inspired theory.

David Howe
Emeritus Professor of Social Work
University of East Anglia, Norwich

What others say about this book

This book explains key psycho-dynamic concepts and applies them to cases in ways that illuminate superbly how relationships can be skilfully used to help vulnerable service users. It does this while ensuring workers' own internal lives and experiences of relationships are kept firmly in the picture, drawing out the agonies and ecstasies, joys and sorrows of people's lives when deeply engaged in social work.

Harry Ferguson, Professor of Social Work,
Centre for Social Work, School of Sociology and Social Policy,
University of Nottingham

This book presents a comprehensive and intellectually sophisticated exploration of the emotional contours between social workers and service users. Claudia Megele spells out more precisely than before the dynamics of these relationships, and how they might become more transformative. This is the perfect text to inspire social workers and supervisors wanting to replace bureaucratic and procedurally-led practice with more humane and creative ways of working.

David Shemmings OBE, Professor of Child Protection Research
Co-Director of Centre for Child Protection University of Kent
Co-Director of the ADAM Project

Claudia's writing is a refreshing mixture of theory and strategy, while also provoking the reader to reflect on their application into practice. Megele presents very specific interventions taken by the social worker with very specific responses of family relational and interactive sequences, including conversational exchanges as well as psycho-social contexts. A detailed focus on case studies over time, combines with a review of relevant literature related to theory and strategy, and with challenging questions to the reader. This engaging book is an excellent teaching tool for practitioners to enhance and inform relationship building skills.

Lynn McDonald, Professor of Social Work, Middlesex University

As social work training returns to a more client-centred focus this book will be invaluable for students entering the profession. But it also has much to offer practitioners in other fields such as health and counselling. It is engaging and written with a clarity that will enable readers to feel confident that they understand the theory and the processes and are ready to move these into their practice.

Mary Baginsky, Senior Research Fellow at King's College London,
Past Assistant Director of Children's Workforce Development Council

Acknowledgements

This book has been a challenging and wonderful journey and, therefore, I would like to take this opportunity to thank everyone who took the time to read the book and its different chapters and shared their insights with me.

In particular, I am humbled and deeply grateful to Prof David Howe for his inspirational foreword to this book. You have always been a source of inspiration and infinite knowledge and insight for me and many generations of social work practitioners, students, academics and researchers. Therefore, having your wonderful foreword and endorsement has meant more to me than I can express.

My profound gratitude goes to Prof Harry Ferguson, Prof David Shemmings, Prof Lynn McDonald, and Dr Mary Baginsky for taking the time to read and endorse this book. Your work and research have meant so much and it is an honour to have your kind endorsements.

Also a great thank you to Prof Brigid Featherstone, Prof Donald Forrester, Prof Stephen Joseph, Prof Sue White, Nushra Mansuri and Jenny Simpson for reading different chapters of the book and sharing your thoughts with me. Your positive feedback has been an enormous source of encouragement.

I would also like to thank Dr Peter Buzzi whose profound insights and invaluable feedbacks have infinitely enriched this book.

Finally, I would like to take this opportunity to thank all students, practitioners, academics and researchers who through their everyday generosity give from the self and enrich many lives, knowing well that there is nothing more enriching for the heart and self than giving from the heart and self. So, thank you so much for all you do. This book is dedicated to you and I hope you enjoy reading it.

The structure of this book

This book has been written so that it can be used by students, practitioners, academics and researchers with different levels of experience and expertise. Each chapter can be used to draw on what has been discussed in previous chapters, and the reader is encouraged to do so. However, each chapter is also self-contained and, therefore, can be used on its own as a complete and separate piece of work and/or study.

Excluding the introduction and concluding reflections, the remaining eight chapters are structured to enhance clarity and coherence of content and ease of reading.

Chapter summary presents a brief snapshot of the chapter and its content.

Chapter objectives present the main objectives of the chapter.

Case study narratives are divided into sections, with each section presenting part of the case narrative including: historical backgrounds, events, dialogues, thoughts, and more. Case study narratives are highlighted by a grey bar/line on the left side of the page. Each section includes a case study narrative followed by reflection and discussion sections.

Reflection: Each case narrative section is followed by a few questions to encourage reflection and further discussion. Try to discuss your reflections with your peers and colleagues to validate your thinking and see other people's perspectives.

Discussion: The discussion section offers an analysis of the narrative, and aims to unpack one or two salient and relevant points from the narrative. This ensures that all discussions are focused on specific learning outcomes and are cumulative in nature; however, it also means that discussions are not exhaustive and do not include every point/issue in relation to each section of narrative.

After each case narrative, try to answer each of the questions in the reflection section as completely as you can, and then read the discussion section and reflect back on your earlier answers. Also try to apply the new information and discussion to the entire case while drawing on the previous sections and chapters that you have read.

In line with systemic tradition, after completing each section or each chapter, try to apply everything you have read so far to all the different narratives in the current and previous chapters.

It is always a powerful approach to try to scaffold our knowledge by tapping into other people's knowledge, thinking and expertise. Therefore, one powerful way to help broaden and deepen the learning from the book is to discuss the case narratives and the reflection questions with your peers. Such discussions enhance our knowledge and broaden our perspective.

I hope that you enjoy the book, and that it will contribute toward an eclectic and systemic approach to a robust evidence-informed psychosocial and relationship-based practice in social work, social care and allied professions.

Introduction

In the midst of the second decade of the twenty-first century, social work is faced with unprecedented opportunities and challenges in its development and in definition of its role and mission, as well as practice and interventions (Ferguson, 2011; Howe, 2009). Indeed, in spite of differences in approach, and perhaps intended meaning, there seems to be an increasing unanimity of voices proclaiming the need for evidence-informed and holistic relationship-based interventions.

Social work operates at the sharp end of society's fears, anxieties and traumas, and intervenes in people's lives at times when they may be overwhelmed by dysphoric emotions and distress, when there is a loss of equilibrium and homeostasis in their lives, and when they are struggling with problems/difficulties/issues that are negatively affecting their sense of self and experiences. Therefore, relationships in general, and psychosocial and relationship-based practice in particular are essential core components of social work knowledge and practice.

However, this book does not provide *answers* in a simplistic or definitive sense, the world of practice being far too complex for any such attempts. Neither is this book meant as an exhaustive or single solution, explanation or interpretation of relationships or practice encounters. Instead, this book begins with storied practice narratives combined with reflections and discussions to offer a coherent collection of ideas and a plausible approach, among other plausible approaches, for an enhanced understanding and a deeper appreciation of the intricacies of human relationships and the complexities of practice.

This book therefore aims to highlight the complexities of everyday practice and offer a critical and evidence-informed approach to psychosocial and relationship-based practice. In doing this, the book draws on a range of therapeutic and disciplinary approaches including: psychology, relational psychoanalysis, object relations theory and transactional analysis, narrative therapy, systemic approaches, family therapy, cognitive and behavioural approaches, and others, to present a rich systemic and eclectic approach to integrative contemporary social work and social care practice.

This book offers a collection of case studies that provide an in-depth appreciation, discussion and analysis of the complexities of the lived experiences of users of services and practitioners, as well as the dynamics of relationships and their healing and yet challenging potential in everyday practice.

However, it is important to note that all case studies in this book are storied and narrativised accounts to demonstrate the multifaceted and complex nature of social work and social care practice. Therefore, any similarities with any cases or individuals are purely coincidental.

Objectives and uses of this book

As described above, the main objective of the book is to offer a critical and evidence-informed systemic and integrative approach to psychosocial and relationship-based practice and interventions.

This book uses a narrative case study approach to introduce and unpack theories, concepts and principles, and to demonstrate their application in practice. It is written so that it is relevant to various levels of experience and expertise, and to enable the reader to readily apply the teachings of the book to their own practice, and to learn more about own emotions, thoughts, experiences and self. Furthermore, all the discussions, analysis and arguments in the book are research- and evidence-informed.

Given the above approach, this book may be used in many different contexts and for a variety of purposes. For example, it may be used:

- for in-depth study of extensive case studies and practice examples with relevant analysis;

- as a reference for analysis of your own casework in practice;

- as a reference for analysis of essays, papers, reflections and other coursework in social work pre- or post-qualifying and CPD courses;

- as a reference and case study source for skills development and for professional training courses;

- as a reference for reflection and in-depth discussion;

- as an evidence-informed and practice-oriented reference for psychosocial and relationship-based practice in social work, social care, health and allied professions;

- as a handy reference for practice and education for practitioners, students, academics and researchers.

What is psychosocial and relationship-based practice?

Aware of earlier work on the theme of *relationship-based practice*, especially by Cooper (2014), Howe (1998), Ruch (2005, 2010), Sudbery (2002) and Trevithick (2003), I agree with Ruch's assertion that:

> *none of these authors attempts a discrete definition of the concept of relationship-based practice, so we are content to hold the book open on an absolute definition. In fact, this dilemma properly reflects the nature of the terrain, which is rich and diverse and may always be hard to pin down to a simple formula.*
>
> (2010, p 10)

Notwithstanding the above, psychosocial and relationship-based practice and interventions take place at the intersection of the individual's psychological/internal world and subjective states (eg happiness, sadness, depression, etc) and their social/external world and objective statuses (eg age, race, poverty, unemployment, etc). Therefore, they are interdisciplinary by nature, systemic in thinking (holistic with cyclical reciprocity) and integrative in approach and practice (drawing upon and integrating multiple approaches).

Indeed, drawing on Howe's (2009, p 12) wisdom:

> *If we are fully to grasp the nature of human experience, we need to understand ourselves biologically and psychologically, sociologically and politically, experientially and spiritually, existentially and interpersonally, artistically and creatively.*

Why a psychosocial and relationship-based practice?

From its inception and the early works of Elizabeth Gurney Fry (1780–1845) for reforms in the British prison system, to Arnold Toynbee's outreach programmes and practical socialism, social work has been, and remains, firmly rooted in relationships and the concern for greater equality, equity and social justice.

At its heart, social work has always been an enabling and empowering relationship-based practice. Therefore, contemporary psychosocial and relationship-based practice may be understood as a systemic and evidence-informed interdisciplinary approach to empowering relationships.

Social work drew upon other disciplines such as existential philosophy, developmental psychology, psychoanalysis, phenomenology, sociology, social policy and critical theory to create a *subject* with essential humanistic values, universal subjectivities and great human and social potential.

By recognising the individual's essential humanity and potential sociability, social work was able to understand the individual's inherent social self. Hence, social work produced an image of the *subject* which was at the same time both subjective and social (Parton, 2008). Indeed, the therapeutic and relationship-based social work was accompanied by increasing theoretical orientation influenced by:

- Neo-Freudianism and the ego-psychology;

- John Bowlby (1951);

- Donald Winnicott (1964); and

- others at the Tavistock.

However, the advent of computers and their application in the mid and late 1900s resulted in a misguided notion of *knowability, calculability* and *predictability* based on increasing information. This made the human *subject* more *knowable* and more *calculable*, and led to an emphasis on eliminating risk with increased information gathering and formulistic models of decision-making which resulted in a shift from relationship-based practice to *form-ulistic* (form-driven) and procedure-driven practice.

One consequence of this has been the MacDonaldisation (Dominelli, 1996; Howe, 2009; Ritzer, 1995) and increasing marketisation of services that change:

> the ethos of the professional intervention from one of trust to that of contract culture where everyone involved from providers and purchasers to customers only related to each other through contractual obligations that had been agreed ... guidelines, manuals act as a defence against the anxiety of 'not knowing'.
> (Aymer and Okitikpi, 2000, p 69)

The above was accompanied with a shift away from therapeutic approaches that individualised problems and pathologised the individual, to social models of practice that emphasised the structural and social aspects of problems. Although these criticisms of relationship-based and therapeutic approaches were important in raising awareness of the social and structural dimensions of individual experience, they generated a pendulum effect where there was a significant shift toward socially oriented practice without sufficient consideration for the individual and psychological dimensions of people's lives.

Indeed, exaggerated swings in professional practice and perspective are invariably unhelpful as they fail to acknowledge the critical balance that is essential for effective practice and interventions.

In contrast to the above, systemic psychosocial and relationship-based approaches to social work practice go beyond passive inclusivity, and offer a message of hope and empowerment through co-production of services and an effective person-centred relationship with users of services with a critical, integrative psychosocial perspective.

Indeed, relationships are foundational to our sense of self and humanity, and human behaviour, and professional relationships are an integral component of any professional intervention. When a practitioner makes a phone call, or meets with a user of services in an interview room, visits a home, or participates in a multi-professional meeting, they are engaging in professional relationships that embody *social work*.

However, although building positive relationships with others is an important element of relationship-based practice, to think that relationship-based practice is limited to building good relationships with users of services, or that relationship building with users of services is an end to itself, is to miss the point.

> *While it is true that people do not come to us looking for a relationship, and while it is no substitute for practical support, nevertheless we are one of the few groups who recognize the value of relating to others in a way which recognizes their experience as fundamental to understanding and action.*
>
> (Coulshed, 1991, p 2)

Empowering psychosocial and relationship-based practice requires both self- and other-awareness and a mindful embodied practice of social work theories, values, principles and capabilities that result in the creative and thoughtful art of relationship. By being *present*, practitioners demonstrate commitment and offer containment and a holding relationship that is empowering for users of services and enables positive change.

However, relationship-based principles encompass intrapsychic (within people) and interpersonal (between people) dimensions of human experience and interrelations/interactions. Indeed, the avoidance of recognising the complexities of practice and relationships can itself be understood as a defence mechanism to mask the anxieties, complexities and uncertainties associated with social work practice and interventions.

Human relationships are complex and multifaceted, and relationships are not simply calculative and rational. They are instead enwrapped in affective, conscious and unconscious emotions, memories and experiences that enrich and deepen as well as complicate relationships and relationship-based practice.

Indeed, as suggested by various authors such as Howe, Ferguson, Cooper, Ruch and others, the challenge of good and effective social work practice/interventions is to maintain *respectful and safe uncertainty* of *not-knowing* and to defend the *complexity* and contain the anxiety of emotionally charged human encounters and lived experiences. This can then guide and transform relationships into a key powerful resource in social work practice and interventions.

There are a number of factors that uniquely enrich and at the same time complicate social work practice and interventions. These include:

1. Social work bridges the individual's internal subjective states such as pain, want, suffering, love and hate, and their objective statuses such as old age, crime, debt, illness and health.

2. Social work interventions involve both practical/instrumental as well as developmental dimensions.

3. Social work practice encompasses the range of human experience including its:

    a. objective statuses such as unemployment, old age, crime, etc;

    b. cognitive aspects such as thoughts, values, beliefs and attitudes;

    c.   affective, emotional and subjective aspects such as happiness, sadness, depression, etc;

    d.   behavioural aspects such as externalising behaviour, etc;

    e.   social aspects such as community action and cohesion, social inclusion and social transformation;

    f.   political aspects such as influencing policy and aspiring for greater social justice and equity.

4.   Social work practice straddles the public and private spheres and impacts the personal, professional, organisational, societal and global dimensions of people's lives and experience.

The interdependent and intertwined nature of internal (psychological) and external (social) worlds of individuals cannot be neatly separated. Therefore, it is important to adopt integrative and systemic psychosocial responses to structural inequities and social imbalances and problems.

Each social work intervention is a unique human encounter that should be appreciated in its rich detail. Hence, a collaborative and co-productive relationship-based approach to interventions with a psychosocial perspective and a reflective and effective *use of self* are foundational to empowering practice that can enable and maintain positive change. Such an approach to interventions hinges on recognition and respect for individuals and their preferred narratives and honours the autonomy, expertise and experiences of users of services.

It is important to note that the above is not a passive stance. On the contrary, effective psychosocial and relationship-based practice in social work and social care is a deeply engaged experience that is systemic in thinking and *person-centred* yet persuasively *directive* in practice.

Indeed, as suggested by Winnicott (1975[1953]), human experience and *reality* take place within an in-between space between self and the *Other*, mother and child, internal and external *worlds*, '… *the thumb and the teddy bear* …' (p 2), and between what has been and what is unfolding and yet to be. Therefore, a holistic/systemic and integrative psychosocial understanding of relationships and relationship-based practice is indispensable for effective and empowering interventions and to bring about and maintain positive change.

Terminology

Language is the medium of human thought and its expression. Through language we make sense of our experiences, construct meaning and generate and maintain an identity narrative and a sense of self and *reality*. Language is not neutral, and as Derrida (1976) and Saussure (1998) argue, meaning is not derived from a link between a word and what it describes, meaning is generated based on difference and a dynamic web of relations, symbols and meanings including social, cultural, religious and political pretexts. Therefore, taking note of the power and importance of language and considering the controversies and the *traces* associated with the terms *client* and *service user* in the context of social work and social care, in this book we will use the term *users of services* which does not carry the same *traces*.

Content

This book has been written so each chapter can draw on what has been discussed previously, and the reader is encouraged to use this reflection. However, each chapter is also self-contained and, therefore, can be used on its own as a complete and separate piece of work and/or study.

Chapter 1: **Colour of love: thinking of Jack**

This chapter covers: attachment and potential space.

Chapters 1 and 2 introduce some basic concepts and theories in relation to understanding of the individual and their intrapsychic and interpersonal experiences and growth. Specifically, Chapter 1 offers an introduction to the concepts of emotional labour, mentalisation, attachment and potential space as some of the fundamental ideas that will be used and that we will build on throughout the book.

An explicit recognition of emotional labour offers us the opportunity to better manage the emotional toil and demand of everyday practice. We will expand on this with the concept of secondary trauma and the importance of good supervision for effective practice. However, the concept of emotional labour is also aimed at rendering this emotional labour and the challenging journey of our users of services visible in practice. At times it may seem that a user of services is not exerting sufficient effort to achieve a given objective; however, it is important to consider that they may be experiencing significant emotional labour that exhausts their resources, energies and capabilities for physical or psychological labour or for tasks that may otherwise seem simple, routine or trivial.

The discussion of mentalisation, attachment and potential space lay the foundation for further chapters in the book and are essential for a better appreciation of individual experience, motivation and behaviour, and for understanding of relationships and relationship-based interventions.

Chapter 2: **Colour of love: it's all about Jack**

This chapter covers: validation, motivation, respectful challenge, splitting, diversity and social identity, parenting and role-modelling.

Following on from Chapter 1, this chapter examines *feeling stuck* and the question of validation and *respectful challenge* in relationships with users of services. This includes a discussion of object relations and Melanie Klein's concept of splitting. We will also clarify the difference between, and emphasise the importance of, not internalising *problem narratives* while internalising locus of control.

The second section of the chapter is focused on social identity in practice. This section begins by highlighting the importance of continuity in life narratives and follows with a discussion of diversity and the need for an anti-discriminatory and anti-oppressive stance.

This chapter concludes with a discussion of parenting, parental capacity and the importance of positive role models.

Chapter 3: **Why not me?**

This chapter covers: psychological and ego defences.

This chapter introduces the concept of ego defences and examines some examples of how they may be used in practice. Specifically, this chapter discusses: suppression, repression, reaction formation, displacement, sublimation, denial, rationalisation, projection and projective identification.

The concluding section of the chapter discusses projective identification and its importance and vast application in practice, highlighting how projective identification is the basis for bias and stigma.

Chapter 4: **Finding a home for Alice**

This chapter covers: psychological and ego defences: schema, stereotypes, cognitive schema and bias, transference and countertransference, and belonging and identity.

This chapter introduces the concepts of cognitive schema, stereotype and cognitive bias. The chapter also discusses how the different consonant and dissonant information may reinforce or challenge our schemas and how through the processes of assimilation and accommodation we reconcile the new information with our model of the external world.

The chapter then proceeds to explore the concept of transference and countertransference and concludes with a brief discussion of belonging and identity.

Chapters 3 and 4 set the foundation for greater understanding of our own and others' emotions and behaviours and the dynamics of relationships.

Chapter 5: **The long shadow of the past**

This chapter covers: trauma, post-traumatic growth, touch and listening to children's voices.

Trauma is a major source of individual and societal distress and a central issue in practice. Therefore, this chapter explores trauma, vicarious or secondary trauma, and post-traumatic stress, and their effects. The chapter also introduces post-traumatic growth as well as examining the concept of developmentally appropriate communication with children.

The chapter begins with an introduction to the concept of trauma, its intergenerational transmission and some of its effects. This is followed by a discussion of vicarious/secondary trauma and its impact. This section also includes a discussion of touch in social work and social care practice.

The chapter highlights some of the challenges in interpreting children's narratives from a developmental perspective, followed by an exploration of play and role play and their significance, and the importance of developmentally appropriate communication with children.

The chapter concludes with a discussion of post-traumatic growth, and the importance of a trauma-informed psychosocial and relationship-based practice.

Chapter 6: **A broken narrative**

This chapter covers: transactional analysis and narrative approaches.

This chapter introduces narrative approaches and transactional analysis. Specifically, the chapter begins by introducing the person-centred approach of reflecting back and externalisation of *problems*. This is followed by an example of re-authoring narratives and shifting to the person's preferred narratives.

The chapter then introduces transactional analysis and how it can be used to reflect upon our own thoughts, emotions and behaviour, and to support our users of services.

The chapter concludes with a discussion of loss and grief, and by introducing remembering conversations as an effective narrative intervention that relocates the person/lost object in the life of the user of services and allows continuity of the bonds between them.

Chapter 7: **Searching for love in all the wrong places (Part 1): family therapy and systemic approaches**

This chapter covers: family therapy and systemic approaches.

This chapter offers an introduction to systemic family interventions.

The chapter begins with a brief reflection on domestic violence followed by a discussion of systemic thinking and systemic family approaches. This includes:

- structural family interventions, examining family organisation/hierarchies and relationships;
- strategic family interventions, brief solution-focused interventions; and
- family life cycle model.

The above intervention approaches enable practitioners to work collaboratively with the family, agree the definition of the family and the scope of interventions, and to visualise its boundaries and the type and quality of relationships between its members. By modifying relationship boundaries, practitioners can support families to effect changes in behaviour that can address the family's concerns/*problems*/difficulties.

The chapter concludes with a discussion of the use of *outsider witness* and *definitional ceremonies* to support users of services in initiating and sustaining positive change. This is an especially powerful approach to enabling users of services to adopt a new narrative and to address *problems*/challenges.

Chapter 8: **Searching for love in all the wrong places (Part 2): that's the way I feel about myself**

This chapter covers: motivational interviewing, and cognitive and behavioural approaches.

This chapter begins with a brief note about gangs and gang membership followed by a discussion of rape and multiple perpetrator rape. The chapter then continues with a brief note on self-harm, before introducing motivational interviewing and demonstrating its application in practice with a fully annotated example of a motivational interview in a home visit.

The chapter then introduces cognitive and behavioural interventions and approaches.

The concluding section offers a discussion of unresolved trauma and its impact. This section offers an example of unresolved trauma and its transmission through projective identification between father and child. The chapter concludes by emphasising the importance of identifying and assessing such dynamics in practice.

Chapter 9: **Concluding remarks**

This chapter offers a brief personal reflection and perspective about the current status of social work and social care and the prospect of psychosocial and relationship-based practice.

Examining the relationship between science and society, in the latter quarter of the last century, we note a significant shift from science setting the stage for society, to society setting the agenda for science. Indeed, the focus of knowledge and knowledge generation changed from the application of knowledge to the knowledge produced in the context of application. This led to a significant shift from a search for causality and objectivity to an appreciation of context and subjectivity. However, the increasing emphasis on evidence-based approaches based on bio-medicalised models of research and intervention has re-inverted this balance toward more objectifying practices that see '*people with problems and people as problems*' (Howe, 1987, p 56). Howe (2009) eloquently captures this divide:

> *Relationship-based social work is not necessarily hostile to science, but it believes that experience rather than experiment underpins our shared humanity.*
>
> (p 12)

This highlights the importance and urgency of evidence-informed psychosocial and relationship-based approaches for contemporary social work and social care practice. Furthermore, social work has always adopted an applied interdisciplinary approach to its interventions and research. Therefore, the recent and increasing demand and recognition for interdisciplinary approaches to research and practice offer unprecedented opportunities for greater appreciation of social work and social care practice and research in general and psychosocial and relationship-based practice in particular.

Taking inspiration from Howe's insight, this book inverts the traditional approaches to writing that begin with an explanation of theory followed by examination of case studies. Instead, this book begins with practice narratives and case studies followed by reflection and a discussion that draw on and ground theories within the context of practice.

This book is for practitioners, students and academics, or anyone with an interest in evidence-informed and critical psychosocial and relationship-based practice.

Whether read throughout in its entirety or as single chapters, or any other order, I hope that you enjoy reading the different stories and reflections as well as the discussions. I also hope that this book can inspire practitioners to defend complexity and the systemic nature of human relationships, and to serve as a companion to shed light on your journey of discovery and the thoughtful art of evidence-informed psychosocial and relationship-based practice.

References

Aymer, C and Okitikpi, T (2000) Epistemology, Ontology and Methodology: What's That Got to Do with Social Work? *Social Work Education*, 19(1): 67–75.

Bowlby, J (1951) *Maternal Care and Mental Health*. Geneva: WHO.

Cooper, A (2014) Making Space: Relationship Based Practice in Turbulent Times. [online] Available at: http://cfswp.org/education/paper.php?s=making-space-relationship-based-practice-in-turbulent-times (accessed 9 August 2014).

Coulshed, V (1991) *Social Work Practice*. UK: Palgrave Macmillan.

Derrida, J (1976) *Of Grammatology*. Baltimore: The Johns Hopkins University Press.

Dominelli, L (1996) Deprofessionalizing Social Work: Anti-Oppressive Practice, Competencies and Postmodernism. *Journal of Social Work Practice*, 26(2): 153–75.

Ferguson, H (2011) *Child Protection Practice*. UK: Palgrave Macmillan.

Howe, D (1987) *An Introduction to Social Work Theory*. Aldershot: Gower.

Howe, D (1998) Relationship-based Thinking and Practice in Social Work. *Journal of Social Work Practice*, 16(2): 45–56.

Howe, D (2009) *A Brief Introduction to Social Work Theory*. UK: Palgrave Macmillan.

Parton, N (2008) Changes in the Form of Knowledge in Social Work: From the 'Social' to the 'Informational'? *British Journal of Social Work*, 38: 253–69.

Ritzer, G (1995) *McDonaldization of Society: An Investigation into the Changing Character of Contemporary Social Life*. Thousand Oaks, CA: Pine Forge; 2nd Revised edition.

Ruch, G (2005) Relationship-based Practice and Reflective Practice: Holistic Approaches to Contemporary Child Care Social Work. *Child and Family Social Work*, 10(2): 111–25.

Ruch, G (2010) *Relationship-based Social Work*. London: Jessica Kingsley.

Saussure, F de (1998) *Course in General Linguistics*. Chicago: Open Court Publishing Co.

Sudbery, J (2002) Key Features of Therapeutic Social Work: The Use of Relationship. *Journal of Social Work Practice*, 16(2): 149–62.

Trevithick, P (2003) Effective Relationship-based Practice: A Theoretical Exploration. *Journal of Social Work Practice*, 17(2): 163–76.

Winnicott, D W (1975[1953]) Transitional Objects and Transitional Phenomena, in *Through Paediatrics to Psychoanalysis*, London: Karnac Books.

Winnicott, D W (2000[1964]) *The Child, the Family and the Outside World*. London: Penguin.

1 Colour of love: thinking of Jack

Attachment and potential space

Chapter summary

This chapter offers an introduction to the concepts of emotional labour, mentalisation, attachment and potential space. These are fundamental concepts that are essential for understanding relationships and are used throughout this book.

An explicit recognition of emotional labour offers us the opportunity to better manage the emotional content and demand of everyday practice. We expand on this with the concept of secondary trauma and the importance of good supervision for effective practice. However, the concept of emotional labour is also aimed at rendering the emotional labour and the challenging journey of our users of services visible in practice. At times it may seem that a user of services is not exerting sufficient effort to achieve a given objective; however, it is important to consider that they may be experiencing significant emotional labour that exhausts their resources, energies and capabilities for physical or psychological labour or for tasks that may otherwise seem simple, routine or trivial.

The discussion of mentalisation, attachment and potential space lay the foundation for further chapters in the book and are essential for a better appreciation of individual experience, motivation and behaviour, and for understanding of relationships and relationship-based interventions.

Chapter objectives

1. Introduce the concept of emotional labour and its relevance in practice.

2. Introduce attachment theory and the different attachment styles as related to children's development.

3. Introduce the concept of *potential space* and its significance and implications for individual experience and development.

The case transfer

CASE STUDY

Jenny: *Jeff has a difficult time with things but he is better to work with than Summer ... The real problem is that neither one thinks of Jack as their responsibility ... I feel sorry for the little lad stuck in the middle it's like he doesn't exist. He is a sweet boy, you will like him and I will miss him when I leave here.*

Jenny, a black social worker in her mid forties, was talking to Sophie, a white social worker in her mid twenties, while typing up her case notes and taking occasional spoonfuls of soup.

Jenny: *Jack has three more days and then he's back with Summer. I think he will miss Whitmore. It gives him the structure that he needs. It was difficult for him at first but now he loves it.*

Jenny notices that Sophie is taking notes on her notepad and adds: *Don't worry, I will write everything up in my handover notes ... It will be a big change for me ... no longer doing this. Remember to look after yourself and don't be like me, last one out and first one in. You will end up with no life and burnt out.*

Jenny is leaving the social work profession after ten years as a qualified social worker with seven of those years as a child protection social worker and five with this particular team. She is an advanced practitioner within the team and takes on the more complex cases as well as supporting the younger, more inexperienced staff members with difficult or challenging cases. Some senior managers view Jenny as being *highly opinionated* and not a team player, and this has led to conflicts between Jenny and senior managers.

Jenny's cases will be distributed amongst the team and Sophie will be allocated some including Jack and his family.

Jenny and Sophie discuss the case as part of the handover process

Jack is an 11-year-old boy with Asperger's syndrome, a syndrome which is on the autistic spectrum. Jack displays certain characteristics indicative of this, for example he has some difficulty with social interactions and can display restricted and repetitive patterns of behaviour and interest. When speaking with children and adults he can become fixated on his point of view and does not allow for other viewpoints or ways of thinking that contradict his thinking. Jack can find it difficult to show or interpret emotion, and he also finds it difficult to distinguish between being an adult or a child and often speaks to other children in an authoritative manner which causes irritation and conflict with them. Teachers and other key adults who interact with Jack have noted that Jack is a very intelligent child with a strong character.

Children's Services have been involved with this family on and off for most of Jack's life. A referral was initially made to them when Jack was two years old. Summer, his mother, reported that she was concerned that Jack may have been sexually abused as he displayed sexualised behaviour. Nursery staff supported Summer's concerns noting that he frequently masturbated in the corner of the nursery. A child protection investigation was initiated; however, it was deemed inconclusive due to lack of evidence and no further action was taken.

Over the next few years Children's Services dipped in and out of their lives. When Jack was six years old he set fire to his room. The blaze was significant and severe and this resulted in Jack's room being completely burnt out. The fire and the fumes also resulted in Jack and Summer needing to move out of their flat for the damage to be repaired and to make the flat habitable again. The fire brigade referred Jack and Summer to Children's Services with serious concerns for Jack's emotional state and concerns around Summer's ability to parent and support Jack. This resulted in a section 47 investigation and Jack being put on a child protection plan. A team of professionals worked intensively with Jack and Summer to provide support and initiate change. A number of positive changes were noted. Summer started to access support from the community mental health team and Jack started receiving support from a psychiatrist. In light of the progress made, the case was closed with the understanding that the psychiatrist, as the lead professional, would continue to work with Jack, and Summer would continue her engagement with the community mental health team.

Sophie: *The case was closed after Summer's engagement with community mental health services and after Jack started to see a psychiatrist and began attending school more regularly. Wasn't it a bit premature to close the case?*

Reflection

1. *Our thoughts and emotions have a great influence on our decision-making and the way we interact with others.*

2. *Think about what you have read so far and note down some of your thoughts and feelings about Jack, Summer and Jeff.*

3. *If this case was assigned to you with only the information you have read so far, what would be your approach and some of the steps you would plan to take?*

4. *Reflect on Jenny's words:* 'It will be a big change for me ... no longer doing this. Remember to look after yourself and don't be like me, last one out and first one in. You will end up with no life and burnt out.' *What do they mean to you?*

5. *Read the discussion below, and reflect on your own feelings and motivations for joining this profession. What are some of the ways you can safeguard and enhance your own health and well-being as well as personal and professional growth?*

Discussion

Reflecting on Jenny's words ('*It will be a big change for me ... no longer doing this. Remember to look after yourself and don't be like me, last one out and first one in. You will end up with no life and burnt out'*) offers a hint into the challenging and yet rewarding world of social work, and highlights the importance of maintaining a professional outlook and clear professional boundaries. Indeed, throughout this book we will explore the different facets and dynamics of relationships and various approaches to different practice situations. However, social work is a highly demanding profession, and one of the greatest challenges inherent in social work practice is rooted in its dual mandate of support/care and safeguarding/control.

Indeed, although often it is necessary to empower the family and caregiver(s) in order to ensure sustainable and effective care for users of services, however, at times there may be a conflict between the best interest of users of services and their caregiver(s). In such cases practitioners experience substantial tension between the elements of care and control in their role. Indeed, this is perhaps one of the most significant sources of stress and emotional toil for social work practitioners.

This situation is further complicated by a host of other factors as reported by various authors. These factors have traditionally resulted in dissatisfaction, excessive stress and burnout among practitioners (Acker, 1999; Anderson, 2000; Egan, 1993; Gerits et al, 2005; Gilbar, 1998; Hamama, 2012; Sze and Ivker, 1986; Um and Harrison, 1998).

Social work is a relationship-based profession with practitioners often involved in complex and emotionally charged situations. Therefore, social work practice often entails significant emotional labour and considerable tensions between different stakeholders and competing variables in its interventions (Cournoyer, 1988; Gerits et al, 2005; Hamama, 2012; Pines and Kafry, 1978; Soderfeldt et al, 1995).

Emotional labour is defined by the expenditure of intellectual, physical and emotional resources, time, effort and energy to identify/understand and fulfil one's own and other's emotional needs.

Emotional labour often is accompanied with physical labour. However, it differs from physical labour in that emotional labour is aimed at producing specific feelings, or meeting specific emotional needs/goals (eg self-validation and feelings of being wanted, belonging, love, being cared for, etc). For example, a mother holding her baby to comfort her/him is exerting physical effort/energy/labour to hold/carry the baby; however, this is with the intention of meeting the emotional needs of the baby (eg to comfort her/him).

Emotional needs are often unspoken, unknown or even unconscious, and therefore, in spite of its importance, emotional labour is often unrecognised, discounted or invisible to those who benefit from it. This invisibility is partly due to the social norms that require disguising the emotional labour one is doing for the other. Hence, recipients of emotional labour may not admit its existence because they cannot, or do not wish to, admit their emotional needs, while performers of emotional labour may be complicit in such denials to save recipients from the pain of recognising their repressed emotional needs. Furthermore, based on gender, age or other demographic characteristics, social norms may impose specific expectations in relation to emotional labour. For example, social norms may require a blind reaction to emotional labour and instead focus on physical labour that actually produces goods and services rather than the emotional services that produce feelings of well-being, being loved, appreciated, cared for and wanted.

Emotional labour is inherent in all relationships and personal expressions. Therefore, relationship-based practice and interventions entail emotional labour. Hence, it is essential that practitioners are able to recognise emotional labour and its dynamics, drivers, motivations and outcomes.

A central objective of this book is to shed light on the drivers and underlying dynamics of relationships in general, and relationship-based practice and interventions in particular. It is hoped that this can enhance the quality, outcomes and effectiveness of practitioners and interventions, and can enable effective expressions of practitioners' creative self in terms of '*the combination of attributes that each of us forms to make a unique place among others in our social interactions*' (Myers and Sweeney, 2005, p 485) and that this supports practitioners' well-being and leads to thriving and strengthening of their '*coping self*' (Lawson, 2007).

Discussing the case transfer and the family background

CASE STUDY

Jenny: *This isn't a difficult case, but it just doesn't seem to move. The whole thing is stuck in a loop, repeating the same cycle over and over again ... Summer neglecting Jack, we go into child protection, then some improvement and then the case is closed just to be reopened in a few months and the whole thing starts all over again.*

Sophie: *Yes, it seems really stuck. So what do you think I should do?*

Jenny: *There's not much you can do, aside from watching out for signs of deterioration and trying to intervene as soon as you feel things are heading in the wrong direction again. But when the case is closed, we need the school and health workers to report problems like Jack's absences, poor performance, and change of mood or behaviour earlier.*

Sophie continues going through case notes and observes that:

A few months later, when Jack was seven, the case was reopened due to concerns around neglect. Jack missed a number of dental and mental health appointments and it was noted that he barely attended school. When he did attend school he arrived looking dishevelled and hungry. A strategy meeting was convened and it was agreed that there was a likelihood of Jack experiencing significant harm due to neglect. The case went to a child protection conference and it was agreed that Jack should be put on a child protection plan under the category of neglect. Jack stayed on a plan for two years after which the plan was discontinued as professionals agreed that the situation seemed to have stabilised and that positive work with the family was achieved. It was agreed that all services would remain engaged and provide intensive support for the family.

During the assessment process it was noted that Summer has a number of emotional and physical difficulties. Historical notes highlight that she was diagnosed with bipolar disorder when Jack was two and medication helped her to stabilise her mood. However, Summer has always strongly denied this diagnosis. She was later diagnosed with personality disorder which was subsequently revised to indicate an undefined/unknown diagnosis of mental health and emotional difficulties.

Summer has revealed some awareness of her mental health and emotional difficulties to her psychiatrist, explaining that she believes many of her difficulties stem from a childhood filled with physical and sexual abuse and neglect. However, she has never shared this information with Jenny. Summer has told her GP that she attributes her illness to Jeff and the stress he caused when he left her for someone else.

Currently, Jack is on a child in need plan due to concerns around Summer's parenting ability and Jeff's infrequent and sporadic contact with Jack. These concerns combined with Jack's increasingly challenging and risk-taking behaviour result in a decision in consultation with Summer and Jeff that Jack should be sent to a children's in-patient centre for assessment.

Reflection

1. *Read the discussion below and think about some of the challenges and difficulties in terms of mentalisation for Summer.*

2. *What is the impact of Summer's mentalisation difficulties on Jack's overall development, attachment and mentalisation capacity?*

3. *Based on the information so far, do you think Jenny and Sophie have an accurate understanding/appreciation of Summer's mental states, thoughts and emotions?*

4. *Based on the information so far, do you think Jenny and Sophie have an accurate understanding/appreciation of Jack's emotions, thoughts and behaviours?*

Discussion

Mentalisation and child development

Fonagy et al (1991) refer to the attitudes and skills involved in understanding our own and others' thoughts and mental states and their connections with and implications for emotions and behaviour.

As human beings we attribute mental states that might have motivated a given action to individuals and their actions. Mentalisation is a recursive process that helps us understand and make sense of our own and other's thoughts, emotions, actions and behaviours by imagining ourselves in their place/position. We also use mentalisation to *predict* others' actions and emotions.

Our capacity to mentalise is gradually developed from our infancy, based on our interactions with our primary caregivers, and continues to evolve and develop increasing sophistication throughout our lives. Mentalisation capacity is linked to our ability for reflection and self-awareness. Indeed, self-awareness can be thought of as mentalisation applied to our self, and is a prerequisite for understanding others (Fonagy et al, 2002; Harris, 2009).

Furthermore, in line with systemic perspective, thinking of mental states as the motivators/generators of actions and behaviours underlines the social origin of self. Indeed, as suggested by Allen et al (2008) the ability to recognise/imagine oneself in the mental state of the other is at the heart of the relational conception of self and the individual's sense of selfhood.

An adequate recognition and perception of one's own state of mind and its congruence with individual's emotions and behaviour are essential for a harmonious and balanced *inner life*. Indeed, one may experience a lack or loss of calibration of such internal state and/or experience, leading to a lack or loss of appreciation and connection with our own subjectivity, and this can result in distress and even mental ill-health.

Recognising mental states, and our awareness of them, is interlinked with and can lead to social emotions such as embarrassment, jealousy, pride, shame and guilt. In this sense, mentalisation enables us to transcend physical *reality* and bodily limitations and to step beyond our physical experience and experience our self as social.

Our preferences and our notions of what is acceptable, valuable or desirable are influenced by our cultural values and social norms. Culture and society influence our behaviour and language and this includes the extent of recognition and the manner of expression of our own and others' emotions and thoughts. In this sense, social and cultural are closely interlinked with personal and developmental aspects of identity and its expressions and representations. Hence, to a great extent the social psyche influences, structures, contains and constrains the individual psyche and its developments and expressions.

However, mentalising is not only the capacity to accurately read our own and others' states of mind, thoughts and emotions, it also conditions our lived experience and relationships. We can facilitate our growth and enhance our experience by assuming an inquiring and respectful stance towards others' thoughts, emotions and behaviours, and by learning about others' mental states and taking into account their perspectives, needs, feelings and preferences. This is similar to the systemic stance of '*curiosity*' (Cecchin, 1987) and takes place at the boundary of one's knowledge, requiring awareness of one's sense of self.

Given that we can never be certain about other people's states of mind, mentalisation is an approximation and, by definition, it is an inexact, developmental and complex process that requires constant social verification.

Attachment and mentalising are cyclical processes that are positively correlated with (ie positively reinforce) one another. In other words, the child who is better understood will better understand the parents. This will facilitate parents' understanding of the child's needs and feelings, and will increase the accuracy of their reactions to the child, which will in turn enhance the child's mentalising capacities. Such an interpretation of mentalisation within the family is in line with systemic thinking that envisions the family as a system that offers both the content and the context for the child's development (ie the development of the child's mentalisation capacity and emotional and behavioural capabilities). In this sense, children's development and their evolving attachment and mentalisation capacities are helped or hindered by their relationships and experiences with their attachment figures and by the relationships, behaviours and emotions of the members of their family system.

Therefore, given the interlinks and interdependencies of attachment and mentalising capacity, Summer's mental health challenges and attentional difficulties as well as her inability to reflect and represent her own mental state and to understand and relate to the mental state of others, create developmental vulnerabilities that disrupt Jack's attachment relationships and undermine his mentalising capacity (Fonagy and Luyten, 2009) and his ability to develop complex metacognitive capacities (Fonagy and Target, 1997).

Throughout this book we will draw on various sociological, psychological, psychodynamic, object relation and other relevant theories to explore the dynamics of human relationships and different developmental processes and their healing and empowering potential. This includes exploring the importance of attachment and mentalising and the different factors that influence their development.

Children's in-patient centre (Whitmore)

CASE STUDY

Jack was placed in a children's in-patient centre which specialises in the assessment of children with additional needs, disabilities and severe mental health difficulties. The assessment process took 12 weeks, and although Jack was initially upset at being separated from Summer, he became fond of Whitmore and established strong links/bonds with staff. During his stay there was a marked improvement in Jack's self-care skills and social skills. The assessment highlighted that Jack thrived there due to the structure and routine in place.

As part of the assessment process, Summer had weekly sessions with Jack and the staff at Whitmore and staff noted a strong attachment between Summer and Jack. However, areas of concern were also highlighted. There were difficulties in how Summer related to Jack, she often attended sessions very late and found it difficult to focus on Jack during the sessions and instead focused many sessions on her own emotional needs and difficulties.

During the assessment process it was identified that Jack had an additional diagnosis of Attention Deficit Hyperactivity Disorder (ADHD), and Jack was prescribed Ritalin. Professionals at Whitmore recommend that Jack attend a specialist school provision where he will be able to develop peer relationships with children who have similar needs and shared interests.

Education and Children's Services agree that a specialist residential school will be most suitable for Jack and allow him to return home on the weekends. However, Summer and Jeff can't agree upon an appropriate specialist residential school. Jeff would like Jack to attend an *Ivy League* boarding school and not a specialist residential school while Summer would prefer that Jack attends a Catholic school.

Jeff has applied to a number of *schools with calibre* for Jack; however, all schools indicated that they don't have the needed facilities to cater for Jack's additional *complex needs*. Jeff started to apply to schools without including Jack's additional needs and this resulted in a number of unsuccessful interviews with many head teachers making reference to Jack's lack of social skills.

Reflection

1. Are Jeff and Summer looking for a school for Jack or themselves?

2. Are Jeff and Summer in effect putting Jack in a position where he cannot/ does not live up to expectations? If yes, why?

3. Jack's behaviour improved when at Whitmore. What can we learn from this experience? And how can Jack be better supported?

4. It seems that Summer and Jeff find it difficult to remain focused on Jack's needs. Why is this the case and how can Sophie work with the parents to help them consider and prioritise Jack's needs?

Discussion

Attachment

John Bowlby (1958) was a British child psychiatrist and psychoanalyst who became interested in the experience of infants who had been separated from their parents. He noted that these children would try different strategies (eg clinging, shouting, crying, frantically searching, etc) to avoid separation or to reunite themselves with their attachment figure. At that time, psychoanalysts attributed such children's behaviours as *immature* defence mechanisms that were used to repress these children's emotional pain.

John Bowlby's interest in theoretical and intergenerational transmission of attachment was evident from his paper in 1940 where he suggests that for mothers with parenting difficulties:

> a weekly interview in which their problems are approached analytically and traced back to childhood has sometimes been remarkably effective. Having once been helped to recognize and recapture the feelings which she herself had as a child and to find that they are accepted tolerantly and understandingly, a mother will become increasingly sympathetic and tolerant toward the same things in her child.
>
> (Bowlby, 1940, p 23)

Although they were developed independently, Fairbain's (1952) object relations theories and Winnicott's (1965) observations offered support for Bowlby's ideas.

Using an ethological approach and observing the behaviour of the children of other species, Bowlby (1958) noticed the similarity of the pattern of attachment behaviour among them. Therefore, he argued that children's crying, searching and other strategies were adaptive responses to separation from their primary attachment figure. Bowlby thought that a motivational system (*Attachment Behavioural System*) was gradually developed by children that regulated their relationships and their desire for proximity to an attachment figure. In spite of the Kleinian perspective, Bowlby continued his work with children and families (especially mothers). Indeed, in his 1949 paper, known as the first published paper in family therapy, he explains how he achieved clinical breakthroughs by interviewing parents in the presence of their children with challenging behaviour or attachment difficulties.

In follow-up of her work in the 1950s as part of Bowlby's research team in London, in the 1960s Mary Ainsworth (Ainsworth et al, 1978) developed the *Strange Situation* test. Although Ainsworth was influenced by her work with Bowlby, she developed this test independent from Bowlby's work. This was designed as a laboratory-based separation and reunion test to determine the different types of attachment and maternal care that infants received at home.

Bowlby's seminal papers presented to the British Psychoanalytic Society in London laid the foundations of attachment theory as: 'The nature of the child's tie to his mother' (1958), 'Separation anxiety' (1959) and 'Grief and mourning in infancy and early childhood' (1960). However, he was heavily criticised by his peers as he questioned some of the dominant ideas and theories of his time. For example, contrary to Anna Freud's claim that due to their insufficient ego bereaved infants cannot mourn, Bowlby (1960) suggested that grief and mourning processes, both in the case of children and adults, appear whenever attachment bonds are activated in the absence of the attachment figure.

There are four basic types of attachment patterns:

Secure attachment: Children who experience consistent and good enough care develop secure attachment. Because of the consistency and reliability of their caregiver behaviour these children develop trust in themselves and others, and are confident to explore their environment knowing that in case of need, their primary attachment figure will be available to them to comfort, protect and support them. In case of *Strange Situation Test* these children become upset when their parent or caregiver (attachment figure) leaves the room, but, when the parent or caregiver returns, they actively seek their parent or caregiver and are easily comforted by them.

Avoidant attachment: The children whose caregivers are emotionally unavailable or are insensitive to the needs of the child, develop insecure and avoidant attachment. Such caregivers discourage crying and encourage independence. They have little or no response to their children's needs. Therefore, children learn to develop independence and an avoidant attitude to remain as self-contained as possible. In *Strange Situation Test* these children don't seem too distressed by the separation from their parent or caregiver, and when reunited, they seem to actively avoid contact with the parent or caregiver, for example by continuing to play or focusing on a toy or other play objects.

Ambivalent/anxious attachment: When caregivers are inconsistent in their response to the child's needs (eg at times they respond appropriately and in a timely manner and at other times they seem insensitive or intrusive) then the child may develop an ambivalent or anxious attachment. In this case, the child is not certain about the caregiver's reaction and, therefore, remains anxious and ambivalent to seek refuge with the attachment figure. In the *Strange Situation Test* these children are often ill-at-ease and upon separation from their parent or caregiver, they become quite distressed. More importantly, when reunited, these children are not easily soothed, and instead exhibit conflicting behaviour that on the one hand suggests that they want to be comforted, but on the other hand they seem to want to *punish* the parent or caregiver for leaving them.

Disorganised attachment: When the caregiver or attachment figure is abusive to the child, the attachment figure who is supposed to be the source of care and comfort instead becomes the source of pain and distress. These children develop disorganised attachment. In this case the child experiences an agonising and terrible dilemma when facing distress as on the one hand the child's survival instinct drives them to seek safety with the attachment figure; however, the attachment figure is terrifying and punishing. Unable to deal with or resolve this dilemma, these children may detach from self and the experience of what is happening to them by blocking it from their consciousness. Continued experiences of such splitting and strong repression/suppression of their experience can lead to a number of negative outcomes including mental health challenges. In the *Strange Situation Test* these children present a mix of avoidant and resistant behaviours and may seem confused or apprehensive in the presence of their parent or caregiver.

Adult attachment: Although Bowlby argued that attachment behaviour affects our experience throughout our lives, it was Hazan and Shaver (1987) who applied Bowlby's ideas to adult romantic relationships, and suggested that adult romantic relationships operate based on the same motivational system and emotional bonds as the attachment system between infants/children and their parents or caregivers. Examining the similarities between children's and adults' attachment, Hazan and Shaver found that both securely attached children and securely attached adults:

- feel safe when their attachment figure is available (nearby) and is responsive;
- seek closeness and engage intimate contact;
- feel insecure or miss the attachment figure when the attachment figure is absent;
- show mutual interest and preoccupation with one another;
- share experiences and discoveries with each other;
- engage in *baby talk*.

Both the attachment between children and their primary attachment figure and the attachment in adult romantic relationships can be classified based on the two dimensions of avoidance and anxiety. Those who score high on avoidance prefer not to rely on others while those who score low on avoidance are comfortable with establishing relationships and being intimate, and tend to be more secure in depending on other people and allowing others to depend on them. Those who score high on anxiety tend to worry about their attachment figure's availability, attentiveness, responsiveness, etc, and whether their emotions would be reciprocated by their partner. In contrast, those who score low on anxiety feel more secure about their relationships and the availability and responsiveness of their attachment figure (see Figure 1.1).

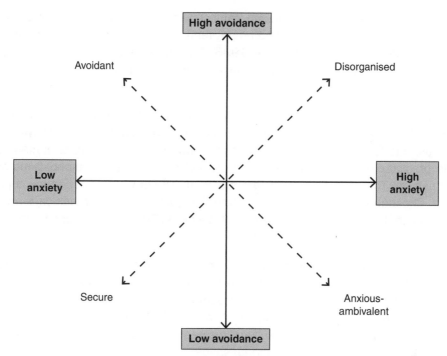

Figure 1.1 *Two-dimensional model of attachment (source: Brennan et al, 1998)*

Both children and adults with secure attachment patterns are usually well adjusted and are rather resilient. They seem to get along with others and are usually liked by their peers, and generally seem more satisfied with their relationships. More specifically, in adult relationships this translates into greater trust, commitment and mutual dependence, and generally longer-lasting relationships. Adults with secure relationships tend to use that relationship as their secure-base to explore the world. In this sense, good enough care and a secure, satisfying and responsive adult relationship can help the individual develop trust and more positive relationships and, therefore, provide healing or mitigate some of the consequences of insecure childhood attachment.

It is important to note that attachment behaviour is influenced by individual differences. Furthermore, Brennan et al's (1998) research (Figure 1.1) implies that differences in attachment styles/behaviours are dimensional differences rather than categorical ones. In other words, different attachment styles are about varying degrees of the same variables (ie attachment-related anxiety and attachment-related avoidance) rather than being about different variables.

Research indicates that in general, when facing distress, securely attached adults are more likely to seek support from their partners, and they are more likely to be responsive and provide support to their distressed partners. This influences the stability and longevity of their relationships. Attachment styles and their associated emotional and behavioural patterns can create a self-reinforcing cycle. In other words, the way individuals interpret and attribute value to their partner's behaviour tends to reinforce their attachment pattern. For example, in case of disagreements or relationship conflicts, the attributions and interpretation of events by individuals with insecure attachment tend to exacerbate, rather than mitigate or alleviate their insecurities (Simpson et al, 1996). Furthermore, Frazier et al (1996) suggest that people end up in a relationship with partners who confirm their existing beliefs about attachment relationships.

Jack received good and appropriate care at Whitmore and the consistency of care and the structure/routine made his environment predictable and reliable, hence allowing him to develop trust and form strong bonds with staff. Routine and consistent care made others' reactions predictable and this helped diminish Jack's anxiety and enhanced his mentalisation capability. This also developed Jack's trust in others while boosting his confidence in himself. Consequently there was improvement in Jack's behaviour, self-care and social skills as noted in the assessment (Granot and Mayseless, 2001; Ranson and Urichuk, 2008; Schuengel et al, 2013; Tharner et al, 2013).

Summer's mental health challenges and her inability to focus on Jack may be due to a host of difficulties. However, this could also be attributed to Summer's experiences of abuse in her childhood resulting in disorganised attachment which subsequently could have led to her mental health difficulties (Schuengel et al, 2013; Sweet, 2013; Zilberstein, 2014). Furthermore, her lack of attention to Jack and his needs and her continued focus on self may be a reflection of Summer's lack of *potential space*.

We will explore the concept of potential space later in this chapter, and will revisit attachment and mentalisation and their relevance, significance and application in practice later in the book. However, if you are interested in greater understanding of attachment, David Howe's *Attachment across the Lifecourse: A Brief Introduction* (2011) would be an excellent place to start while David Shemmings (2011) and David Wilkins (2012) offer a good discussion of disorganised attachment and its application in practice.

Meeting the family and taking the case forward

CASE STUDY

Jack and Summer missed a number of appointments before Sophie was finally able to meet them. Sophie rings the buzzer and a woman with a European accent answers the telecom and buzzes Sophie in. Sophie is met by a woman with dark hair and blue eyes and behind her stands a small boy with dark hair and blue eyes. Summer greets Sophie with a friendly smile and invites her into the flat. The flat is heavily cluttered with boxes, clothing, books and DVDs. The lounge area is completely taken over by clutter and there is no space to sit apart from a small patch on the sofa and a wooden stool. Summer sits on the wooden stool, Jack on the floor and Summer motions for Sophie to sit on the small area not yet taken over by the clutter.

Summer explains that her fatigue does not allow her to clean the flat as frequently as she would like.

Summer and Jack clearly enjoy each other's company as they laugh and joke around. However, they relate to each other as friends rather than mother and son, and Jack calls Summer by her name instead of mummy, mum or mother. Jack tells Sophie that he has watched all the episodes of *Family Guy* and *American Dad*, both adult animation series which are known for their social stereotypes, satire and intentional humour. Sophie listens to Summer talk about the various difficulties she has experienced over the past few years. Summer speaks at length for almost an hour non-stop with Jack chipping in now and again.

Sophie feels she is building a positive rapport with the family and Jack even showed Sophie some of his favourite toys.

Sophie asks to speak with Summer alone and Jack goes to his room stating that he is going to tidy it up. Sophie speaks with Summer and tries to be as sensitive as possible when bringing up the home environment. However, Summer becomes upset and asks Sophie:

Summer: *Do you have any kids, Sophie?*

Sophie: *I am here for you and Jack to support your parenting.*

Summer angrily replies: *Don't think so … barely know me and you are judging me.*

Summer starts to cry and goes to the kitchen and lights up a cigarette. Sophie is taken aback at how angry Summer became. A few minutes later and Summer returns less angry and apologies stating that she is having a difficult time at the moment and asks Sophie to leave.

Reflection

1.	*As we receive new information our feelings, judgements, reactions, etc are either reinforced or modified. Therefore, what are some of the steps that you would take if this case was assigned to you?*

2.	*Compare your current thoughts, feelings and plan of action to the one you developed at the beginning of this chapter. Are they the same or different? Why?*

3.	*Why do you think Summer and Jack relate to each other as friends rather than mother and son? Is this a reflection of the strength of their feelings and relationship?*

4.	*Why did Summer react sharply to Sophie?*

Discussion

The potential space and the not-me *transitional object*

In his paper, 'Transitional objects and transitional phenomena', Winnicott speaks of a '*potential space*' that represents the developmental area of individual experience. Winnicott argues that this potential space precedes and exists next to emotions and cognitions (Winnicott, 1975[1953], p 230).

Winnicott's concept of potential space has no specific location or physical attributes, and represents the third dimension of experience in addition to the intra-psychic *reality* of the individual, and the external/actual world (Winnicott, 1989[1967], p 103). In his words:

> The place where cultural experience is located is in the potential space between the individual and the environment (originally the object) … For every individual the use of this space is determined by life experiences that take place at the early stages of the individual's existence.
>
> (1989[1967], p 100)

> The potential space between baby and mother, between child and family, between individual and society or the world, depends on experience which leads to trust. It can be looked upon as sacred to the individual in that it is here that the individual experiences creative living.
>
> (Winnicott, 1974a, p 121)

Drawing on the above we can state that we live neither entirely within our inner world, nor fully in an external *reality*, but, rather our lived experiences are positioned and take place in a space between the two.

Therefore, the potential space is a space in which the distinctions between rational and affective modes are put into play. Winnicott (1974b, pp 47–8) suggests that infants create *'transitional objects'* to act as a surrogate symbol for the bond between the infant and the primary caregiver at the times when such bond is missing or lacking. The transitional object may take a variety of forms (eg rags, dolls, or other toys/objects or even a word, or the *Linus blanket*). Through the creation of the transitional object the infant creates its first *not-me* object that functions at the will and control of the child. The transitional object offers a symbolic medium (ie a symbolic potential space) that serves as the locus for projections of the child's affections, insecurities and anxieties, and offers an *illusion* of the attachment bonds that can attenuate the infant's anxiety.

Through experiences of play and creative discovery with another (usually the primary caregiver) the potential space becomes an area that holds and contains the world of symbols, thoughts, images, sounds, emotions and the ongoing lived experiences of the infant. This is where the infant's needs, desires, hopes and creativity are expressed through the child's ability to play, and this is the foundation of *future adults'* ability for reflective capacity, creative living and adaptive sense/solution making (Winnicott, 1989[1967], p 101; 1974b).

In Winnicott's (1975[1953]) words this developmental process happens between mother and baby in the transitional space, an 'intermediate area of experience' between inside and outside, between the subjective and the objective, between '*the thumb and the teddy bear … between primary creativity and projection of what has already been introduced*' (p 2).

Like most psychic developments, the potential space can better be traced by its absence. For example, the lack of potential space in children may show in their inability to play, lack of curiosity, lack of imagination or desire or will, while in adults it may be reflected in a variety of forms such as feelings of insecurity or being attacked, feelings of being criticised and invaded by others' opinions, difficulty in thinking or meditating, feelings of being compelled to do something by an other.

Drawing on the above developmental notion and the above discussion we may consider that perhaps Summer's angry reply to Sophie *'didn't think so ... barely know me and you're judging me'*, followed by her crying and going to the kitchen, and her subsequent return in a less angry mood, may be reflective of the lacking development and/or absence of the above-mentioned potential space. Summer has not had the care, containment and the positive experiences that allow the creative and secure development of that potential space, and this results in her difficulty in accurately mentalising others' (in this case Sophie's) thoughts, emotions and motivations. We will explore defence mechanisms such as projection and project-ive identification later in the book, and that may shed further light on Summer's reaction.

Unfortunately, in everyday practice, there are instances in which the interaction between social workers and users of services resemble the dynamic of the above interaction between Summer and Sophie.

Therefore, it is important to note that often in order to protect and promote the child's (Jack's) best interest we need to support the family and enable the caregiver (Summer) to provide the necessary attention and care to the child (Jack). This means that Sophie needs to be able to contain Summer's anxiety and emotional turmoil to enable her to (re)create/(re)build that potential space and to be able to separate the past from present before she is able to move forward into a more supportive and harmonious future with her son. This highlights the challenge and opportunity in terms of the empowering and healing potential inherent in psy-chosocial and relationship-based interventions. We explore this latter point throughout the different chapters and case scenarios in this book. The next chapter offers an example of how Sophie can use psychodynamic approaches to facilitate positive change.

Reflection

1. *What are some of the implications of mentalisation and attachment for social work interventions, and assessment?*

2. *Reflecting on the above, what could Sophie have done differently?*

3. *Is there a conflict between Jack's and Summer's best interests?*

4. *Given the complex and multilayered difficulties in this case, how can Jack and Summer be best supported?*

References

Acker, G (1999) The Impact of Clients' Mental Illness on Social Workers' Job Satisfaction and Burnout. *Health and Social Work*, 24: 112–19.

Ainsworth, M D S, Blehar, M, Waters, E and Wall, S (1978) *Patterns of Attachment*. Hillsdale, NJ: Erlbaum.

Allen, J, Fonagy, P and Bateman, A (2008) *Mentalizing in Clinical Practice*. Washington, DC: American Psychiatric Press.

Anderson, D (2000) Coping Strategies and Burnout Amongst Veteran Child Protection Workers. *Child Abuse and Neglect*, 24(6): 839–48.

Bowlby, J (1940) The Influence of Early Environment in the Development of Neurosis and Neurotic Character. *International Journal of Psycho-Analysis*, 21: 1–25.

Bowlby, J (1949) The Study and Reduction of Group Tensions in the Family. *Human Relations*, 2: 123–8.

Bowlby, J (1958) The Nature of the Child's Tie to its Mother. *International Journal of Psycho-Analysis*, 39: 350–73.

Bowlby, J (1959) Separation Anxiety. *International Journal of Psycho-Analysis*, 41: 1–25.

Bowlby, J (1960) Grief and Mourning in Infancy and Early Childhood. *The Psychoanalytic Study of the Child*, 15, 3–39.

Brennan, K A, Clark, C L and Shaver, P R (1998) Self-reported Measurement of Adult Attachment: An Integrating Overview, in Simpson, J A and Rholes, W S (eds) *Attachment Theory and Close Relationships* (pp 46–76). New York: Guilford Press.

Cecchin, G (1987) Hypothesising, Circularity and Neutrality Revisited: An Invitation to Curiosity. *Family Process*, 26: 405–13.

Cournoyer, B (1988) Personal and Professional Distress Among Social Caseworkers. *Social Casework: The Journal of Contemporary Social Work*, May: 259–64.

Egan, M (1993) Resilience at the Front Lines: Hospital Social Work with AIDS Patients and Burnout. *Social Work in Health Care*, 18: 109–25.

Fairbairn, W R D (1952) *An Object-relations Theory of the Personality*. New York: Basic Books.

Fonagy, P and Luyten, P (2009) A Developmental, Mentalization-based Approach to the Understanding and Treatment of Borderline Personality Disorder. *Developmental Psychopathology*, 21: 1355–81.

Fonagy, P and Target, M (1997) Attachment and Reflective Function: Their Role in Self-organization. *Development and Psychopathology*, 9: 679–700.

Fonagy, P, Steele, H and Steele, M (1991) Maternal Representations of Attachment During Pregnancy Predict the Organization of Infant-Mother Attachment at One Year of Age. *Child Development*, 62: 891–905.

Fonagy, P, Gergely, G, Jurist, E L and Target, M (2002) *Affect Regulation, Mentalization, and the Development of the Self*. New York: Other Press.

Frazier, P A, Byer, A L, Fisher, A R, Wright, D M and DeBord, K A (1996) Adult Attachment Style and Partner Choice: Correlational and Experimental Findings. *Personal Relationships*, 3: 117–36.

Gerits, L, Derksen, J, Verbruggen, A and Katzko, M (2005) Emotional Intelligence Profiles of Nurses Caring for People with Severe Behaviour Problems. *Personality and Individual Differences*, 38(1): 33–43.

Gilbar, O (1998) Relationship Between Burnout and Sense of Coherence in Health Social Workers. *Social Work in Health Care*, 26: 39–49.

Granot, D and Mayseless, O (2001) Attachment Security and Adjustment to School in Middle Childhood. *International Journal of Behavioral Development*, 25: 530–41.

Hamama, L (2012) Differences Between Children's Social Workers and Adults' Social Workers on Sense of Burnout, Work Conditions and Organisational Social Support. *British Journal of Social Work*, 42(7): 1333–53.

Harris, P L (2009) Simulation (Mostly) Rules: A Commentary. *British Journal of Developmental Psychology*, 27: 555–9; author reply 561–7.

Hazan, C and Shaver, P (1987) Romantic Love Conceptualized as an Attachment Process. *Journal of Personality and Social Psychology*, 52(3): 511–24.

Howe, D (2011) *Attachment Across the Lifecourse: A Brief Introduction*. UK: Palgrave Macmillan.

Lawson, G (2007) Counselor Wellness and Impairment: A National Survey. *Journal of Humanistic Counseling, Education, and Development*, 46(1): 20–34.

Myers, J E and Sweeney, T J (2005) The Wheel of Wellness, in Myers, J E and Sweeney, T J (eds) *Counselling for Wellness: Theory, Research, and Practice* (pp 15–28). Alexandria, VA: American Counseling Association.

Pines, A and Kafry, D (1978) Occupational Tedium in the Social Services. *Social Work*, November: 499–507.

Ranson, K E and Urichuk, L J (2008) The Effect of Parent-Child Attachment Relationship on Child Biopsychological Outcomes: A Review. *Early Child Development and Care*, 178: 129–52.

Schuengel, C, Clasien de Schipper, J, Sterkenburg, P and Kef, S (2013) Attachment, Intellectual Disabilities and Mental Health: Research, Assessment and Intervention. *Journal of Applied Research in Intellectual Disabilities*, 26: 34–46.

Shemmings, D (2011) *Understanding Disorganized Attachment: Theory and Practice for Working With Children and Adults*. London: Jessica Kingsley.

Simpson, J A, Rholes, W S and Phillips, D (1996) Conflict in Close Relationships: An Attachment Perspective. *Journal of Personality and Social Psychology*, 71: 899–914.

Soderfeldt, M, Soderfeldt, B and Warg, L (1995) Burnout in Social Work. *Social Work*, 40: 638–46.

Sweet, A (2013) Aspects of Internal Self and Object Representations in Disorganized Attachment: Clinical Considerations in the Assessment and Treatment of Chronic and Relapsing Substance Misusers. *British Journal of Psychotherapy*, 29(2): 154–67.

Sze, W and Ivker, B (1986) Stress in Social Workers: The Impact of Setting and Role. *Social Casework: The Journal of Contemporary Social Work*, March: 141–8.

Tharner, A, Dierckx, B, Luijk, M, van Ijzendoorn, M H, Bakermans-Kranenburg, M, van Ginkel, J, Moll, H, Jaddoe, V, Hofman, A, Hudziak, J, Verhulst, F and Tiemeier, H (2013) Attachment Disorganization Moderates the Effect of Maternal Postnatal Depressive Symptoms on Infant Autonomic Functioning. *Psychophysiology*, 50(2): 195–203.

Um, M Y and Harrison, D F (1998) Role Stressors, Burnout, Mediators, and Job Satisfaction: A Stress-Strain-Outcome Model and an Empirical Test. *Social Work Research*, 22: 100–15.

Wilkins, D (2012) Disorganised Attachment Indicates Child Maltreatment: How is this Link Useful for Child Protection Social Work? *Journal of Social Work Practice*, 28: 15–30.

Winnicott, D W (1965) *The Maturational Process and the Facilitating Environment*. New York: International Universities Press.

Winnicott, D W (1974a) The Location of Cultural Experience, in *Playing and Reality* (pp 112–21). Harmondsworth: Penguin Books.

Winnicott, D W (1974b) Playing: A Theoretical Statement, in *Playing and Reality* (pp 44–61). Harmondsworth: Penguin Books.

Winnicott, D W (1975[1953]) Transitional Objects and Transitional Phenomena, in *Through Paediatrics to Psychoanalysis*. London: Hogarth Press.

Winnicott, D W (1989[1967]) The Location of Cultural Experience, in *Playing and Reality*, New York: Brunner-Routledge.

Zilberstein, K (2014) The Use and Limitations of Attachment Theory in Child Psychotherapy. *Psychotherapy*, 51(1): 93–103.

2 Colour of love: it's all about Jack

Validation, motivation, respectful challenge, splitting, diversity and social identity, parenting and role modelling

Chapter summary

Following on from Chapter 1, this chapter examines *feeling stuck* and the question of validation and *respectful challenge* in relationships with users of services. This includes a discussion of object relations and Melanie Klein's concept of splitting. We also clarify the difference between, and emphasise the importance of, not internalising *problem narratives* while internalising locus of control.

The second section of the chapter is focused on social identity in practice. This section begins by highlighting the importance of continuity in life narratives and follows with a discussion of diversity and the need for an anti-discriminatory and anti-oppressive stance.

The chapter concludes with a discussion of parenting, parental capacity and the importance of positive role models.

Chapter objectives

1. Introduce the dynamics of validation and emphasise the need for respectful challenge in practice.

2. Introduce the concept of splitting and its relevance in practice.

3. Clarify the difference between and the importance of internalising locus of control and non-internalising *problem narratives*.

4. Discuss diversity and social identity and the importance of anti-discriminatory and anti-oppressive practice.

5. Highlight parenting and parental responsibility and the importance of positive role models.

Validation and respectful challenge

CASE STUDY: FEELING STUCK

Over the next three months Sophie visits Jack and Summer every two weeks hoping to build a positive relationship and ensure that the situation is moving along. During each visit Sophie listens to Summer's account of her difficulties and makes sure to speak with Jack separately. Sophie is supportive and encouraging and seems to have gained Summer's and Jack's trust as they confide in her, sharing their experiences and Summer's challenges. However, Sophie is feeling uncertain about the progress and raises the issue in supervision with her team manager. Sophie explains to her manager that although she has been able to build a good relationship with Summer and Jack, she feels stuck. There is no real change in Summer's behaviour and she feels like something may go wrong the moment she stops visiting the family. Sophie's manager challenges Sophie to use a task-centred or a solution-focused approach and to agree clear milestones with Summer.

A few days later, the school alerts Sophie that Summer and Jack had a very loud argument outside of the school gates, and Jack's attendance has dropped again. When staff talk to Summer about it Jack intervenes and states that it's his fault and not Summer's. Staff notice that Jack is very protective over Summer and becomes angry if any of the teachers talk to Summer about her neglectful behaviour.

A series of events happen over the weekend which Sophie is not aware of. Summer takes Jack to a pub and, while socialising, loses sight of Jack. Jack becomes bored and leaves the pub at about 9pm and wanders over to the park opposite the pub where he finds a discarded ball which he plays with for a while before picking it up and taking it back to the pub with him. In total Jack is away from Summer for about 30 minutes. However, Summer does not notice Jack's absence. The following day (Sunday) Summer spends most of the day in bed and Jack starts experimenting with the matches he got from the pub. Jack lights a small fire in his room and the flame becomes large quickly. He is not sure how to put it out and uses his shoe and a bucket of water to put out the fire, and in the process ends up burning a hole in his shoes and hurting his hand.

On Monday morning Margaret, the teaching assistant, notices that Jack's hand is red and blistered. She also notices that he has a large hole in his shoe. It is a rainy day and Jack's socks are drenched with water. Margaret has a very good relationship with Jack and asks him about his hand and shoes, and Jack tells her what happened.

Margaret contacts Sophie with concerns that the situation at home seems to be deteriorating:

1. Jack's attendance is at 55 per cent.

2. He is frequently late for school.

3. Staff have observed Summer having loud arguments with Jack outside of the school gates.

4. Teachers have observed that Summer and Jack have more of a same-age-friend relationship than a parent-child relationship.

5. Jack often arrives at school without having had breakfast and needing to have a piece of toast before he can concentrate.

A strategy meeting is convened and, after careful examination of the case and the relevant needs and risks, it is recommended that Jack needs to be placed with a foster carer who can provide for his needs. The parents are unable to agree upon a residential school for Jack and given the continuous neglectful parenting a Section 20 (Children Act, 1989) foster placement with a specialist foster carer is recommended.

Reflection

1. *Have you been in a similar situation to Sophie? And have you felt stuck? What were the dynamics of the situation, and what did you do?*

2. *Noting Summer's reaction as described at the end of the last chapter, Sophie has worked hard to build a relationship with Summer. Can she challenge Summer without negatively affecting their relationship?*

3. *From a relationship perspective, how can Sophie empower Summer to initiate positive change in her life?*

Discussion

In the case transfer process between Jenny and Sophie, Jenny made reference to the case saying '*This isn't a difficult case, but it just doesn't seem to move. The whole thing is stuck in a loop, repeating the same cycle over and over again ...*' and it seems that Sophie is also stuck in the same predicament.

Morrison (1997) explains that '*anxiety is like a vein that throbs throughout the child protection process*' (p 196), while Munro's research (1999a, p 748) places the professionals' failure to revise old risk assessments at the top of the list of common errors of reasoning in child protection work. This is in spite of increasing risk for children. Given that the fear of child death is perhaps the greatest fear among child protection social workers, from a psychoanalytic perspective, Munro's research (1999a) seems to imply that social workers' greatest fear may be also their most repressed fear.

Morrison and Munro attribute this dilemma to different organisational and cultural factors (Morrison, 1997, 2005; Munro, 1999a, 1999b, 2004, 2005), and Morrison (1997) goes on to argue that the greatest source of stress for professionals is the work culture where normative emotional responses to child protection work are pathologised (p 206). Hence, Morrison suggests that professionals become victims of '*professional accommodation*' which in effect is a reflection of the workers living out their fears in sequences of secrecy, helplessness, entrapment, delayed disclosure and retraction (Morrison, 1997, pp 203–5).

Could this be the reason for Sophie's and Jenny's feelings of being stuck?

Looking at the situation from a psychodynamic perspective, the difficulty seems to be firstly on the part of Sophie. During her home visits and conversations with Summer, Sophie had tried to be reassuring, hoping that by offering containment for Summer's anxieties it would be possible to establish a positive relationship between them. Summer is seeking validation (Linehan, 1993) and Sophie's *accommodation* (Morrison, 1997) of her experiences and narrative offers a space where Summer can evacuate her anxieties and can find validation.

Sophie's acknowledgement of Summer's difficult past and current challenges validates Summer's perception of her experience, and research suggests that such a validation can support positive change (Koerner and Linehan, 2000). However, there seems to be no positive change. Instead the situation seems to be stuck in a cycle similar to what Jenny had described when transferring the case to Sophie: '*This isn't a difficult case, but it just doesn't seem to move. The whole thing is stuck in a loop, repeating the same cycle over and over again ...*' The difficulty is that Summer is longing to be understood rather than to understand (Steiner, 1993).

Here we can see the dynamics of projective identification where both Jenny and Sophie have identified with Summer's projection of her helplessness and, therefore, feel unable to influence the situation. In Jenny's words: '*There's not much you can do, aside from watching out for early signs and trying to intervene as soon as you feel things are heading in the wrong direction again.*'

Summer is able to describe the negative consequences of her past experiences and their detrimental effect for herself and Jack, and yet she does not seem to feel that she is able to do anything to change the situation. Therefore, Sophie needs to help Summer to feel enabled and to find the motivation to be able to turn her cognitive knowledge into action and to initiate positive change. However, motivation is closely related to the concept of self-determination and the question of locus of control.

Although motivation is often treated as a single construct, motivation is a complex multifaceted phenomenon and although our exact understanding of motivation continues to evolve (Kanfer et al, 2008), it is evident that people are motivated by a wide range of factors. Drawing on self-determination theory Ryan and Deci (2000) and Vallerand (1997) offer a nuanced discussion of motivational regulation and state that '*Motivation concerns energy, direction, persistence and equifinality – all aspects of activation and intention.*' However, for practical purposes, in this chapter we consider a simplified notion of motivation by dividing motivation into extrinsic and intrinsic. Extrinsic motivation is driven by the prospect of instrumental gains or loss (eg incentives or coercion), while intrinsic motivation is not instrumental toward other outcomes and instead is driven by the individual's values, preferences or interest, etc.

Motivation is closely related to an individual's sense of self-determination (Ryan and Deci, 2000; Vallerand, 1997) and locus of control (Rogers, 1961). Therefore, for Summer to move from cognition (ie being able to articulate her difficult experiences and their impact) to action (ie make a positive change in her life) she needs to understand and believe that she and her actions matter and that her actions/behaviour can influence and change the course and outcome of events and her life experiences. Hence, she needs to feel able and empowered to shape her own experiences. This highlights the importance of an anti-oppressive and empowering practice.

Motivational interviewing is an example of an intervention strategy that uses motivational techniques to enable and support positive change. We will explore motivational interviewing in the last chapter of the book. However, at this stage let us consider the situation from a psychodynamic and object relations perspective.

Splitting

Melanie Klein (1946, 1955) argues that the newborn infant is quite fragile and experiences a great deal of anxiety caused by the death instinct and the trauma experienced at birth as well as the infant's basic needs and experiences of hunger, frustration, pain, etc and reliance on external sources for protection and for meeting those needs. Therefore, given their fragility and vulnerability the infant experiences a paranoid state. At this stage the infant does not have a clear conception of the mother/caregiver and given their limited ability to make sense of the *world* and their experiences, the infant simply divides her/his experiences and feelings into *good* or *bad*, and uses schizoid mechanisms to split both her/his ego and the figure of the mother into separate *good* and *bad* objects.

Hence, when the infant receives *good enough care* and their needs are met in a timely and appropriate manner the infant experiences positive feelings and a sense of soothing and satisfaction and associates such good feelings with the *good* and loving mother, while when the infant's needs are not met in a timely manner the infant experiences frustration and anxiety and associates these *bad* feelings with the *bad* and hating mother. In Kleinian terms, the maternal object is divided into a *good breast* (mother that is loved and felt to be loving and gratifying) and *bad breast* (mother that is felt to be frustrating, persecutory and is hated). Both the *good* and *bad* objects are projected externally and introjected internally in cycles of re-projection and re-introjection and based on the infant's experiences of anxiety and *good* and *bad* feelings.

As the infant grows and develops physically and emotionally, they come to realise that both the *good breast* and the *bad breast* belong to the figure of the mother/caregiver. At this stage the infant begins to integrate their fragmented perceptions of the mother/caregiver and develop a more integrated sense of self. This allows the infant to have a better understanding, and a better approximation of the world and their experiences. We all may experience a paranoid-schizoid position at different stages in our lives. When we are faced with feelings, anxieties or fears that we are unable to contain and/or process, we use schizoid mechanisms to split our feelings and/or experiences into *good* and *bad* and engage in cycles of projection and introjection. This leads to *omnipotence* (whenever possible *bad* feelings and experiences are omnipotently denied) and *idealisation* (*good* feelings and experiences are exaggerated and idealised as a protection against anxieties and fears). Such splitting of one's feelings, experience, self and *reality* into *good* and *bad* is the characteristic of the paranoid-schizoid position, and leads to the so-called *black and white thinking* or *binary thinking*.

Klein explains that both constitutional factors (balance of life and death instincts) and environmental factors (love and care) affect the course of the paranoid-schizoid position, and considers this *binary splitting* as essential for the infant's healthy development. For Klein, it is through the schizoid mechanism that the infant is able to take in enough *good* to construct a central core around which they can begin to integrate the split objects. However, the infant faces a significant challenge when there is not *enough good* to construct this *central core* that allows the infant to integrate the split object, and their view of self and the world.

We will explore projective identification and the use of other defence mechanisms in the next chapter. At this time, suffice it to say that bringing together our conflicted feelings of love and hate and good and bad experiences enables us to gain a more accurate understanding and approximation of our self and the external world. However, such object integration requires the ability to contain anxiety and recognise that *good* and *bad* can reside in the same object. Indeed, Klein argues that, for children, integration of the *good breast* and *bad breast* into the single figure of the mother/caregiver leads to anguish and a sense of guilt which at times is accompanied with a desire to repair. These cycles and feelings can recur and are revisited at different stages in our lives.

Paranoid-schizoid position

Drawing on the above analysis, we can see that Summer is stuck in a paranoid-schizoid position, projecting all her *bad* feelings and anxieties onto Jeff without considering her own role in maintaining the familial dynamics and what she is projecting onto him and Jack.

Therefore, Sophie needs to offer respectful challenge to refocus Summer's attention on her agency and ability to change the course of events. This will empower Summer to find the self-confidence to initiate positive change. The continued experiences of adversity, life challenges and negative outcomes can generate feelings of hopelessness and/or helplessness, and change our world view and the way we feel about ourselves. Summer's life experiences may have made her feel that she cannot change or influence the outcome of events and her life. This leads to a feeling of despair and loss of hope, and without hope there can be no motivation for change. This feeling of lack of control over one's life and its outcomes can make us feel subjugated and subjected to change and life events. We may then begin to think of ourselves as victims of circumstances and deprived of agency. This is referred to as an external locus of control. People with internal locus of control tend to think that they can influence the course of events in their lives and this can motivate them to initiate and maintain positive change. Here I should emphasise that we need to be careful to distinguish between a narrative that reflects an external locus of control and a narrative that externalises the problem. The first one is negative while the second one can be helpful for positive change. While internalising one's locus of control is about enhanced self-esteem, confidence, positive self-concept and feelings of empowerment, internalising problems is about blame and personalising and pathologising the problem and the individual. For example, think about these three sentences: *Jenny is mentally ill* or *Jenny has mental illness* or *Jenny experiences mental health difficulties*. The first sentence assumes that people are their *illness* so Jenny is *mentally ill* and the word *mentally ill* pathologises mental health and illness. The second sentence depicts mental ill health as something people *have* and pathologises *mental illness*. The third sentence externalises the problem *mental health difficulties* as something that is *not Jenny* and not *owned by Jenny* but something external that Jenny is experiencing. Furthermore, the third sentence does not pathologise mental health or illness and instead has an emphasis on mental health (ie positive emphasis) while acknowledging the difficulties. Indeed, a central objective of this book is to provide an interdisciplinary appreciation of the multilayered and complex nature of relationships and lived experience. Hence, the learnings from this book should help us better understand rather than pathologise our own and others' interactions or challenges in everyday life and professional practice.

Demonstrating empathy and understanding for our users of services and their experiences is foundational to developing an effective relationship-based intervention. However, although such empathic acceptance of users of services is a necessary condition for good practice, it is not always sufficient to initiate positive change. Indeed, by simply accommodating Summer's experiences, Sophie may be validating Summer's lack of agency and her lack of taking ownership of her own experience.

Therefore, while appreciating the effect of social and structural constraints and inequalities and their implications for the individual's choice, Sophie should offer *respectful challenge* to enable Summer to recognise her role as an active agent who is able to influence her life events and their outcomes. This means that when Summer articulates her experiences of childhood abuse or Jeff leaving the family, Sophie should facilitate the conversation by accompanying validation with *respectful challenge*. Sophie can do this by moving from a description of the problem to exploring its effect and implications. For example, in reply to Summer, Sophie can ask: '... *that must have been very difficult for you, and how do you think that is influencing Jack?*' or she can ask Summer how she felt about her mother, and then question her about how she thinks Jack is thinking about her. These sorts of replies go beyond simple validation. They invite the person to think reflectively about themselves and their actions and emotions and how these are impacting others.

This can shift the focus of discussion and offer Summer an opportunity to think about her role in what is happening. Recognising that we are all participants and active agents in shaping our own experience is fundamental for empowering Summer to begin to reflect and consider the possibility for positive change. This can also be examined from the perspective of Eric Berne's transactional analysis and Karpman's drama triangle, which suggests that people see themselves and assume one of the three roles of victim, persecutor or rescuer. We will explore transactional analysis and the drama triangle in Chapter 6. Such an approach can help Summer re-examine and reconnect with her experience and recognise that Jeff could not be the repository of all that is bad in her life. Summer should be supported so she is able to reintegrate the split-off good and bad objects and recognise that the same object can be the source of both good and bad.

Gaining the parents' consent

CASE STUDY

How was Sophie to discuss the issue with Summer?

Sophie contacts Summer and Jeff to discuss the situation and to seek permission for accommodation under Section 20 of the Children Act 1989. Initially, Summer agrees but Jeff disagrees and states that he will only communicate with Sophie through his lawyer.

Later Jeff contacts Sophie to tell her that he agrees for Jack to go into foster care. Both parents sign consent forms and it is agreed that Jack will be placed in foster care in a week's time. This will provide Jack with time to meet the foster carer and for everyone to agree upon a routine for Jack. It is also agreed that Jack can go home on the weekends with the provision that Jeff will share this responsibility with Summer. After establishing a clear understanding with the parents and obtaining everyone's agreement, Sophie focuses on finding a suitable foster carer for Jack.

Finding a foster carer for Jack

Sophie and the placement officer find it difficult to identify a suitable foster carer who meets the full list of criteria which the parents had requested which includes being Catholic and Polish, living locally and ideally close to Jack's school.

The two incidents of playing with fire combined with Jack's special needs and some very specific requirements such as the foster carer living close to the school for the school commute make the matching process rather difficult.

There is only one foster carer, Alma, willing to provide a placement for Jack. She lives locally, is Catholic, has previously worked as a special teaching assistant for children with special needs and comes from India. She is a warm woman with a kind and gentle manner about her. A lengthy discussion ensues about the cultural and ethnic difference; however, it is agreed that she would be the best person for Jack, and it is noted that her knowledge, skill set and experience with children with special needs can be particularly helpful in this case.

Speaking with Summer and Jeff about Jack being placed with Alma

Summer and Jeff are hesitant and Jeff is derogatory towards Alma. However, eventually they agree to meet Alma before they decide.

The meeting is arranged for the following day at Sophie's office. Summer and Jack arrive, Jack is fiddling with his shoes, first pulling up his socks and then redoing his shoe laces. Summer encourages him to come into the room; however, she seems anxious and in a high state of alert. She scans the room and sits down next to Sophie and starts talking non-stop first about the weather, then the chair and her cab ride over to the office.

Sophie takes a back seat to give Summer and Alma space to talk and to get to know each other. Alma is very reassuring towards Summer and tells her not to worry and talks about some of the schools she has worked with and her interest in education. This reassures Summer. Alma likens the situation to a special residential school except tailor-made for Jack. Summer confirms that she is in agreement with the placement. Although Jeff does not attend the meeting, he later phones Sophie to confirm that he is in agreement for Alma to be Jack's foster carer.

Reflection

1. *What are your views with regards to interracial and/or intercultural placements and adoptions?*

2. *What is your understanding of diversity, race, ethnicity and culture and their place and importance in practice?*

3. *Reflect on a situation when you were involved in, observed or experienced discrimination in practice? What were the dynamics of the situation? And what have you learnt from that experience?*

Discussion

Due to Alma's cultural identity, Summer and Jeff were hesitant about her ability to care for Jack, and Jeff was even derogatory when speaking about her. Therefore, let us briefly examine the question of belonging, race, ethnicity and cultural diversity.

'The sense of continuity in individual and collective narratives is an important element for anchoring of identities and cultures' (Buzzi and Megele, 2011a, p 234). In fact, Derrida argues that an unbroken narrative of identity offers *'a reassuring certitude … and on the basis of this certitude anxiety can be mastered'* (1978, p 279). Therefore, for children, identity and belonging are about developing a positive sense of self and who they are, and feelings of being valued, loved and cared for as part of their family and community.

Broken narratives, such as those of refugees, adoptees, migrants and diasporic populations, create dissonance and incertitude and, therefore, generate tension and anxiety (Buzzi and Megele, 2011a). Transracial adoption expert Joseph Crumbley (1999) states that all foster children wonder and worry about *'Will I be accepted in this home, even if I am from a different family?'* and interracial adoptions pose an added challenge of ensuring continuity of the child's cultural identity and its development.

However,

> *narratives, and dynamics of identity, belonging, authenticity and legitimacy of race, ethnicity, gender, blood, and culture escape simplistic categorizations or fixed legislative responses, nor are they appropriately addressed by discourses and dichotomies of (post)colonization vis-à-vis benevolence/humanitarianisms.*
>
> (Buzzi and Megele, 2011a, p 238)

As social work practitioners, we should adopt an anti-discriminatory and anti-oppressive stance, and this means that it is not sufficient to be non-discriminatory; instead professionals and organisations have the added obligation to be proactively anti-discriminatory. This means taking a positive and proactive stance against all kinds of discrimination. Indeed, professionals and organisations are held accountable not only for their acts of commission but also for their acts of omission and this requires proactively challenging discrimination and oppression.

Given the importance of an anti-discriminatory, anti-oppressive and empowering practice in social work, let us briefly examine the meaning of race and ethnicity.

Race can be considered both a biological/genetic as well as a social construct maintained through social processes. Race can refer to people with distinct groups of common geneti-cally inherited physical characteristics, associated mainly with appearance. Ethnicity, on the other hand, is a broader concept which identifies a group of shared characteristics or factors (eg race, religion, language or culture).

Geertz (1993) defines culture as a *'historically transmitted pattern of meanings embodied in symbols, a system of inherited conceptions expressed in symbolic forms by means of which men communicate, perpetuate, and develop their knowledge about and their atti-tudes toward life'* (p 89). Therefore, culture can be considered as *webs of significance* spun between people through their actions and interactions. Through this dynamic, identities, actions, practices, communities, subjects and objects become cultural through more or less structured webs of significance and this is the foundation of subjective understanding and cultural identity (Buzzi and Megele, 2011a).

People shape their cultures and are also shaped by them or as Geertz (1993[1973], p 5), drawing on Weber, suggests *'man is an animal suspended in webs of significance he himself has spun'*. Therefore, culture defines and structures language and people's expressions. Indeed, given the close link between culture and language and between language and think-ing, Hofstede (1980) defines culture as *'the collective programming of the mind which dis-tinguishes the members of one human group from another'* (p 25).

The existence and influence of race is a reflection of our capacity to form communities and to be shaped by them (Markus and Hamedani, 2007). However, it is also an indication of our desire to categorise and classify and to seek affinity based on actual or perceived similarities. Such actual or perceived similarities and differences lead to power differences. Indeed, from ancient history to recent news headlines, race and ethnicity have been used to divide and rally one group against another and to subjugate, and even dehumanise others. Therefore, whether it is possible to create and observe difference among individuals or groups without establishing a hierarchy remains a contested question (Sidanius and Pratto, 1999).

People often speak of race and ethnicity as if these were a characteristic, trait or property that people possess, and then use these *characteristics*, *traits* and *properties/attributes* to categorise people into groups. This social construction of race and ethnicity involve social processes that include both in-group and inter-group relations and are essential components of individual identity. Goffmann (1959) argues that the *self* is not a fixed entity *owned* by social actors; it is rather dynamically and collaboratively (re)enacted, (re)constituted and (re) performed in social actions and interactions, and as such remains a fluid and ever-evolving phenomenon (Buzzi and Megele, 2011b). This is in line with Tajfel's (1981) social identity theory suggesting that the social groups to which we belong help define who we are and thus constitute an essential part of our identity.

One fundamental assumption of social identity theory is that people strive to maintain or increase their self-esteem. However, self-esteem does not depend only on individual attributes, but also on the attributes of the groups with which we may identify. Therefore, discrimination and stigma can have detrimental effects on self-esteem, identity, thinking, behaviour and performance.

The way we think and act about social identities depends on how we make sense of and reconcile/integrate our commitments to different groups within a given context. From this perspective racial and ethnic identities are only one component/dimension/type of social identity among other psychologically equivalent ones (eg gender). Nonetheless, racial and ethnic identities are the '*single component [that] is consistently positively related to an individual's self esteem*' (Umana-Taylor, 2004, p 139).

Jeff's derogatory remark about Alma presents an ethically complex and professionally challenging situation, where from an anti-discriminatory stance Sophie needs to challenge Jeff's remark while she is also aiming to work collaboratively with Jeff and Summer to secure the best interests of Jack. Sophie's good practice is evidenced in her ability to challenge Jeff and navigate this difficult situation to eventually obtain everyone's understanding and collaboration to place Jack with Alma. We will elaborate on this in the section that follows.

Preparing for transition

CASE STUDY

Preparation for a child to be looked after begins the moment a social worker is aware that the child will be looked after; this planning and preparation contributes greatly to making the placement positive.

During the pre-placement planning meeting, Jack's routine is discussed, as are his favourite toys and food and what he should bring with him to the placement. Contact with Summer is discussed and it is agreed that he will see Summer on the weekends and stay overnight on Fridays and Saturdays. Jack will phone Summer every evening at 7pm to say goodnight.

Sophie is under a lot of pressure to complete all the required paperwork before the placement starts.

On the agreed first day of the placement, Sophie helps Summer to take Jack to Alma's. Both Summer and Jack look worried; however, Summer tries her best to reassure Jack. As part of the planning for the placement it was agreed that Jack will talk to Summer every evening at 7pm, and Summer uses this to reassure him that she will only be a phone call away.

Sophie visits Jack twice during his first week in placement and during the first week the IRO (Independent Reviewing Officer) convenes the first placement meeting.

Learning life skills, new friendships and attachment bonds

Jack starts to settle into the placement and starts building a relationship with Alma. The evening calls to Summer were often difficult and problematic. Jack would phone

Summer at 7pm and there would be no answer. Summer would return Jack's phone call much later than 7pm and then insist on speaking with him. Jack would come to the phone and Summer would start talking non-stop, not allowing Jack to get a word in edgeways, about her day and this really frustrated Jack as he wanted to share his stories with Summer. This would result in a shouting match and both would hang up frustrated and angry.

Alma noticed that Jack also had a tendency to talk non-stop and would often become fixated on this. Alma managed this by listening to Jack and allowing him to speak without interruption. If someone else tried to interrupt or talk she would say '*but Jack is talking*'. When others were talking and Jack wanted to interrupt she would ask Jack to wait until the person finished.

Jack started to listen curiously to Alma's conversations with her mother, and although they spoke a different language to each other, there was a phrase that Alma would always say in English: '*Goodnight Mummy, I love you*'. Jack asked Alma why every time she had to tell her mother that she loved her? Alma thought about the best way to explain it to Jack, and said: '*Because I love her, and if you love someone you should let them know.*'

After a while, the phone calls between Jack and Summer stopped ending in screaming matches. Alma noticed that Jack would allow Summer to talk non-stop and sometimes Summer remembered to ask Jack about his day and sometimes she didn't, but their conversations no longer ended in a screaming match.

Alma: *The conversations you have with your mummy have changed.*

Jack: *Yes.*

Alma: *You are listening to your mummy more.*

Jack: *Yes, because you taught me how to listen.*

Jack also started to call Summer mummy and at the end of their phone calls started to say: '*Good night Mummy, I love you*'.

Reflection

1. *Jack's placement seems to have had a very positive effect on his behaviour and emotional development. What are some of the dynamics and drivers of this positive change?*

2. *Transitions require careful planning and support. Can you think of a time when you planned or experienced a transition? What were the circumstances? And what support was in place or needed for that transition?*

3. *What are some of the transitions you have experienced in your personal or professional life? And what support did you need for those transitions?*

Discussion

Our narratives of identity are rooted in time and place and, therefore, changes such as a placement, adoption, transfer to a new home, etc can be a difficult moment for the individual as they affect our life narrative and sense of belonging and identity. This highlights the importance of careful planning and of the period of support and transition. Indeed, the positive outcomes of Jack's placement are partly due to Sophie's planning to ensure a smooth transition for Jack.

Social work and social workers do not receive much appreciation for their delicate, challenging and critically important role in society, and often it is when things go wrong that social work is paraded online and in the media, and becomes the subject of public scrutiny without a real understanding of the dynamics of the case. However, Jack's narrative highlights how placement of children when appropriately planned can offer them the possibility to find healing and flourish.

From the perspective of attachment theory, children's positive relationships with their primary caregiver(s) with *good enough care* enable them to develop self-regulation skills (Ainsworth et al, 1978; Main and Solomon, 1990) that are lacking in children with ADHD. Furthermore, low emotional regulation skills can influence children's ability to develop appropriate attention processes and behavioural inhibition which can then lead to hyperactivity and attention deficit (Franc et al, 2009).

Attachment patterns and ADHD have been linked to children's temperament, and difficult temperament presents a risk factor for ADHD and for the development of an insecure attachment (eg, Franc et al, 2009; Howe, 2006, 2011). Children with ADHD need a balanced, proactive and emotionally containing optimal parenting style that can allow the child to establish secure attachment bonds and develop emotional- and self-regulation. Parents who try to manage their children's behaviours by adopting intrusive control or permissive parenting styles may actually contribute to consolidating their children's difficulties and insecure attachment patterns (Finzi-Dottan et al, 2006).

Hence, Alma's experience and capabilities have been a crucial factor in Jack's positive behavioural change and emotional containment. Indeed, Alma's sensitivity and ability are evident from the first encounter with Jack and Summer when she *likens the situation to a special residential school except tailor-made for Jack*. Such an analogy recognises the bond between Jack and Summer and allows them to maintain and develop their *potential space* as discussed in the previous chapter. It is respect for this *potential space* that mitigates Jack's and Summer's anxieties as they recognise that they are accepted and their bonds respected, giving them the *potential space* to *be*. This is complemented by Alma's caring, clear and consistent routines that foster a sense of clarity and stability (Baumrind, 1971). Research suggests that when parents of children with anxiety difficulties have the ability to anchor themselves and their children, safeguarding daily routines and family structure from the child's anxious demands, it has a positive effect in reducing and managing the child's distress and the symptoms of anxiety (Lebowitz and Omer, 2013).

Jack's experience of Alma's flexibility, emotional containment, availability, responsiveness, consistency and sensitivity to his full range of emotions enabled him to begin to develop a more secured attachment bond.

This example highlights the importance of positive role models for children's development. Jack quickly mirrored Alma's conversations with her mother by starting to tell his own mother '*Goodnight Mummy, I love you*'. This was not only pleasant for Summer, it was also important for Jack's own psyche. After all, what we say and do about others says much more about our self than the other.

Baumrind (1966) conceptualised parenting on a continuum defined by *responsiveness* versus *demandingness*. Responsiveness refers to the extent to which parents foster the child's individuality and self-assertion by being attuned, supportive and sensitive to the child's needs, while demandingness refers to the extent to which parents demand their children's behavioural regulation through discipline and supervision with the objective of becoming integrated in society through social conformity.

The conversation between Jack and Alma highlights the importance of positive role modelling and the significance of listening, containment and potential space:

> Alma: *The conversations you have with your mummy have changed.*

> Jack: *Yes.*

> Alma: *You are listening to your mummy more.*

> Jack: *Yes, because you taught me how to listen.*

Children's experiences enable them to make sense of their world and to learn and develop. It is only by listening to children that they can learn to listen. Indeed, we need to find the space within/internally before we can share it without/externally. We will revisit this concept in later chapters.

No longer going home for the weekend

CASE STUDY

Time was going by very quickly and Jack had been on placement for four months when Sophie contacted Alma to ask whether Jack could stay with her for the weekend instead of going home to Summer. She briefly explained to Alma that Summer had just informed her that she was going away with her new boyfriend and wanted Alma to have Jack for the weekend also. Jeff too was unable to have Jack as he had also planned a trip away.

Alma: *I don't have any problem with it and I like having Jack. The only problem is that Jack is going to ask for his mummy and then I don't know what to tell him. I treat Jack like he is my own ... he knows I love him and he is always welcome ... Whatever you think is best. I just want him to know he has a home here. He has been talking about Summer and what they have planned for this weekend ... he will be disappointed.*

Sophie: *I know, it is very difficult, but your help will be really crucial.*

Alma: *I am really sorry about this situation. I wish somehow things were different for him. He is such a bright boy.*

Sophie: *Alma, this is Summer's decision. I wish it was different and I have spoken to her about how unhappy Jack will be, however, she is really clear that there isn't enough space for Jack this weekend.*

Alma: *I know but it seems like she is a child herself in so many ways. I feel like she needs a mother also.*

Alma asked whether she should cut the picnic with the children short so that they could be home for Sophie to talk with Jack.

Sophie: *No, enjoy the picnic and let the children have a good time. I will come out as soon as I can. I have a meeting and a home visit so I will be there straight after.*

Reflection

1. *Jack will clearly be very disappointed to hear that he cannot go home. If you were Jack's social worker, how would you communicate this message to him?*

2. *Have you been in a similar situation? What did you do? Is there anything that Sophie can do to minimise the disappointment for Jack?*

3. *How do you think this may affect Jack? And is there a risk that this news may jeopardise the positive achievements so far?*

Discussion

According to Hardy (2002), '*The most egregious form of rejection that anyone can ever experience is parental rejection.*' Whether real or imagined, parental rejection can lead children to evaluate themselves and their future negatively, and can have important developmental, emotional and behavioural consequences. Indeed, the ways parents respond to their children's emotional experiences is associated with youth emotion regulation competencies (Eisenberg et al, 1998; Sheffield Morris et al, 2007).

Summer doesn't seem to have the awareness or capacity to consider Jack's feelings and developmental needs, and this may lead to feelings of rejection and even greater pain and difficulties for Jack. Consequently this can precipitate the situation and damage all that has been achieved by Jack and Alma.

Children have limited ability to separate their view of themselves from their negative view of their rejecting parents, which they still see as part of themselves (Hamilton, 1989). Indeed, given their limited ability to see beyond their role in their relationships, when experiencing parental/caregiver rejection children can only blame themselves and assume that somehow they are *bad* and *unworthy* of their parents'/caregiver's acceptance, love and care, leading to intense feelings of guilt and shame (Thomas, 1999). Such feelings of guilt and shame have long-term effects on children's development, identity, emotional capacity, relationships, self-esteem and confidence.

Therefore, children who experience parental/caregiver rejection, neglect, abuse, trauma or other harm may direct their negative feelings toward the self or externally, resulting in internalising behaviour, when they direct their negative and challenging reaction toward the self, or externalising behaviour, when they turn their negative and challenging reaction toward others. In essence, people with internalising or externalising behaviours have difficulty coping with stressful situations and negative/dysphoric emotions, therefore, they direct their feelings and actions/reactions either inward or outward. For example, a person who has suffered sexual abuse may isolate themselves from groups or may experience feelings of guilt or fear, may have nightmares and changes in sleeping patterns, or may experience negative self-talk and changes in behaviour, depression or other psychosomatic reactions such as headaches, stomach ache, nervousness, physical pains or other medical conditions. Externalising behaviour includes physical aggression, destruction of property, substance misuse (eg excessive drinking, addiction, etc), or other behaviour such as gambling, running away, etc. Whereas externalising behaviour is observable (eg you can easily notice when someone is speaking aggressively to another person) internalising behaviour may be more difficult to identify (eg you can't hear someone's negative self-talk). Furthermore, some children may show both internalising and externalising behaviour. These children are at higher risk of negative outcomes such as experiencing mental health difficulties.

Jack has exhibited externalising behaviour such as aggressive behaviour toward his peers, playing with fire, lack of emotional and behavioural regulation, etc, as well as internalising behaviour such as experiencing a great deal of anxiety, guilt and fear, nervousness, psychosomatic pain, etc. He is, therefore, at a high risk of experiencing further negative outcomes.

This is clearly a difficult situation where Jack is looking forward to the weekend with his mother and the change in plans may register as a further rejection. Therefore, Sophie needs to have one of those difficult conversations with Jack, and needs to draw on her best communicative (Buzzi and Megele, 2012), relationship-based and emotional knowledge and capabilities. Difficult conversations such as this are about connecting on an emotional level to hold and contain others (Jack) while wrapping words around painful feelings to communication a difficult message.

The beginning of a new dynamic

CASE STUDY

Sophie got out of her car and walked toward the park. She thought about how easy it was to spot Jack – he was always the most animated and lively person in a group and of course today was no different. He was making animated gestures and his dark hair glistened in the sun. As Sophie walked down Alma and the children saw her and everyone welcomed her warmly. *Come and eat some fruit with us.* Sophie sat down and they all chatted about their day. Jack spoke about how he sung in the choir and that he pushed Sabine on the swings and she started to scream because it was too high. Sabine pretended to box Jack and they both started to laugh.

Jack: *I wasn't expecting to see you today, cause I'm going home today.*

Sophie: *Well, I always like coming out to see you. Plus, I have been asked by mummy to come out and see you today to make sure you are ok and having a good time. Mummy also asked me to come out and talk to you today about this weekend.*

Jack: *What about this weekend?*

Sophie: *There is a change of plans for this weekend and you will stay with Alma. Mummy needs a rest this weekend.*

Jack's body seemed to freeze and his eyes darted from one side to the other.

Jack: *She has had a break the whole week … she promised I could come home on the weekends.*

Sophie: *She wants to see you but she feels very tired and needs a break.*

Jack: *It's just two days. She has a break the whole week.*

Sophie: *I am sorry. But the next weekend will come around very quickly again.*

Jack: *What about Jeff, can't he take me?*

Sophie: *I am sorry Jack, he is out of the country. I tried him on his mobile and also sent him an email … Are you unhappy with Alma? Has something happened? Alma is happy to have you for the weekend.*

Jack: *No and that's not the point. They are my parents and should be looking after me.*

Jack was confused, panicked and angry and although Sophie could understand Jack's frustration she did not fully understand the underlying dynamics and its profound and powerful significance for Jack. However, from that point the course of events took a much more difficult turn.

Jack felt he was losing his family, his identify and his sense of belonging. Alma was kind and loving; however, Alma was not his mother. Sophie recalled that in one of her conversations with Jack, he had told her that he wished things could be different, that Alma could be his mother. He wished that they were the same skin colour so people would confuse her with his mother. Sophie thought about Jack's feelings and his experience of parental neglect. Jack felt scared and alone. He felt abandoned, and they reached home, he went to his room without saying another word. He refused to allow Sophie or Alma to enter his room as he sank in his sorrow, but was not sure how to talk about his fear and pain and the difficult feelings inside.

During the seventh month of placement Summer began finding it difficult to keep up with the arrangements of picking Jack up on Fridays and returning him to Alma on Sundays. This resulted in new arrangements being put in place: Jack went home on Saturday mornings and returned to Alma's on Sunday evenings. However, this arrangement did not work well as Jack and Alma would spend most Saturdays waiting for Summer to arrive.

The change in weekend home visits coincided with Jack displaying regressive behaviour. Jack stopped cleaning up after himself. He would use the toilet and not flush, he refused to have a shower and displayed a very negative attitude towards everything.

Sophie made an unannounced visit to Summer's home and the home environment had deteriorated significantly.

By the ninth month, Summer's difficulty with timekeeping and failure to pick Jack up on agreed dates and times combined with the deterioration of the home environment resulted in Jack's weekend visits being changed to twice-monthly supervised home visits.

The sharp contrast between the two home environments was causing tension and conflict between mother and son, as Summer came to Sophie's office complaining that Jack thought she was a bad mother as everything was about Alma.

Summer: *It's all about her [Alma] … all I hear is Alma this and Alma that from Jack. Alma's house is clean, Alma gives me fruit for dessert, Alma takes me to choir practice, Alma bought me shoes, Alma takes me swimming. Well you know what, if I had the kind of money Alma gets for looking after Jack I would be doing all of these things for Jack also.*

Sophie felt upset about Summer's reaction and wanted to tell Summer *'No, it's not about Alma. It's not about you or me … It's all about Jack.'* But she reflected in action and answered: *'No, I understand this is a difficult moment for you. But, it is really about Jack.'*

Reflection

1. *Was it the event of a single weekend that turned the cycle of positive change into a negative one?*

2. *What are your reflections and analysis of the conversation between Sophie and Jack as well as the overall narrative? What can we learn from this?*

3. *Read the last paragraph about Sophie feeling upset about Summer's reaction. Have you been in a similar situation? How did you react? What was your reflection in action? And what have you learnt from that experience?*

Discussion

Looking at the above narrative it seems that the weekend when Summer went away and Jack stayed with Alma was a turning point in Jack and Summer's lives. Was this an over-reaction on the part of Jack? What were some of the underlying dynamics that influenced Jack and why was there such a significant turn of events?

Summer's unresolved childhood trauma and subsequent life experiences have conditioned her relationship with Jeff, her mothering with Jack and present life circumstances.

Summer's life may seem a continuous repetition of incomplete narratives and unsuccessful attempts at achieving positive change. However, notwithstanding her agency, this may be attributable to her childhood experiences of abuse and trauma. Indeed, her continued focus on her past traumatic experiences is an indication of her unresolved trauma and represents her attempts at resolving traumatic memories. In everyday life we reconcile our new experiences and information with the meaning and significance of our past experiences and life story so that they weave into our life narrative and become part of our self-concept and system of meanings. However, the experiences of trauma disrupt this process and each attempt at reconciling *what is* with *what was* gratifying may produce various responses and emotional states including fear, anxiety, rage, panic or guilt, etc. In case of traumatic experiences such responses may exceed the individual's capability for their processing and may overwhelm the person's state of mind. Therefore, the individual may resort to various control or defence mechanisms to modify their cognitive processes in order to avoid entering into such states of mind (Horowitz et al, 1979). We will discuss the dynamics of trauma and its impact in greater detail in Chapter 5. However, Summer's focus on self and inability to meet Jack's needs can be attributed to her unresolved trauma and her past experiences of abuse. This is not to justify Summer's actions or reactions, it is just to offer an added perspective and greater understanding of the psychosocial and relationship-based dynamics that influence those actions and reactions.

Therefore, although the weekend when Summer went away without Jack may have marked a clear turning point for Jack, to attribute the course of subsequent events to that single weekend is to miss the point. Jack has suffered years of parental neglect which led to him developing an avoidant attachment and his experience of ADHD (Finzi-Dottan et al, 2006). This is in contrast to Alma's sensitivity to Jack's emotional needs, and her thoughtful approach and responsive care that helped Jack begin to form more secure attachment bonds. This was evidenced in marked improvements in his behaviour and well-being and had an overall positive effect even on Summer. Alma's likening '*... the situation to a special residential school except tailor-made for Jack*' demonstrates her sensitivity and understanding of the challenges involved. Alma's analogy enabled a continuity of mother-and-son narrative between Summer and Jack, and mitigated Jack's fears of losing his mother. However, Summer's trip resulting in Jack not being able to see either of his parents during that weekend reawakened his worst fears of losing them and of losing his identity:

> *Jack felt he was losing his family, his identity and his sense of belonging. Alma was kind and loving, however, Alma was not his mother. He wished things could be different, that Alma could be his mother, that they were the same skin colour so people would confuse this woman who cared about him for his mother instead of the woman who didn't seem to care about him.*

However, things were as they were, and Jack felt rejected and abandoned. This was a reaffirmation of the fragility of his *dream* and a reminder of his *disposability* as he insisted:

> *Jack:* 'She has had a break the whole week ... she promised I could come home on the weekends', *and again:* 'It's just two days, she has a break the whole week.' *Jack goes on hoping Jeff can be there for him:* 'What about Jeff, can't he take me?'

> *However, any dim hope is completely extinguished:* 'I am sorry Jack, he is out of the country. I tried him on his mobile and also sent him an email …'

Sophie attempts to capitalise on Jack's bond with Alma and to refocus his attention to his positive relationship with her: '*Are you unhappy with Alma? Has something happened? Alma is happy to have you for the weekend.*'

Jack's response to Sophie's attempt is as simple as it is powerful, and reflects parental neglect and his feelings of rejection: '*No, and that's not the point. They are my parents and should be looking after me.*'

Jack's reply highlights the main issue which is Jack's parents' inability to care for him. Indeed, even when things were going well Summer had little space for Jack's needs although because of his relationship with Alma Jack was calm and more secured:

> *Alma noticed that Jack would allow Summer to talk non-stop and sometimes Summer remembered to ask Jack about his day and sometimes she didn't, but their conversations no longer ended in a screaming match.*

Here is an example of parents with low self-efficacy (self-efficacy is the extent to which one believes they are able to complete a task or to achieve a goal), while research (Jones and Prinz, 2005) suggests a strong link between parental self-efficacy and parenting competence, even when faced with challenging child behaviour.

We saw positive change and marked improvement in Jack's behaviour, emotional capacity and other developmental areas for as long as everyone did their part. We also noticed how at times one member of the family can upset the family equilibrium, and how such loss of equilibrium can lead to a negative cycle of events and outcomes. This highlights the systemic nature of many familial challenges. We will examine family and systemic approaches in Chapter 7.

When unable to deal with fear, anxiety or stress, we may resort to using defence mechanisms to protect ourselves. Although such strategies may provide a temporary respite, they tend to mask deeper challenges and can become an obstacle to sustained positive change and healthy growth. Therefore, in the next chapter we'll explore psychological defence mechanisms followed by a discussion of cognitive schema, stereotypes and cognitive bias as well as transference and countertransference, to conclude with the question of identity and belonging.

In the next chapters we will further explore the above dynamics and related concepts. We will also draw on a number of behavioural, systemic, psychodynamic, narrative and other approaches and discuss different psychosocial and relationship-based intervention skills and strategies.

References

Ainsworth, M D, Blehar, M C, Waters, E and Wall, S (1978) *Patterns of Attachment: A Psychological Study of the Strange Situation*. Hillsdale, NJ: Laurence Erlbaum.

Baumrind, D (1966) Effects of Authoritative Parental Control on Child Behavior. *Child Development*, 37: 887–907.

Baumrind, D (1971) Current Patterns of Parental Authority. *Developmental Psychology Monographs*, 4 (1, Pt 2): 1–103.

Buzzi, P. and Megele, C (2011a) Cyber-Communities and Motherhood Online – A Reflection on Transnational Adoption, in Moravec, M (ed) *Motherhood Online*. UK: Cambridge Scholars Publishing.

Buzzi, P and Megele, C (2011b) Reflections on the 21st Century Migrant: Impact of Social Networking and Hyper-reality on the Lived Experience of Global Migration, in German, M and Banerjee, P (eds) *Migration, Technology and Transculturation: A Global Perspective*. Centre for International and Global Studies, St Charles, MO: Lindenwood University Press.

Buzzi, P and Megele, C (2012) Honne and Tatemae: A World Dominated by a 'Game of Masks', in Christopher, E (ed) *Communication Across Cultures*. UK: Palgrave Macmillan.

Crumbley, J (1999) *Transracial Adoption and Foster Care: Practice Issues for Professionals*. [online] Available at: http://www.ifapa.org/pdf_docs/TransracialParenting.pdf (accessed 17 December 2014).

Derrida, J (1978) *Writing and Difference*. Chicago: University of Chicago Press.

Eisenberg, N, Fabes, R A, Shepard, S A, Murphy, B C, Jones, J and Guthrie, J K (1998) Contemporaneous and Longitudinal Prediction of Children's Social Functioning from Regulation and Emotionality. *Developmental Psychology* 34: 910–24.

Finzi-Dottan, R, Manor, I and Tyano, S (2006) ADHD, Temperament, and Parental Style as Predictors of the Child's Attachment Patterns. *Child Psychiatry and Human Development*, 37: 103–14.

Franc, N, Maury, M and Purper-Ouakil, D (2009) ADHD and Attachment Processes: Are They Related? *Encephale-revue de psychiatrie clinique biologique et therapeutique*, 35(3): 256–61.

Geertz, C (1993[1973]) *The Interpretation of Cultures: Selected Essays*. London: Fontana Press.

Goffman, E (1959) *The Presentation of Self in Everyday Life*. New York: Doubleday.

Hamilton, G N (1989) A Critical Review of Object Relations Theory. *American Journal of Psychiatry*, 146: 1552–60.

Hardy, K (2002) Parental Favoritism. [online] Available at: http://abcnews.go.com/sections/2020/DailyNews/2020_favoritism_020503.html (accessed 12 July 2014).

Hofstede, G (1980) *Culture's Consequences: International Differences in Work Related Values*. Newbury Park, CA: Sage Publications.

Horowitz, M, Wilner, N and Alvarez, W (1979) Impact of Event Scale: A Measure of Subjective Stress. *Psychosomatic Medicine*, 41(3): 209–18.

Howe, D (2006) Disabled Children, Parent–Child Interaction and Attachment. *Child and Family Social Work*, 11: 95–106.

Howe, D (2011) *Attachment Across the Lifecourse: A Brief Introduction*. UK: Palgrave Macmillan.

Jones, T L and Prinz, R J (2005) Potential Roles of Parental Self-efficacy in Parent and Child Adjustment: A Review. *Clinical Psychology Review*, 25(3): 341–63.

Kanfer, R, Chen, G and Pritchard, R D (eds) (2008) *Work Motivation: Past, Present, and Future*. New York: Taylor & Francis Group.

Klein, M (1946) Notes on Some Schizoid Mechanisms. *International Journal of Psycho-Analysis*, 33: 433–438.

Klein, M (1955) On Identification, in Klein, M, Heimann, P and Money-Kyrle, R E (eds) *New Directions in Psycho-analysis*. London: Tavistock.

Klein, M (1975) *Envy and Gratitude and Other Works 1946–1963*. London: Virago Press.

Koerner, K and Linehan, M (2000) Research in Dialectical Behavioral Therapy for Patients with Borderline Personality Disorder. *Psychiatric Clinics in North America*, 23: 151–67.

Lebowitz, E and Omer, H (2013) *Treating Child and Adolescent Anxiety*. Hoboken, NJ: John Wiley & Sons.

Linehan, M M (1993) *Cognitive Behavioral Treatment of Borderline Personality Disorder*. New York: Guilford Press.

Main, M and Solomon, J (1990) Procedures for Identifying Infants as Disorganised/ Disorientated During the Ainsworth Strange Situation, in Greenberg, M T, Cicchetti, D and Cummings, E M (eds) *Attachment in the Pre-school Years: Theory, Research and Intervention* (pp 121–60). Chicago: University of Chicago Press.

Markus, H R and Hamedani, M G (2007) Sociocultural Psychology: The Dynamic Interdependence Among Self Systems and Social Systems, in Kitayama, S and Cohen, D (eds) *Handbook of Cultural Psychology*. New York: Guilford Press.

Morrison, T (1997) Emotionally Competent Child Protection Organizations: Fallacy, Fiction or Necessity?, in Bates, J, Pugh, R and Thompson, N (eds) *Protecting Children: Challenge and Change*. Aldershot: Arena.

Morrison, T (2005) Chapter 2: Supervision and Outcomes in a Turbulent World, in *Staff Supervision in Social Care: Making a Real Difference for Staff and Service Users*. London: Pavilion.

Munro, E (1999a) Common Errors of Reasoning in Child Protection Work. *Child Abuse and Neglect*, 23(23): 745–58.

Munro, E (1999b) Protecting Children in an Anxious Society. *Health, Risk and Society*, 1(1): 117–27.

Munro, E (2004) A Simpler Way to Understand the Results of Risk Assessment Instruments. *Child and Youth Services Review*, 26(9): 873–83.

Munro, E (2005) A Systems Approach to Investigating Child Abuse Deaths. *British Journal of Social Work*, 35(4): 531–46.

Rogers, C R (1961) *On Becoming a Person: A Therapist's View of Psychotherapy*. Boston, MA: Houghton Mifflin.

Ryan, R M and Deci, E L (2000) Self-determination Theory and the Facilitation of Intrinsic Motivation, Social Development, and Well-being. *American Psychologist*, 55: 68–78.

Sheffield Morris, A, Silk, J S, Steinberg, L, Myers, S S and Robinson, L R (2007) The Role of the Family Context in the Development of Emotional Regulation. *Social Development*, 16(2): 361–88.

Sidanius, J and Pratto, F (1999) *Social Dominance: An Intergroup Theory of Social Hierarchy and Oppression*. New York: Cambridge University Press.

Steiner, J (1993) *Psychic Retreats*. London: Routledge.

Tajfel, H (1981) *Human Groups and Social Categories*. Cambridge: Cambridge University Press.

Thomas, H E (1999) *The Shame Response to Rejection*. Sewickley, PA: Abnel.

Umana-Taylor, A (2004) Ethnic Identity and Self-esteem: Examining the Role of Social Context. *Journal of Adolescence*, 27: 139–46.

Vallerand, R J (1997) Toward a Hierarchical Model of Intrinsic and Extrinsic Motivation, in Zanna, M P (ed) *Advances in Experimental Social Psychology* (Vol 29, pp 271–360). San Diego, CA: Academic Press.

3 Why not me?

Psychological and ego defences

Chapter summary

This chapter introduces Freud's structural model of the mind followed by the concept of ego defences and examines some examples of how they may be used in practice. Specifically, this chapter discusses: the conscious, the preconscious, the unconscious, the id, the ego, the superego, as well as psychological defences such as: suppression, repression, reaction formation, displacement, sublimation, denial, rationalisation, projection and projective identification.

The concluding section of the chapter discusses projective identification and its importance and vast application in practice.

Chapter objectives

1. Introduce the concept of ego defences.

2. Introduce some examples of ego defences in practice.

3. Discuss projection and projective identification.

4. Explore the importance and diverse applications of projective identification.

Meeting Alice

CASE STUDY

Late on Friday evening the emergency duty team at Children and Families Services receives a notification from the police informing them that they have taken Alice MacAndrew, a 14-year-old white British girl, into police protection and that she needs accommodation for the weekend. The emergency duty team arranges for Alice to be placed in foster care for the weekend.

The police report faxed to the children and families' team outlines the events briefly as follows:

Alice returned home on Friday evening to find the lock of the front door smashed, blood on the door and the flat empty. Alice attempted to reach her mother by calling her mobile phone, however, it went straight to voicemail. Alice informs the police that her mother has a history of mental health difficulties. The police, concerned for her welfare, placed Alice in police protection.

Previous police notifications:

- Verbal disturbance reported at home. No arrests made as father agrees to leave.

- Verbal disturbance reported at home. No arrest made as father agrees to leave.

- A year ago Ms MacAndrews reports Alice missing. Alice returns home after the intervention of Children and Families Services. NFA (No Further Action).

On Monday morning the duty team picks up the information and during the duty team meeting this case is allocated to a duty social worker (Jacklyn Robertson). Shortly thereafter at 9:15 the social worker receives a message from reception. The foster carer (Charlotte) and Alice are in reception wanting to speak with the duty social worker.

Jacklyn goes out to meet Alice and the foster carer. The reception is very busy although it is only 9:20; this is fairly typical for a Monday morning in this borough. Jacklyn looks around the reception area and notices a short middle-aged woman with curly brown hair and a young petite girl who looks about 12 years old sitting next to her. The girl's head is down and she's playing on her iPhone. Jacklyn approaches the woman and the girl and introduces herself to them. The woman gets up and shakes Jacklyn's hand. Jacklyn turns and says hello to Alice; however, Alice remains fixated on her iPhone. The foster carer turns to Alice:

'Alice stand up this is your social worker'.

Alice stands up reluctantly and says hello. Alice looks younger than 14 years old, she is very slim and her excessive use of make-up creates an almost mask-like appearance – that of a child who has raided her mother's make-up stash. Her face is caked with heavy foundation three shades darker than her natural skin tone which creates a stark colour contrast between her face and neck. Her bright red blush looks like two round balls on her face, and her false eyelashes are coated with a heavy dose of mascara. However, despite all the make-up her face looks tired and her eyes weary.

The foster carer asks the social worker:

'Will you need me for the week or she is going home?'

Jacklyn asks for the foster carer's availability. She is available for the week and is willing to take Alice if need be. The foster carer says goodbye to Alice; however, Alice barely acknowledges her as she leaves. Jacklyn takes Alice into an interview room and Alice sits down with her arms and legs folded.

Jacklyn tries to put Alice at ease by offering her something to drink and eat. Alice looks away and looks around the family room which has a lot of toys mostly for toddlers and younger children. Jacklyn starts the interview by acknowledging that the situation must be difficult for Alice ... Jacklyn asks Alice to tell her about what happened on Friday evening.

In a softly spoken voice Alice starts to explain the events that took place.

On Friday afternoon dad came over to the flat with lager saying he wanted to watch telly. His telly at his mum's had broken and he wanted to watch the football. At first mum said no. But, then he said she was a 'sorry old cow' and she never helped him none with anything. He called her a 'bitch and a cunt' and then she agreed that he could watch the football. I went to my room and I could hear him unpacking his lager and opening his first can. He seemed to be ok.. But I don't really know what was going on in there. About an hour later I heard him talking really loudly and singing along with the telly at the top of his voice. Mum was worried about the neighbours and asked him to keep his voice down. He just swore at her and said she was a useless cow. They started shouting at each other and mum told him that the neighbours would call the police if he kept on shouting. He said he will give everyone something to shout about and then I heard a crash like something was smashed. That's when I came out of my room he had taken the television and thrown it on the ground and cracked the screen. He also kicked the dining room table over and left.

Mum was crying and I told her to go to bed, she asked me to sit with her but I didn't want to. I don't like it when she gets like that. She went to bed and I went to my room. I was on the internet for a while and then I got hungry and called a mate. We met up for McDonalds and when I got home the lock was smashed and no-one was home. I did not know what to do so I called the police and they put me with Charlotte.

Jacklyn: *Have you had any communication or contact with your mother since the incident took place?*

Alice: *Yes I called her on Friday night and let her know where I was. We spoke on the phone on Saturday again.*

Jacklyn: *Has this happened before? Your mum and dad fighting like this?*

Alice (with a resigned voice): *Yeah ... kind of ... they have fights and makeup and get back together. She is always giving him second chances. I don't really care ...*

Jacklyn: *A lot has happened over the weekend – how do you feel about everything?*

Alice (with an assertive tone): *I don't want to go home I want to be placed in foster care. My mother is a 'nut case' and my dad's a drunk. I don't want to go home, there is nothing there for me. I want to go into care.*

Jacklyn: *Well we need to think things through to make sure it's the best fit for you ...*

Alice (with an angry tone): *You don't know me. You don't know anything about me. I was in care before and it was fine. I don't want to be around my dad, he is a 'dead-beat alcoholic' and my mum feels sorry for him. She always lets him in even when she promises that she won't. She is so pathetic, she is a real nut case. I don't want anything from her. I'll go anywhere ... what about my aunts? Can one of them take me? ... I don't want to go home ... if I go home, I'll run away.*

Jacklyn contacts the mother, Siobhan MacAndrews, and discusses the situation briefly and informs her that Alice is angry and upset, and that she does not want to return home. Siobhan is quiet and makes no objection when Jacklyn suggests that Alice stays with a family member until she can assess the situation and risks involved. Siobhan agrees and states that she thinks it is the most reasonable way forward. Siobhan suggests that perhaps one of her two older sisters will be able to take Alice for a few days until the situation is resolved. Before the call ends Siobhan tells Jacklyn *'Please tell Alice I love her'.*

Reflection

1. *What are some of your observations so far?*

2. *What do you think of the different individuals in this case so far? List down your observations, feelings and any reflections about the people, events or interactions so far. As we proceed these notes will be an important source of learning and reflection for yourself.*

3. *Alice speaks harshly about her parents and states that she doesn't care. What are some of your thoughts about Alice's account and description of her parents, and her relationship with them?*

Discussion

Exploring psychological and ego defences and Freud's structural model of the human psyche

In previous chapters we have used the terms consciousness and the unconscious, so let us briefly consider their meaning and significance.

From Cicero's invitation *nosce te ipsum* (*know thyself*) inscribed on the Temple of Apollo at Delphi to the present day, humans have been fascinated by, and have tried to understand, their own and others' minds, thoughts, emotions, behaviours, desires and intentions. In fact, attribution theory aims to describe how humans as *social perceivers* use information to arrive at causal explanations for events. In other words, it explores what information is gathered and how it is combined to establish a causal judgement (Fiske and Taylor, 1991).

However, about a century ago, Sigmund Freud used Joseph Breuer's ideas about the conscious, the preconscious and the unconscious to describe the state of the human mind (see Figure 3.1). Breuer is considered the grandfather of psychoanalysis and played a paternal role for Freud both in terms of theoretical foundation of psychoanalysis as well as supporting Freud financially to establish his family life. In fact, *Anna O.*, whose case study greatly influenced the development of Freud's thinking, was a patient of Breuer. It may be of interest to note that *Anna O.* was Bertha Pappenheim who became a pioneer social worker and in 1904 founded the League of Jewish Women (*Judischer Frauenbund*), a Jewish feminist movement and a modern social work organisation to help illegitimate girls and Jewish women endangered by prostitution.

The *conscious* mind or consciousness comprises our awareness (ie everything that we are aware of) in a given moment. For example, you are aware of your environment, or whether it is day or night or warm or cold, or of your breathing, or whether you are hungry or thirsty.

The *preconscious/subconscious* consists of information, thoughts and desires which are not in our conscious awareness at a particular moment, but which are accessible to us and which we can become aware of by directing our attention to them. We can think of this as information that is at the fringes or margin of our consciousness, but which is available for recall and can become conscious. For example, you can be busy in a phone conversation with a friend while walking home without losing your way. The location of your home in this case is an example of preconscious information that is available for cognitive processing but which currently lies outside your conscious awareness.

The *unconscious* consists of thoughts, desires, memories, affects and processes of the mind that are not accessible to our consciousness or to introspection. Therefore, we have no awareness of the unconscious, but it contains our instinctual desires and needs. Freud suggested that although the unconscious lies under the surface of consciousness and out of our awareness, it influences our thoughts, emotions and behaviours. For example, during our childhood we acquire countless experiences and memories that form the foundation of who we are today. However, we cannot recall most of those memories.

Therefore, the influence of unconscious and preconscious are quite significant in understanding relationships and relationship-based practice, as they are important forces (unconscious thoughts, emotions, beliefs, patterns, desires, etc) that form our subjective maps of *reality* and attribute meaning to our experiences, hence, influencing our judgement and behaviour. The unconscious may find symbolic expression in our dreams, the so-called slip of the tongue or in jokes.

The unconscious and preconscious can help us to understand where our own and others' strong emotions, thoughts or beliefs may come from. For example, they may help us to understand how experiences of neglect from one's parents can influence one's relationships or parenting skills and behaviour in the present. Furthermore, we need to explore and try to understand our own motives, and the origins of our own emotions, as we interact and react to the experiences, challenges and pains of our users of services.

Freud also presented a structural model of the human *psyche* composed of three parts – the id, the ego and the superego – and argued that mental activity, and psychological states, are the result of interaction between these parts. It is important to note that these psychic structures are theoretical constructs. In other words, the human brain is not divided into equivalent discrete areas, although there are some indications of similar processes in the brain.

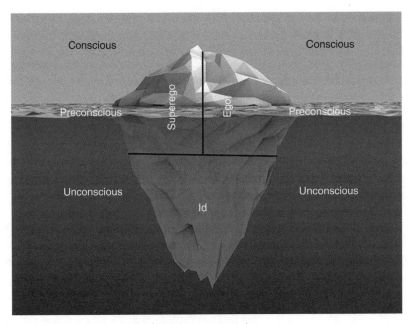

Figure 3.1 *Freud's structural model of the human psyche*

The *id* is the unorganised part of the psyche/personality that contains our basic and unrestrained drives (eg drive to reproduce or to survive), desires, emotions and feelings (eg love, hate, rage, etc). The id is self-centred and functions based on the *pleasure principle* (instinctually seeking pleasure and avoiding pain) without morality. Children are born with the id and it helps them to meet their basic biological and emotional needs.

The *ego* is the organised, thinking and deciding part of the personality/psyche and functions based on the *reality principle* (the ability to assess and act upon the *reality* of the external world). Therefore, it mediates between our internal and external *world/reality*. The ego protects itself from external threats (eg threat to survival or safety, competition, aggression, etc) while controlling the instinctual desires and drives of the id and satisfying the demands of the superego. Freud suggests that the ego often covers the unconscious desires, demands and commands of the id with its own preconscious rationalisations to hide the id's conflict with *reality*.

In contrast to id, the *superego* acts as the conscience, or morality, and reflects the internalisation of social expectations, rules, norms, cultural values and others that are mainly taught by parents, caregivers, teachers and other significant relationships in our childhood. This includes '*the internalisation of parental prohibitions and demands*' (Laplanche and Pontalis, 1973, p 436). The superego sits above the ego and performs judgemental self-observation. The superego is our exacting inner critic that punishes *misbehaviour* with feelings of shame and guilt.

Childhood experiences can result in underdevelopment or overdevelopment of one or more of these psychic structures. For example, an underdeveloped superego can lead to insensitivity toward others and unacceptable social behaviour (eg antisocial behaviour) while an overly developed superego can be too exacting and too punishing resulting in excessive prudishness or excessive guilt. A weak ego can result in a weak sense of self, low self-esteem and poor self-efficacy or poor self-control and feelings of inadequacy.

A large part of our psyche and mental activity, including most of our superego and id operate at the unconscious level, while most of the ego, but not all, operates at the conscious level.

For example, a child who experiences trauma or neglect may grow up to feel unlovable, or may find it triggering and difficult to respond to some of the needs of their own children, although they may not be able to recall the traumatic experiences in their own childhood. Or the experiences/witnessing of domestic violence in childhood may generate an unconscious fear of close relationships in adulthood.

The dynamics and the inner tensions between ego, id, superego and external *reality* generate anxiety which further threatens the ego. To mitigate these anxieties the ego uses a number of defence mechanisms to avoid the *reality* and maintain some sort of *balance* between these competing demands.

Exploring psychological and ego defences

Sigmund Freud in his psychoanalytic theory argued that defence mechanism is a tactic/strategy used by the human ego to protect itself against anxiety and is therefore meant to safeguard the mind against feelings and thoughts that are unwanted, too difficult or perceived as inappropriate, for the conscious mind.

For instance, if you are faced with a particularly unpleasant or difficult task that you find overwhelming, your mind may try to focus on other priorities or activities in order to avoid thinking about the dreaded task. There are many different defence mechanisms such as rationalisation, intellectualisation, repression, denial, dissociation, projection, projective identification, displacement, rejection, reaction formation, and more ... and we will examine some of them in this and the next chapter.

The American Psychiatric Association defines defence mechanisms as mental processes that operate unconsciously to protect individuals against anxiety or awareness of internal threats and external stressors. However, although defences operate primarily at an unconscious level, individuals may be aware of their *residuals*.

Take a few minutes and re-examine the story so far. Can you identify any defence mechanisms?

To answer that question, let us consider Alice's response to Jacklyn's question of whether Siobhan and Tim have fought before.

> *Alice (with a resigned voice):* Yeah ... kind of ... they have fights and make up and get back together. She is always giving him second chances. I don't really care ...

Alice ends her response with *I don't really care* and this may be a good example of a defence mechanism. Is this a sign of Alice being in denial of her feelings for her parents and that she actually cares how they feel and behave?

This is an example of reaction formation. *Reaction formation* is when one takes the opposite feeling because what they are actually feeling creates anxiety. Alice is using reaction formation as a defence mechanism to hide her true feelings by showing indifference and behaving in the exact opposite way. In other words, Alice could be suppressing her desire for love and care from her parents, and instead through reaction formation, acting or claiming that she does not care: '*I don't really care …*' Indeed, the word *really* may be an indication of such a defence mechanism and of Alice's effort to suppress her actual feelings.

Suppression is another defence mechanism whereby the person suppresses/pushes an unwanted, or distressful, or unacceptable feeling, thought or experience out of their conscious memory. Suppression is a conscious act of trying to forget or trying not to remember or deal with an emotion, feeling, event or experience. This is different from *repression* which is when the individual unconsciously blocks such emotions, feelings, experiences, etc, repressing them into the unconscious. For instance, sometimes as a consequence of a major trauma the person does not remember the details of the event. In such cases usually the person has unconsciously repressed the details of the traumatic event into their unconscious. Because repression is an unconscious process, the individual may not have any conscious memory of the traumatic event.

Another example of an ego defence mechanism may be Alice's response to Jacklyn in the following exchange:

JACKLYN: *Well, we need to think things through to make sure it's the best fit for you …*

ALICE (WITH AN ANGRY TONE): *You don't know me. You don't know anything about me. I was in care before and it was fine …*

Alice's angry voice could be a sign of displaced anger. *Displacement* is when we redirect or express our frustrations, feelings or impulses toward a person or object that poses no threat or is less threatening. For instance, you might displace your anger or frustration with a colleague or with your boss, by being abrupt or by getting angry with your friend, or family. In the above extract, Alice may find it easier to displace her frustration, anger or anxiety by assuming an angry tone toward Jacklyn rather than expressing the same feelings directly with her parent.

Displacement, repression, suppression and reaction formation are only a few examples of different defence mechanisms that we may encounter in everyday situations. It is important to remember that resorting to defence mechanisms may not always be a negative thing. For instance, a person experiencing anger may take up kick-boxing, and use this sport as a channel to displace and release their anger. This is an example of *sublimation* when a person acts out an unacceptable emotion or impulse by converting their reaction or behaviour into a more socially acceptable form. Freud believed that sublimation was a sign of individual maturity and allowed the individual to function in a socially acceptable manner. For instance, a married person may suppress their sexual attraction or desire toward another person, and may displace those feelings toward their partner as they may find/perceive this as a more *appropriate*, and a more socially acceptable, behaviour.

Can you give some examples of these or other defence mechanisms from your own experiences?

Can you identify any other instances of displacement, suppression, repression, sublimation or reaction formation in the above narrative or in what follows?

Meeting Alice's aunts and mum

CASE STUDY

Jacklyn contacts Siobhan's oldest sister (Kay Nicholas) and briefly outlines the situation. Kay comes across as having an authoritative tone and a *no nonsense* attitude, and states that it is simply out of the question, and that she will not be able to accommodate Alice for a few nights. Although she would like to, she does not want to have Siobhan and all of Siobhan's problems in her life and asks not to be contacted again.

Jacklyn contacts Julie Shepard who seems more open to the idea of accommodating Alice for a few days. Julie seems anxious for her sister and Alice's welfare and asks:

What is Siobhan's mental health like? Do you think these may be the first signs of a relapse? I knew this would happen. Do you know the history of the case? Do you know we have been down this road before? The last time Siobhan was admitted, we wanted Alice to stay with us and to become her guardians ... Alice was in foster care while the case was in court and then she ended up going back to her mother under a supervision order.

It was very painful for everyone and at the time these social worker said to us she believed that the judge made the wrong decision and that things would break down when Alice became a teenager ... we went through the assessments and interviews and we got our hopes up and then it all came crashing down. We have been down this road before, and it was very difficult for us, very heart-breaking for us. We made significant changes to accommodate Alice and we really wanted her to stay to have a better life. Alice needed stability, love, warmth and care.

Julie agrees to take Alice but only for four days as her oldest son is preparing for his exams. This provides Jacklyn with some time to speak with the parents and undertake initial checks and assessment of the situation.

Meeting with Siobhan MacAndrews

Siobhan opens the door and is dressed in brown corduroy trousers and a polo neck. The flat is on the third floor of a tall council block. Some youths are riding their bikes bare-chested and shouting out in the distance. Siobhan is a soft-spoken woman anxiously turning her hands around in her lap.

I miss and love Alice very much and I want the best for my daughter, I love her incredibly. I would do anything for her as she means so much to me. She is the only one I have left. I love all my babies, but she will always be my baby girl.

The incident on Friday night was an isolated incident, a one-off event. You can check the notes on your file you will see there has been no involvement for a long time.

Tim and I are no longer in a relationship, I was just helping him as a one-off favour to his mum as their television was broken. Me and Alice have been very happy together and I am sorry about Friday evening but the whole thing has been a bit of a misunderstanding.

Yes, Tim was wrong for losing his temper and he understands that. He is usually a very calm and mild-mannered person. However, when he has had a drink he becomes a different kind of person. We have had verbal incidents in the past but it has never been physical. Tim was feeling upset and frustrated on Friday as he lost his benefit entitlements, and he overacted and he is sorry for his behaviour. But he did leave when I asked him to.

The blood on the door and smashed lock was a misunderstanding. I went to bed after the incident as it left me upset and emotional. Alice was going to lie down also but when I woke up she was not in. So I rushed out to go and find her and realised that I left my key at home and had locked myself out of the house. I then broke the lock to get into the house and hurt my hand and that is how the whole incident happened.

The police rang me on Friday night to inform me of the situation, and Alice called me on Saturday. She told me she was fine and that she wanted more clothes. I would like my daughter to come home.

Jacklyn is not sure what to make of the visit.

Reflection

1. *Thinking about the earlier discussion about defence mechanisms and examining the above text, can you identity any defence mechanisms at play?*

2. *Siobhan is acknowledging the difficulties of the weekend and admits that Tim should not have been in her home. Is this good enough for Alice and her needs?*

3. *There seems to be a clear contradiction between Alice's and Siobhan's description of Tim and the situation. Why do you think the mother and daughter have such different views about Tim and the incident?*

4. *What should Jacklyn do and what do you think should be the next steps forward?*

Discussion

Exploring psychological and ego defences

Siobhan describes Tim as '... *a very calm and mild-mannered person*'. However, this is in contrast to Alice's description of Tim. Why do you think there is such a contradiction between the mother's and daughter's perspectives?

Referring back to our earlier discussion, Siobhan is using *denial* to minimise her anxiety. But what is the source of her anxiety and what can Jacklyn do to help? How can Siobhan and Alice reconcile their different views about Tim?

These are difficult questions that we will try to answer later; however, for now, we are focusing on identifying the different defences that influence interpersonal relationships.

In her description of events, Siobhan seems to be very protective over Tim, by depicting him as '… *a very calm and mild-mannered person*' and by trying to explain and rationalise his anger and behaviour. *Rationalisation* is a defence mechanism that aims to explain away an unacceptable feeling, emotion or behaviour by offering what seems to be a logical and good explanation without addressing or acknowledging the actual feeling, emotion or behaviour or the reason and the dynamics behind it. For instance, a student who fails an exam due to poor performance may blame the tutor for being biased rather than their own lack of preparation.

Rationalisation is a commonly used ego defence that aims to protect self-concept and self-esteem while minimising anxiety. In fact, people tend to attribute positive outcomes, such as success and achievement, to their own qualities and abilities, while blaming failure on others or circumstantial or outside factors.

There are other defence mechanisms that we will explore in this chapter and later in the book.

One of the main objectives of this book is to use case studies for introducing and unpacking theories and concepts, and to demonstrate their application in practice. Another important objective is to apply this learning to our own practice and to enable us to learn more about our own emotions, thoughts, experiences and self, and their impact on relationships and relationship-based practice. Therefore, at this point, take a few minutes to reflect about why you chose this specific profession. How did you feel about it before, and how do you feel about it today?

These are important questions that allow us to reflect on ourselves and our own desires, preferences, practice and hopes. These notes are for you, and are meant to help you develop a more in-depth understanding of self and your identity as well as your strengths, fears, biases, insights, vulnerability and inner beauty. So be as open and honest as you can. Do this as you go along and complete each section and each chapter. You will have the opportunity later in the book to re-examine these notes and that may shed further light on your own thoughts and emotions, and their consequences for your practice.

Speaking with dad and meeting the grandma

CASE STUDY

Talking with father (Tim Lawson)

Jacklyn contacts Tim to hear his perspective.

What do you want social? I'm not interested … I heard you been harassing Siobhan … it is just like you lot putting your noses where it's not wanted. Back off …

Tim tells Jacklyn not to call again and hangs up the phone. Jacklyn allows Tim to calm down and contacts him the next day. Jacklyn calls Tim at midday. Tim answers the phone and his speech is slurred.

Just what I need … you lot again, like I said … I don't want to talk to you. You bring nothing but trouble and you are the reason for my family breaking up. I am very busy and don't have time to talk to you.

Meeting with paternal grandmother

Jacklyn undertakes an unannounced visit to Tim Lawson's home. His mother Phyllis opens the door and asks what she wants. Jacklyn explains that she has come to talk to Tim and Phyllis indicates that Tim is not doing well. He was taken to hospital in the evening of the same day he spoke with Jacklyn due to alcohol poisoning. Phyllis is angry with Jacklyn, telling her that it has been some time since she has been asking for help for Tim, but none is forthcoming. She is afraid that Tim will drink himself to death if he continues on this path.

Phyllis tells Jacklyn that she should not be so quick to blame Tim for everything, and that Siobhan also has her part to play. She adds that Siobhan met Tim when he was too fresh to know what was going on. '*You know, Siobhan is 17 years older than Tim, and she is the one that took advantage of him … not the other way around.*'

Meeting with the headteacher

Jacklyn meets with Alice's headteacher.

The problem as I see it is simply … it's a matter of too little too late. We have been asking you guys, not you personally, but social services to intervene for months and we have received nothing.

It is clear Siobhan can't cope with Alice and it's a pity as Alice is a bright girl. She just needs stimulation, the right kind of approach and she will do very well. Alice is a quiet shy girl. She packs all this make-up on her face but our strategy at the school is not to say anything that will put more pressure on her. Instead we are giving her positive reinforcement and encouraging her. That is what she needs at the moment because she does not have much going on in her life.

She is popular and lots of the pupils are friendly with her, and this helps her. But, one of the main problems is that she attends school very irregularly. She usually attends three to four days a week.

It is clear that Siobhan can't do this, and in the meantime while she is trying to get her life back on track and in shape, Alice is growing up without a parent. I understand that her father has not been much support to her either. She seems to be embarrassed about her parents and has told us that she prefers it if her mother does not attend parents' evenings.

Reflection

1.   Consider the phone conversation between Tim and Jacklyn. Can you identify any defence mechanisms at play? How are they being used and why?

2.   What are your reflections so far? Do you see any common thread in the above conversations? How does this relate to our earlier discussion about emotional labour, mentalisation and potential space?

3.   Initially Siobhan did not want to let Tim into the house, so why did she change her mind? What are some possible and plausible explanations for Siobhan's change of mind?

Discussion

Exploring projection and projective identification

Alice's description of events on Friday, and her depiction of her parents reflect deep-rooted and long-term dynamics that we will examine in later chapters. For now, let us consider the following phrase from Alice's account of Friday's events: '*At first mum said no but then he said she was a "sorry old cow" and she never helped him none with anything. He called her a "bitch and a cunt" and then she agreed that he could watch the football.*'

Why did Siobhan agree that Alice's dad '*... could watch the football*' – what made her change her mind?

This is a good example of projective identification, and represents an important dynamic that we encounter in many other situations and in everyday practice.

Projective identification is a defence mechanism that was first described by Melanie Klein (1946). However, before exploring projective identification let us first consider the concept of projection.

Sigmund Freud (1924[1905]) argued that psychological *projection* is a defence mechanism in which the individual ascribes their own unacceptable feelings, emotions or attributes to other objects or people in the external world. For example, a person who may be anxious or litigious may accuse other people of being anxious or litigious. In other words, projection is an unconscious defence mechanism in which the person uses other people or objects as a hook upon which to hang their own unacceptable or unwanted emotions. Although projecting our unwanted qualities and emotions onto others may be considered an *immature defence*, on a small scale, this is a common occurrence in people's lives and interactions.

Projective identification, however, does not just hang the cloak of our unwanted emotions or attributes onto others, it makes the other person wear it. In this sense it is a way of controlling or soliciting others. For example, a person may project their own anxiety onto another person, resulting in the other person behaving anxiously.

In observing children at play, Melanie Klein found that in the play of children a common fantasy was that a part, or parts, of the self could be located in the external world, in other objects, or in other people. Klein called this projective identification (Klein, 1946).

Therefore, we can define projective identification as the projection of one person's state of mind into another person, or another object. This allows the individual to externalise or expel their emotions and attributes, as well as both *good* and *bad* parts of the self (as seen from the person's subjective point of view) into others.

Projective identification occurs in everyday interactions, and is not necessarily a negative thing. In fact, Bion (1962) suggests that projective identification is the basis of communication between babies and their mothers/carers. For instance, a baby may cry when hungry or distressed, and their crying may evoke anxiety or distress in the mother/carer. In this manner the baby is able to communicate his or her feelings, emotions and state of mind to the mother/carer. If the mother/carer is able to manage (contain) that anxiety or distress and respond in a timely and appropriate manner to the baby, then in that instance, the mother/carer is able to offer good enough mothering, and meet the needs of the baby. However, if the mother is unable to manage or contain the anxiety and distress evoked by her baby and does not respond in an appropriate and timely manner to the baby then in that instance, the mother does not show/have the parental capacity necessary to meet the needs of the baby. Can you think of how this relates to our discussion of mentalisation, attachment and potential space in Chapter 1?

As described above, projective identification often has an evacuative element (ie the subject evacuates a part of the self or their own emotion or state of mind into someone else), and an acquisitive element (ie the object induced to experience what the subject is wishing to expel) (Britton, 1998, p 5), and plays an important role in everyday life. Prejudice, discrimination or stigma may be considered as forms of projective identification, aiming to externalise the individual's own feelings of inadequacy, fear or anxiety, eg discrimination against older people, or stigma associated with ageing may be considered as a reflection of one's own fear of death, or anxiety about one's own frailty and weakness. A well-known example of such a dynamic is when Freud at the age of 48 made the notorious claim that '... *near or above the age of fifty the elasticity of mental processes, on which the (psychoanalytic) treatment depends, is as a rule lacking*' (Freud, 1924[1905], p 264). Freud's ageism is particularly striking given that he himself showed great productive capacity to develop and revise his own theories until he died in his eighties. Have you heard an older person say '*I am old, but I'm not like the others*'? That is an example of projective identification.

We will continue Alice's story in the next chapter. See if you can identify any projective identification in the remainder of this case study.

References

Bion, W R (1962) *Learning from Experience*. London: Karnac.

Britton, R (1998) *Belief and Imagination*. New York: Taylor & Francis.

Fiske, S T and Taylor, S E (1991) *Social Cognition* (2nd edn). New York: McGraw-Hill.

Freud, S (1924[1905]) On Psychotherapy, in *Collected Papers* (Vol. 1). London: Hogarth Press.

Klein, M. (1946) Notes on Some Schizoid Mechanisms. *International Journal of Psychoanalysis*, 27: 99–110. Reprinted in *The Writings of Melanie Klein* (Vol 3, pp 1–24). London: Hogarth, 1975.

Laplanche, J and Pontalis, J (1973) *The Language of Psychoanalysis*. London: Karnac.

4 Finding a home for Alice

Psychological and ego defences: schema, stereotypes, cognitive schema and bias, transference and countertransference, and belonging and identity

Chapter summary

This chapter introduces the concepts of cognitive schema, stereotype and cognitive bias. The chapter also discusses how the different consonant and dissonant information may reinforce or challenge our schemas and how through the processes of assimilation and accommodation we reconcile the new information with our model of the external *world*.

The chapter then proceeds to explore the concept of transference and countertransference and concludes with a brief discussion of belonging and identity.

Chapter objectives

1. Introduce the concept of schema and assimilation versus accommodation of dissonant information.

2. Discuss stereotypes and cognitive bias.

3. Briefly introduce transference and countertransference and explore the importance of belonging and identity.

Finding a home for Alice

CASE STUDY: REVIEWING THE HISTORICAL CASE NOTES

Siobhan MacAndrew has a history of mental health difficulties which dates back to her early twenties. She became pregnant two years after her diagnosis and her first child was taken into care and adopted a few months after birth.

Siobhan became pregnant again the following year and when she was pregnant her mental health deteriorated, and she was admitted into a psychiatric ward. Her second child was born in a psychiatric unit and placed on child protection before birth under the category of neglect. When the child was born he was placed on an emergency protection order as Siobhan refused to take her medication and left the hospital without him and without informing anyone. Later an interim care order was granted and he was adopted shortly after that.

Alice was born a year later and was placed on the child protection register due to concerns regarding Ms MacAndrews' mental health difficulties and relationship with Tim Lawson. Alice stayed on child protection for two years. During this time support was in place from mental health and Children's Services and Ms MacAndrews made a number of positive changes including engaging with mental health staff, taking her medication and attending child care management groups, resulting in a stable family situation for her and Alice. The situation remained stable for a number of years. However, Siobhan's mental health deteriorated when she stopped taking her medication and there were concerns due to the *unhygienic* state of the home. Siobhan was hospitalised while Alice stayed with a family friend and later she was taken into care. At the time the social worker made an application for an interim care order. The application was unsuccessful and Alice returned home under a supervision order. Children's Services continued to support Alice and Siobhan for two more years after which the family situation was assessed as stable and the case was closed.

Other incidents of Alice running away and the police being called due to arguments at the home between Alice and Siobhan were recorded but the case had not been open for the last ten months.

Michael White (manager)

Jacklyn is worried about the case and seeks advice from her manager. The local authority is piloting a new project that has a strong emphasis on keeping families together, and if possible Jacklyn's manager would like to see Alice move back to her mother's home.

Jacklyn feels there are too many risk factors and thinks that alternative accommodation is necessary.

Jacklyn's manager tells her: '*I have seen a lot of these cases, they always end up going home. You will see, this case will not be any different.*'

School visit to see Alice

Jacklyn visits Alice at school and asks her how things are going. Alice enjoys staying with her aunt and wants to live with her. Jacklyn tells her that this won't be a possibility.

Why, why do you want me to stay with my mother? My brothers were adopted but you still want me to stay with her ... to help her, to fix her ... What about me? What about my life?

If I can't stay with my aunt I want to go into care. If you don't put me in care I will run away.

Jacklyn speaks with Siobhan and describes some of Alice's behaviour. Jacklyn tells Siobhan that given Alice's behaviour and the risk factors she believes that the relationship has broken down and that Alice needs some time away from Siobhan.

Jacklyn outlines the options including Alice being accommodated under Section 20 of the Children Act (1989). Siobhan agrees to this option and Jacklyn contacts Alice and Julie to make arrangements. It is agreed that Jacklyn will pick up Alice later in the afternoon and take her to the foster carer.

Julie has a beautiful home, the kitchen is large and the three youngest children are sitting around the kitchen table finishing up their homework, while the oldest child is sitting in the lounge completing his homework. Each room has a fireplace and the fire in the lounge is on. The home evokes a feeling of love and calm and Jacklyn is sorry to be moving Alice. Jacklyn thinks that Julie is sad for Alice to be going, but sometimes life works out this way, although no-one intended for things to be so.

Jacklyn helps to settle Alice into Charlotte's home and Jacklyn tells Charlotte that Alice needs support, attention and care. Jacklyn is worried about how Alice will get on with the foster carer, as Charlotte is in her late fifties and Alice is 14 years old, and they have such different expectations. Alice wanted to go to Charlotte – she was insistent – and Jacklyn can understand this.

Alice has a small, clean room at Charlotte's home. It is white and Charlotte asks Alice not to hang any posters on the wall.

Reflection

1. *What are the risks and the protective factors for Alice so far?*

2. *What are some of your reflections on the different identities and their stories so far?*

3. *Why is Alice insistent on staying with Charlotte?*

4. *What is the meaning and significance of this phrase: 'Alice wanted to go to Charlotte – she was insistent – and Jacklyn can understand this'?*

Discussion

Exploring cognitive schema, stereotype and cognitive bias

Let us begin by considering the following passage:

> *Jacklyn's manager tells her: I have seen a lot of these cases, they always end up going home. You will see, this case will not be any different.*

Jacklyn's manager sounds pretty sure that Alice will return to her mother. What makes her manager so certain and what is the dynamic of this interaction?

Thinking about the above, one might say Jacklyn's manager has '... *seen a lot of* ...' similar situations and experience tells her manager that in all likelihood Alice will return to her mother. However, the manager's response reflects more than that. The manager goes on to say: '*You will see, this case will not be any different.*' Here there is an emphasis and an assumption of certainty by Jacklyn's manager that Alice will return to her mother. This is an example of a stereotype.

One of our most basic mental processes is *categorisation*. We tend to think of things either in groups or as members of a group, rather than as isolated and unique entities. To categorise things, we compare people, objects and different stimuli to a cognitive *prototype* which is basically an abstraction (ie our idea) of the *typical* or quintessential instance of that group (Michener et al, 2004, p 107). For example, all of us have an idea and image (ie a cognitive *prototype*) of a doctor, or teacher, or a dog, or a birthday party, etc. These are cognitive schemas that facilitate our appraisal of external stimuli and the *world*.

A *schema* is a well-organised structure of cognitions about an entity such as a person, group, role or event (Michener et al, 2004, p 107). Piaget (1947) suggests that the harmony or synthesis of our internal working model of the world and our experiences of the external world are moderated by schemas. By setting our expectations of others and our environment, schemas help make *our world* and the external stimuli more predictable. For example, person schema are cognitive structures that prescribe personalities of others. These can apply to a given individual (eg Barack Obama, or my mother) or a group of individuals (eg extrovert, etc). Schemas can also be about a role (eg CEO, inspector, teacher, police) or an event (eg a graduation, wedding, funeral or birthday); this is also called a script and usually entails a list of expectations and actions, etc.

Schemas have the two functions of assimilation and accommodation. When our experience presents us with new information that is in consonance with our existing schema, this information is assimilated into our internal model of the world and reinforces that schema. However, when there is a dissonance between the new information and our schema then the environment resists the reproduction of the schema, and the individual needs to resolve this dissonance to reconcile the discrepancy. This can be achieved either by modifying the person's schema to incorporate the new information or experience (this allows for *accommodation* of the new information), or by reinterpretation and reattribution of meaning and significance to the new information or experience (eg the individual may discount the new information as a one-off incident and, therefore, not important). For example, imagine your neighbour had a son and you knew him to be a polite and well-behaved young person. One day looking out of your window you see him push another boy to the ground. This is a new piece of information that is dissonant with your belief and, therefore, you may apply the process of assimilation by assuming that the chances are the other boy was rude to him and he may have pushed the boy as a defensive move, or you may assimilate this new information and think of him as a fundamentally good boy who also has a mischievous side to him. Alternatively you may apply the process of accommodation and decide he is not really such a good boy after all otherwise he would not have pushed the other boy to the ground. Accommodation of information requires a greater amount of adjustment on the part of the individual and, therefore, is more difficult to achieve. When the process of accommodation is successful, the new information or experience is assimilated successfully and this restores the harmony between the individual's internal working model and the external *world* (Fischer and Riedesser, 1999).

General schemas which coordinate other schemas are called *scripts*. In a healthy mental state we maintain a variety of inner working models or *cognitive maps* of basic factors and different interactions in our lives. These include our body image, different self-concepts, role relationship models, scripts and agendas, spatial layouts of our repeated social and environmental surroundings, and other schemata that help us organise our perceptions and plan our future actions (Horowitz, 2013).

Schema can also be about a group. This is also called a *stereotype*, associating fixed attributes to the members of a particular social group/category. For example, Jacklyn's manager considered Alice as part of a group with certain characteristics and behavioural attributes: '... *"they" always end up going home*'. We also have schema about our *self* (ie self-concept) which is our idea/conception of our own abilities, qualities, characteristics. Schemas facilitate our thinking; however, whether correct or otherwise, schemas form our impression of others and our environment and, therefore, condition our thinking and influence our behaviour. This can lead to cognitive bias and become a self-fulfilling prophecy. For example, we may use stereotypes to process information and, therefore, organise information around our expectations and ignore/neglect information that is inconsistent/dissonant with our stereotype. This creates what is referred to as *confirmation bias*.

Jacklyn's manager seems to have a stereotype of Alice as a member of a certain group where *they* always end up returning to their mothers. This sort of thinking can lead to confirmation bias where due to expectation of Alice returning home to her mother, there could be insufficient resources allocated to support Alice. This can then become a self-fulfilling prophecy where due to lack of resources Alice is forced to return home to her mother, and this in turn will strengthen the manager's stereotype as yet another confirmation that '*they always end up going home*'.

This is one reason why it is critically important to engage in *active thinking* and critical reflection, and to challenge stereotypes or other cognitive biases.

We will revisit the concept of stereotypes and cognitive bias and their impact in practice in other examples in this book. However, in the meantime, can you think of some other stereotypes? And can you identity any in your own practice or thinking? How about in the thinking of the people around you and your colleagues?

Shifting the blame

CASE STUDY

Jacklyn leaves Charlotte's place and returns to her office to complete the paperwork for Alice's placement, but she continues to worry about Alice. Jacklyn has mixed feelings about Alice staying with Charlotte and hopes that the situation works out. She feels that Alice is deeply hurt and will need a lot of care and attention; however, she doesn't know whether Charlotte has the skills to manage the situation. She tries to refocus on completing the paperwork for the placement.

Alice has not been speaking with Jacklyn and their relationship has been tense. Alice blames Jacklyn for moving her from Julie's home. Jacklyn understands that it is easier for Alice to blame her instead of facing the difficult truth that it was Julie who was only willing to accommodate Alice for four days.

The following morning Jacklyn receives a police notification involving Siobhan and Tim. Siobhan contacted the police last night as Tim refused to leave the flat. He had been drinking and had been staying at the flat for the last few days. Siobhan no longer wanted him there and asked him to leave; he started shouting and threatening her and the police were called and arrested him.

Jacklyn arranges a strategy meeting and given the risk factors believes that the case has met the threshold for a child protection conference. She discusses the case with her manager and the child protection consultant and everyone is in agreement to proceed and take the case to an initial child protection conference.

Siobhan had previously denied Jacklyn consent for inter-agency checks with her psychiatrist. As the Section 47 has been triggered Jacklyn contacts the psychiatrist and asks for further information regarding Siobhan and her current mental health. Jacklyn is able to gather the following information:

1. Mental health from consultant psychiatrist

Ms MacAndrew has a long history of schizoaffective disorder. Her first contact with the mental health services was 20 years ago and subsequently she has had several admissions to hospital, several under sections of the Mental Health Act 1983. Between difficult episodes she often had fairly long periods of managing well in the community. Her last admission was a few years ago and on admission she was thought disordered (disorganised thinking) and very suspicious of mental health staff. She admitted finding it difficult to cope at home and that she was struggling to care for herself and her daughter. Her admission was fairly brief and she responded well to medication.

Relapse indicators for Ms MacAndrew include increasing levels of disorganisation, self-neglect and neglect of her daughter as well as low mood and paranoid thinking.

Current mental state

During Ms MacAndrew's latest review she discussed with me the difficulties she was having with her daughter and the involvement of Children's Services. At that time she appeared quite stressed but seemed to be managing fairly well despite her understandable anxieties. She finds it difficult to parent Alice at times and expressed a real desire to be helped by Children's Services. I did not feel she was relapsing and there was no evidence of depression or psychosis. She continues to take her medication regularly.

She is due to see a cognitive behavioural therapist in a few months.

2. School report

Alice started attending Wood Hill School a year ago as she had experienced problems at St Jude School. Some areas of concern included poor attendance and wearing excessive make-up.

When transferring to Wood Hill School Alice continued to display the same behaviour; however, Wood Hill are more understanding of some of the problems that Alice is facing.

Alice is described as a bright pupil by teachers and her head of year; however, Alice was initially placed in a lower ability group to help her settle in and deal with her emotional problems. Alice finds it difficult to attend school for a full week.

The only time Alice attended Wood Hill for a full week was when she was living with her aunt and while in foster care. School attendance is so poor that despite *social problems* the school is considering taking legal action against Siobhan.

Alice is described as a friendly pupil who is popular and makes friends easily.

Jacklyn also gathers the historical reports about the family.

Reflection

1. *Consider Jacklyn's thoughts and emotions while completing the paperwork for Alice's placement. What is the relationship between this and what we have discussed so far? What is the relationship between this and emotional labour?*

2. *Have you been in a similar situation as Jacklyn? Explore how you felt and what it meant to you. How do you feel about the situation so far?*

3. *Consider a similar case from your own practice and apply the concepts discussed in Chapters 1–3 and this chapter to that case.*

Discussion

Exploring transference and countertransference

We can easily identify the defence mechanism of displacement being used by Alice in the following situation:

> Alice has not been speaking with Jacklyn and the relationship has been tense. Alice blames Jacklyn for moving her from Julie's home. Jacklyn understands that it is easier for Alice to blame her instead of facing the difficult truth that it was Julie who was only willing to accommodate Alice for four days.

However, this is also a good example of transference. Transference is an unconscious redirection of feelings from their actual source to another person or object. For example, in the above passage, Alice is redirecting her anger toward Jacklyn. This could be for several reasons; however, in this case, Alice's anger is an expression of her frustration and anxiety associated with the many difficulties she is experiencing, and she finds it easier and safer to direct that anger toward Jacklyn. Specifically, Alice is angry with Julie for not allowing Alice to stay in her home for a longer period. She is also angry with her parents for not taking care of her and for not offering her the love and care she needs. However, Alice feels she cannot express her feelings toward Julie as that will upset Julie and the consequence may be that Julie will not want Alice in the future. Alice may also feel anger toward her parents, and this may evoke feelings of guilt and, therefore, she finds it easier to displace her anger and redirect it toward Jacklyn. We will revisit this concept later in the book.

Freud referred to such unconscious displacement of repressed emotions and desires onto another person or object as transference. Transference is a common occurrence in everyday communication and interactions and does not necessarily relate to an underlying mental health cause. For example, you may know someone, or meet someone for the first time, who reminds you of someone else, and this may lead to transference. Transference may be related to mental health difficulties only if it leads to maladaptive outcomes.

Carl Jung (1985) suggests that within transference both parties experience various and opposite emotions, and that psychological growth hinges on the ability to endure this tension without abandoning the process. This tension allows the individual to grow by transforming their emotions and desires.

Transference is always an affective relationship and the analysis is not an intellectual but an emotional process. Indeed, for transference to proceed and to lead to growth what is needed is rapport between the transference dyad. It is only when we make direct contact with the affects through empathy that we can interpret them more accurately, and can gain an understanding of how our user of services is feeling. Indeed, accurate empathy is indispensable to effective relationship-based interventions. This involves a combination of intelligent insight and emotional understanding with accurate empathy to correctly identify, analyse, understand and contain the dynamics of emotional encounter that is at the root of relationship-based work.

It is important to note that emotional encounters are a two-way relationship and that no one is a *blank sheet*. Therefore, our experience of transference of the emotions and desires of others is shaded by our past experiences, values, preferences, emotions, desires and identity. The emotions, feelings and desires experienced by the subject of transference are referred to as countertransference. It was Sigmund Freud (1910, 1912) who first spoke about and defined countertransference as therapists' emotions, feelings, attitudes and behaviours that were stirred/evoked by the client; in his words countertransference is '*the result of the patient's influence on [the physician's] unconscious feelings*' (Freud, 1910, p 144).

Freud thought that countertransference was a result of the therapist's own childhood experiences and repressed emotions, and that it represented a neurotic conflict and, therefore, was a disturbance to therapy (Freud, 1910, 1912).

However, Helen Deutsch (1926) and subsequently Paula Heimann (1990[1949–50, 1959–60]) argued that countertransference could be used in a controlled manner to analyse the emotions of the client (Analysand). In fact, Kernberg (1965, pp 38–56) labelled Freud's description as '*narrow*', excluding the relational perspective in individual psychotherapy, and ever since then the interest and understanding of the concept of countertransference has developed significantly, with different thinkers and authors highlighting the important relational aspects of it. For example, Winnicott (1949), when reporting psychotherapy process with a child, described the therapist's negative feelings as a '*normal reaction*', while Sullivan (1953) suggested the therapist's reaction could be understood as a response to the client's invitation to an interpersonal interaction. In psychodynamic and psychoanalytic psychotherapy, countertransference is considered as the most important instrument in understanding the relationship and the emotions and desires of clients/users of services (Heimann, 1950).

As mentioned earlier the paragraph below is a good example of transference and countertransference:

> Alice has not been speaking with Jacklyn and the relationship has been tense. Alice blames Jacklyn for moving her from Julie's home. Jacklyn understands that it is easier for Alice to blame her instead of facing the difficult truth that it was Julie who was only willing to accommodate Alice for four days.

The concepts of transference and countertransference are central to understanding relationships and to effective relationship-based interventions. We will explore these concepts throughout the book, and in greater depth. In the meantime, can you think of some examples of transference and countertransference in your own relationships and in your practice? What were the dynamics of the situation, and how did it make you feel? What was your reaction to what you felt and what did you do?

When there is too much pain

CASE STUDY: CHILD PROTECTION CONFERENCE

Alice refuses to take part in the child protection conference and the relationship between Jacklyn and Alice is very difficult.

The decision is unanimous. Alice will be made subject to a child protection plan. Siobhan is the only member of the family to attend the child protection conference. Siobhan becomes teary during the case conference and accuses Jacklyn of being vicious and insensitive and spreading lies about her.

After the conference Siobhan seems disorientated and unsure of how she will get home. Jacklyn offers to take her home and she accepts. Siobhan tells Jacklyn that she has nothing left in her life.

Jacklyn feels guilty and sorry for Siobhan. She finds it difficult to process her emotions. A huge sense of loss and guilt overcomes her. She wishes she could do more for Alice who seems so lonely and lost and sad. She wishes she could do more for Siobhan but at the same time thinks that Siobhan has been continuing to put Alice at risk.

On the day of the child protection conference Alice returns to her foster carer's home at 10pm. Jacklyn undertakes a school visit in the morning to speak with Alice. They use an empty classroom to talk and Alice answers all of Jacklyn's questions as *'fine'* ... there is a long silence and then Alice tells Jacklyn very matter-of-factly:

You don't know what it's like to stay in foster ... you don't know what it's like to have no-one and nothing. You know nothing about me and my life ...

Strong emotions are stirred in Jacklyn. She wants to help Alice but does not know how, and memories of her own childhood surface. She thinks about the difficult relationship she had with her own mother, and the many times she had felt threatened that her mum was going to throw her out of the house.

Later in the afternoon Alice is caught shoplifting and in possession of cannabis. Two days later the foster carer reports Alice as missing. The police are called and they start searching for Alice. They also contact Siobhan, Tim, friends, extended family and the school.

Alice returns home to Siobhan two days later and tells Jacklyn that she was with her brother whom she met via Facebook.

Alice refuses to return to foster care and calls it a prison, and says that she hates Charlotte.

A legal planning meeting is convened and it is agreed that care proceedings will not be initiated, and instead services will be put in place to help Siobhan manage at home with Alice. Jacklyn should undertake home visits twice a week. Home visits prove difficult as Alice tells Jacklyn that she is intruding and that she just wants to be left alone. Alice shouts at Jacklyn to get out of her house and to leave her alone.

Most of Jacklyn's visits are spend with Siobhan as Alice refuses to see her. Siobhan initially states that all is going well, and that there is nothing to be concerned about; however, later on Siobhan starts to open up more, and tells Jacklyn that things are very difficult as Alice refuses to talk to her.

The case needs to move to the long-term team and Jacklyn feels as though she has let the family down ...

Reflection

1. *The child protection conference seemed to be painful for all concerned. Alice refused to participate in it, and felt angry with Jacklyn, while Siobhan cried and accused Jacklyn of being vicious and insensitive and spreading lies about her. Jacklyn felt guilty and sorry for Siobhan, and found it difficult to process her own emotions. The child protection conference was meant to help protect and support Alice. So, why did everyone feel so bad?*

2. *Why did Alice refuse to participate in the child protection conference?*

3. *Jacklyn has tried very hard to help and support Alice, and has been very honest, open and helpful toward Siobhan. Why did Siobhan accuse Jacklyn of being vicious and insensitive and spreading lies about her?*

4. *Alice had insisted on being placed with Charlotte, so why did she leave without notice and return to her mum? Was Jacklyn's manager right in stereotyping Alice and saying 'they always end up going home'?*

5. *Alice seems to be a young girl with great potential, so why is she engaging in this type of behaviour?*

Discussion

Exploring belonging and identity

Alice has experienced continuous and repeated neglect and rejection, and is deeply hurt. Therefore, she may be experiencing a host of opposite emotions such as anger and guilt, and most importantly a lack of belonging. Indeed, research suggests that some of the more disturbing and detrimental behaviours in placements are hyperactivity, aggression, fire setting, stealing and sexually acting out (Rosenthal, 1993).

From birth, children search for their place in their family, and a child's sense of self and security depend on the child's feeling of belonging in the group. Adler (1931[1992]) suggests that the fundamental motivation of humans is the need to belong, while Dreikurs and Soltz (1964/1992) explain the desire to belong is inherent in children because they are social beings. Children attempt different behaviours, and based on their experiences, and the feedback from their parents, carers and environment, they decide on the repertoire of behaviours, reactions and responses that they adopt. However, the experience of rejection and the feeling of loss experienced by most adoptive children and children in care, means that they may be more sensitive to being *in or out* of the family and, therefore, may overcompensate by trying too hard to belong to any group, good or bad. This may explain why some adolescents become a part of a gang or other undesirable groups. They may be seeking a point of hold and anchoring, and a sense of connectedness and belonging, and in that sense they may feel that it is better to be part of something, whether good or bad, than to be part of nothing and be alone. Blomquist (2001) suggests that they do this in an effort to lose their identity in a group as a way to gain an identity, which otherwise they feel they lack. This puts them at risk of getting involved in harmful activities just to be part of the group. Furthermore, Brodzinsky (2002) cites several studies reporting that adopted children are overrepresented among youth diagnosed with externalising challenges, such as attention deficit hyperactive disorder (ADHD), oppositional disruptive disorder, conduct disorder and substance misuse. Brodzinsky (2002) notes a higher incidence of adjustment difficulties for children and young adults who were placed at a relatively older age, and who had more adverse experiences such as multiple placements, prolonged neglect or multiple abuse.

The impact of the rejection and abandonment affect children throughout their lives; however, children become more conscious of it when their thinking moves from concrete to abstract, roughly the ages of 12–14 or around the time of puberty.

Children at the concrete stage tend to focus on one small aspect of an issue; however, children moving into abstract stage tend to categorise items, and are able to see multiple issues at one time, and begin to question things (Fogarty, 2000). This is the stage when the children may gain a greater appreciation of the impact of rejection and abandonment and begin to question it. Alice is at a critical stage in her life, with repeated experiences of neglect and rejection, and entering her early adolescence she is struggling to make sense of her life and her identity, and to find and develop her potential space to reconnect with herself to grow and to be. So, is she to be blamed for shoplifting or for possessing cannabis?

Without meaning to justify Alice's actions, we need to remember that there is enough blame going around, with teachers who blame parents, parents who blame schools or the social worker, the local authority can be blamed or can blame the parents or the schools for not doing enough, social workers can be blamed for not doing their job, and so on. However, as a relationship-based practitioner it is incumbent upon us to break the cycle of blame, and offer some hope, not in an excessively optimistic way, but from a belief that we can help to understand the meaning of children's and young people's behaviours, and contain the complex emotions and feelings that in turn can provide relief and growth, and help Alice make sense of herself, her surrounding and her experiences, and to reduce the projective and acting-out cycles.

Children are helped in many ways, not least through contained and containing relationships that offer them a chance to escape the projection of being the *bad* and the *unmanageable*, needing exclusion.

We will explore some of these concepts further in the next chapters where we discuss trauma, its meaning, impact, and significance.

References

Adler, A (1992[1931]) *What Life Could Mean to You* (C. Brett, trans). Oxford: Oneworld.

Blomquist, B T (2001) *Insight into Adoption*. Springfield, IL: Charles C Thomas Publisher.

Brodzinsky, D M (2002) Children's Understanding of Adoption: Developmental and Clinical Implications. *Professional Psychology: Research and Practice*, 42(2): 200–7.

Deutsch, H (1926) A Contribution to the Psychology of Sport. *International Journal of Psychoanalysis*, 7: 223-7.

Dreikurs, R. and Soltz, V (1964/1992) *Children: The Challenge*. New York: Hawthorn Books.

Fischer, G and Riedesser, P (1999) *Lehrbuch der Psychotraumatologie (Textbook of Psychotrauma-thology)*. München: Ernst Reinhardt Verlag.

Fogarty, J A (2000) *The Magical Thoughts of Grieving Children*. Amityville, NY: Baywood Publishing.

Freud, S (1910) The Future Prospects of Psychoanalytic Psychotherapy, in Strachey, J (ed; trans.). *The Standard Edition of the Complete Psychological Works of Sigmund Freud*. London: Hogarth.

Freud, S (1912) *The Dynamics of Transference*. SE12 (pp 97–108). London: Hogarth.

Heimann, P (1950) On Counter-transference. *International Journal of Psycho-Analysis*, 33: 81–4.

Heimann, P (1990[1949–50, 1959–60]) *About Children and Children No Longer: The Work of Paula Heimann*. New York: Routledge.

Horowitz, M (2013) *Stress Response Syndromes* (5th edn). New York: Jason Aronson Publishers.

Horowitz, M, Wilner, N and Alvarez, W (1979) Impact of Event Scale: A Measure of Subjective Stress. *Psychosomatic Medicine*, 41(3): 209–18.

Jung, C G (1985) *The Practice of Psychotherapy: Essays on the Psychology of the Transference and Other Subjects* (Bollingen Series XX, Vol 16) (R F C Hull, trans). Princeton, NJ: Princeton University Press.

Kernberg, O (1965) Notes on Countertranference. *Journal of the American Psychoanalystic Association*, 13: 38–56.

Michener, H A, DeLamater, J D and Myers, D (2004) *Social Psychology* (5th edn). Belmont, CA: Wadsworth/Thompson Learning.

Piaget, J (1947) *La Psychologie de l'Intelligence*. Paris: Armand Golin.

Rosenthal, J A (1993) Outcomes of Adoption of Children with Special Needs. *The Future of Children*, 3: 77–88.

Sullivan, H S (1953) *The Interpersonal Theory of Psychiatry*. New York: Norton.

Winnicott, D W (1949) Hate in the Counter-transference. *International Journal of Psycho-Analysis*, 30: 69–74.

5 The long shadow of the past

Trauma, post-traumatic growth, touch and listening to children's voices

Chapter summary

This chapter explores trauma and vicarious trauma, or secondary trauma, and post-traumatic stress and their effects. The chapter also introduces post-traumatic growth as well as examining the concept of developmentally appropriate communication with children.

The chapter begins with an introduction to the concept of trauma, its intergenerational transmission and some of its effects. This is followed by a discussion of vicarious/secondary trauma and its impact. This section also includes a discussion of touch in social work and social care practice.

The chapter highlights some of the challenges in interpreting children's narratives from a developmental perspective, followed by an exploration of play and role play and their significance, and the importance of developmentally appropriate communication with children.

The chapter concludes with a discussion of post-traumatic growth, and the importance of a trauma-informed psychosocial and relationship-based practice.

Chapter objectives

1. Introduce the concept of trauma and its effects.
2. Introduce the concept of vicarious or secondary trauma and its implications.
3. Introduce the concept of post-traumatic growth and its implications.
4. Introduction to the meaning of *touch* and its place in practice.
5. Consider appropriate communication with children from a developmental perspective.

Exploring trauma and its effects

CASE STUDY

It's a cold and rainy day in December and Laura feels worried about the Moffita case. Mother (Ms Teresa Williams) presented at the office today and sat in the reception area for 60 minutes refusing to speak with anyone. Later Laura noticed her sitting outside directly opposite her office staring at the building for some time before leaving.

Working with this family has been difficult due to Teresa's erratic behaviour and at times aggressive attitude. Laura has often felt as though she is picking up the pieces of a broken life that Teresa wants to forget. The fragmented pieces of Teresa's life can be found across case notes documenting life stories, narratives and significant events, family group conference minutes, child protection conference notes and police reports. From the very first piece of information it seems as though Shane's life was marked with intergenerational trauma before he even took his first breath. When Teresa was nine months pregnant she approached Children and Families Services requesting that her baby be adopted at birth, telling social workers that her unborn child was the product of rape. Teresa later changed her mind, and believed that she could look after the baby. Children and Families Services remained involved to monitor Teresa's parenting and emotional state, and as no significant concerns arose the case was closed and with that the family packed their bags and moved. The social worker who was working with the family at that time noted that Teresa hoped for a fresh start wanting to leave painful memories from the past behind.

Family composition

Name: Teresa Williams (Mother)   Age: 38   Ethnicity: White

Name: Shane Williams Moffita (Child)   Age: 6   Ethnicity: White

Name: Jefferson Moffita (Father)   Age: 35   Ethnicity: White

Name: William Allen (ex-partner of mother)   Age: 32   Ethnicity: White

Family background

Teresa's early childhood was chaotic, her mother worked as a prostitute to provide for her and her siblings while her father, a violent man who misused substances, was often abusive to Teresa, her mother and her three sisters with Teresa receiving beatings from her father on a daily basis. At the age of 12 Teresa was raped by her maternal grandfather and this resulted in her and her sisters being removed from the family home. Teresa was placed with a foster family and she lost contact with her siblings, some of whom were young enough to be adopted. Teresa formed a close bond with her foster family and stayed with them until she turned 18, at which time she left to start a new life in the city. Her foster family were always under the impression that Teresa wanted to try and re-establish contact with her mother. As the oldest of four children Teresa tried to protect her younger siblings even if that meant that she received the brunt of the abuse from her father. Previous case notes show that Teresa was always consistently blamed by her mother for tearing the family apart.

Apart from the above information that was faxed from a previous local authority Laura has very little information relating to Teresa's life as a child. Teresa has never spoken with Laura about her childhood or adolescence and refuses to discuss any of her family history with Laura. The only information from her past that she does share with Laura is that Jefferson Moffita raped her and that Shane is the product of that rape. However, historical records indicate that the fact-finding investigation which was completed after Shane's birth concluded otherwise.

Reflection

1. *Teresa clearly had a traumatic childhood. But what is trauma and how does it influence the individual?*

2. *Drawing on the previous chapters can you identify any defence mechanisms?*

3. *Drawing on the previous chapters and your own knowledge and experience, what are your thoughts/reflections about Teresa and Shane?*

Discussion

Reflecting on the above narrative, we can surmise that Teresa's traumatic childhood experiences have influenced her life outcomes, and continue to burden her emotions and behaviour today. Research indicates that childhood trauma can result in negative outcomes in adult life (Hiskeya et al, 2008). Therefore, let us examine the concept of trauma and some of its effects.

Fischer and Riedesser (1999) define trauma as the experience of a vital discrepancy between threatening factors in a situation and our coping capabilities. Here the word *vital* distinguishes trauma from everyday stress or distress. Traumatic events produce profound and lasting changes in psychosocial arousal and the individual's internal model of the external world as well as emotions, cognitions and memory and their processing. '*Moreover, traumatic memories may sever these normally integrated functions from one another'* (Herman, 1992, p 34).

Trauma is not just a situational phenomenon, it is a psychosocial process which develops longitudinally in time and dominates individuals' mental states. The lack or impossibility of an appropriate and adequate response to an existential threat can result in trauma. The urgency of the existential threat combined with the impossibility or perceived impossibility of an adequate/appropriate response on the part of the individual represent an inherent paradox that drives the trauma process.

Drawing on our discussion of schemas in the previous chapter, relationship schemas contain cognitions, emotions, affects, wishes and moods, and moderate the harmony and synthesis of our internal working model of the world with our experiences of the external world. Therefore, traumatic experiences which cannot be integrated into our self-concept and the system of schemas remain as dissociated schemas, contradicting coordination rules and scripts, and may lead to the development of distorted coping or protection mechanisms against the dissonant external world (Fischer and Riedesser, 1999).

Although the processing of traumatic memories is a developing area in neuroscience research, it seems that traumatic memories present distinct neurological difference from *ordinary*, non-traumatising, memory when stored. Traumatic memories seem to be immersed in a sea of emotions and sensory details within the right hemisphere of the brain, which is dominant for unconscious processes, unable to be fully and appropriately integrated within the brain (for a more detailed conceptualisation of memory see Brewin, 2014). In this sense, it seems that traumatic memories are fragmented and splintered, and remain unresolved and unintegrated with the individual's autobiographical memory. Therefore, they remain highly charged within the mind and often unable to be articulated or verbally described (van der Kolk, 1994). These indications are in line with the psychoanalytic and object relational understanding of trauma.

Without resolution of the traumatic experience, the person will devote considerable energy to processing of the trauma after an interval following traumatic experience. Past trauma is then repeatedly handled in the person's active memory and in the context of present time. These repetitions are attempts at resolving the traumatic experience; however, with each reactivation of traumatic memory and the subsequent attempt to reconcile it in the context of the present, new information and material is incorporated in the memory which may either work toward resolution of trauma or its further complication resulting in new psychological *realities*. The repetition of trauma only ceases when the contents held in present, active memory are terminated by the completion of the cognitive processing of the trauma. This understanding of trauma is the basis for therapies such as EMDR (Eye Movement Desensitisation Reprocessing).

Trauma is often accompanied by fear and a feeling of loss of control and helplessness which is attributable to the repeated reactivation of traumatic event without its resolution. The individual feels that they cannot save themselves and, therefore, perceive/experience self as an object of the unpredicted traumatic situation rather than a subject with agency (Fischer and Riedesser, 1999). Basoglu and Mineka (1992) argue that unpredictability and uncontrollability of the stressor are related to the development and maintenance of fear. Therefore, the unpredictability and uncontrollability of traumatic memories and their outcome generate anxiety and fear. The perceived *impossibility* of developing mastery over one's experience may be seen as the main reason that a situation becomes traumatic, and this is often accompanied by anger which may be directed inward (toward the self; eg leading to depression) or outward (toward others; eg leading to aggression).

These circumstances prevent the traumatic experience from being processed. The unprocessed traumatic experience leads to dysregulation of the person's responsiveness and results in polarised behavioural reactions oscillating from unresponsiveness to hyper activity/excessive reactivity. This increases the individual's vulnerability/fragility after the traumatic event and influences their behaviour and relationships. Therefore, some of the more salient consequences of trauma include: loss/lack of temperance, loss of a sense of control and a sense of increased or diminished interpersonal distance.

Traumatic experience and perception of time

Time influences all perceptions, and all experiences occur in and over time. The present moment drives from a past and leads to a future (Levine, 1997; Merleau-Ponty, 1962; Stern, 2004).

Husserl (1989) suggests that the individual's consciousness is structured by retention, primal impression and protension. Retentions are intendings of direct past experiences and events (not representations of past events), primal impressions are anticipations about here-and-now and protensions are intendings of future states. This structure of consciousness and perception of time are at the heart of our historicity and sense of continuity, and help maintain both the continuity of our self and the world around us.

Heidegger (1962) in *Being and Time* highlights the complexity of lived time and argues that when we anticipate a future event, in a sense that future becomes part of our current consciousness, even though it represents intentional awareness of an event that may occur in the future. While Merleau-Ponty (1962) explains how events from the past can lie at the fringes/edge of our consciousness and colour our entire experience and existence.

Thinking of the above we can state that a traumatic situation does not end in the actual/linear time in which the traumatic event takes place and ends. Instead, in each instance that there is an activation of the traumatic memory combined with the attempt to (re)process it, the traumatic memory becomes present and overlays the here-and-now whereas the original traumatic experience remains in the past. In this sense, the traumatic time perception supplants the linear perception of time.

It is the long shadow of trauma and its superimposition of the past over here-and-now and within the present context that darkens and distorts the present and taints the lived experience and *reality* of Teresa with the pain of the past. We will explore this aspect of trauma and its infiltration of the present and future later in this chapter when we discuss the intergenerational transition of trauma.

Listening to children's voices

CASE STUDY

Conversations and interactions with Teresa always seem difficult and awkward and a part of this has to do with how Teresa communicates. She often talks over others and does not maintain appropriate personal distance, this combined with frequent mood changes creates an atmosphere of constant uncertainty and tension when communicating with others.

Father initiates private proceedings to have contact with son

Jefferson Moffita, Shane's father, would like to have regular contact with his son and initiates private proceedings to gain access. The court request that Children and Families

Services complete a Section 7 report under the Children Act 1989 and this is completed by Laura and discussed in supervision with her manager.

This is a difficult time for Teresa and she is concerned that her lengthy and consistent involvement with Children and Families Services as well as Shane being subject to a child protection plan under the category of emotional abuse reflects badly on her and fears that she may lose her son.

History of involvement with Children and Families Services

Teresa and Shane have a history of involvement with social services that dates back to when Shane was a baby. Initially, Children and Families Services became aware of Shane and Teresa because of the allegations of rape and Teresa's request for adoption at birth. However, other incidents also resulted in support or monitoring at one time or another. When Shane was a baby his mother was assaulted by her ex-partner (William Allen). She sustained injuries but refused to stay in hospital and made her way to the police station where William was being held. All attempts to help her were declined and her behaviour and communication made officers believe she may be experiencing some mental health difficulties.

A few years later, William Allen reported Teresa for harassment and produced a number of aggressively worded letters which she had sent him. A few months later Teresa was arrested for harassment following an assault on William Allen and his new girlfriend. Shane was not present at the time; however, he was taken into police protection as there was no one available or able to pick him up from nursery while Teresa was in custody and later Shane was placed with a foster carer while his mother appeared in court the following morning.

When Shane was in overnight emergency foster care, the foster carer noted a mark on his back when he was bathing. When asked how he got it, Shane told the foster carer '*mummy hit me*'. Therefore, Shane was seen alone at nursery by Laura and the assistant team manager and asked about how he got the mark on his back. Shane remarked that his mother pushed him through a door. This later changed to happening at a friend's house and to his mother pushing him into the mud. Laura and her colleague role played the event with Shane and Shane was asked to take on the role of his mum. During the role play Shane acted in a caring manner towards Laura and did not hit her. In a separate meeting, between Teresa and Laura, Teresa explained that she was unsure as to how Shane got the mark and also regretted her actions towards William.

A month later Shane told two members of staff at nursery that Teresa had thrown him against the window and that he had hurt his head. Staff contacted Children and Families Services and Shane was spoken with alone and his head was also checked. No marks, bruises or cuts were present. Teresa was seen alone to discuss the disclosure and, after speaking with Shane and Teresa, Laura thought it was unlikely that Teresa had physically hurt Shane.

Section 7 report from local authority

The Section 7 report outlines that the local authority recommends that Shane deserves an opportunity to have a relationship with his father; however, such action could potentially cause distress and emotional turmoil for Teresa, therefore, contact should be limited to a few times a year. Both parents disagree and contest the recommendation.

Historically Teresa has refused to have a psychiatric evaluation or to receive psychotherapy or counselling support. However, she agrees to meet with a psychiatrist for evaluation of her mental health for the Section 7 report. The psychiatrist's report indicates that Teresa is suffering from behavioural and emotional difficulties and does not have any *mental illness.*

Reflection

1. Teresa talks over others and does not maintain appropriate interpersonal distance from others. If you were Teresa's social worker, how would you ensure better communication with Teresa?

2. What are some plausible explanations for Shane's changing narrative for the mark on his back? What are some of the challenges in communicating with children?

3. Were Laura and her colleague communicating in a developmentally appropriate manner with Shane?

Discussion

Listening to children's voices from a developmental perspective

Communication with others is a complex process that involves an array of verbal and non-verbal cues, symbolisms, significations and meanings. Drawing on our previous discussion of potential space may help us better understand the difficulty in communicating with Teresa and her often talking over others and not maintaining appropriate personal distance. Jack learnt how to listen by observing Alma, as evidenced in his response to Alma: 'you taught me to listen', and by good enough care that made him feel valued, and supported the development of his potential space. Therefore, Teresa's difficult communication and talking over others may be a reflection of the lack of growth in her potential space. Indeed, she seems to try to claim this psychosocial space through verbal and behavioural gestures such as interrupting others or not maintaining appropriate personal distance and interpersonal spaces.

Interpersonal communications can be complicated by a host of factors as different people may attribute different values and meanings to the same word or gesture. This is particularly important when communicating with children. Depending on their age and developmental capabilities, children communicate and make sense of the world differently from adults. Therefore, when communicating with children, special attention is needed to ensure that communication is age-appropriate and is attuned to the developmental and interpretative capabilities of the child.

Reflecting on Shane's changing explanation for the mark on his back (first *'mummy hit me'*, then his mother having pushed him through a door, and eventually that it happened at a friend's house) raises a number of questions regarding effective communication with children and how to interpret the voices of children. Therefore, let us examine the meaning of children's differing narratives.

Given Shane's age (six years old) there could be a variety of reasons for his inconsistent explanation of the mark on his back. Therefore, it is important to consider a number of factors. Firstly, if he has reported something that is factually inaccurate, it is important to find out about its meaning and his motivation. Secondly, we need to consider that children can change their narrative for a variety of reasons ranging from trying to fit in to being fearful. Thirdly, we need to consider children's suggestibility, defined as '... *the degree to which the encoding, storage, retrieval, and reporting of events can be influenced by internal and external factors'* (Ceci and Bruck, 1995, p 44). In their effort to attain validation and positive regard from adults, children can be influenced by suggestions from adults. Furthermore, research suggests that young children are inclined to acquiesce to yes–no questions and rarely ask for clarification (Fritzley and Lee, 2003).

The credibility of information from children's narratives is judged based on children's consistency. For example, in court proceedings jurors rely heavily on children's consistency as a measure of credibility and legal and forensic professionals mostly agree with this perspective. However, Hammond and Fivush (1991) found that preschoolers' reports were highly inconsistent across interviews; however, their inconsistency was not related to accuracy. Furthermore, Quas et al (2007) reconfirm that consistency is not associated with accuracy. In their research, when some children were coached to lie about innocuous touching and some children told the truth, it was the children who were touched and told the truth about it that were the most inconsistent. These contradictory findings suggest that consistency is not a reliable indicator by which to assess credibility (Malloy and Quas, 2009).

Furthermore, research indicates that children's understanding of promise guaranteeing performance varies depending on their age. For example, Astington et al (1988) reported that young children fail to refer to promising as a reason for acting and that it was not until the age of eight when children used the word *promise* as assurance for their performance of a task. Rotenberg (1980) found that five-year-olds (in contrast to seven- and nine-year-olds) who were told stories about children who kept or broke their promises virtually never mentioned whether a promise was kept or broken as the basis for trusting another child. Moreover, five-year-olds focused on the positive actions of individuals rather than on the consistency of their words and actions when choosing which individuals they would trust.

However, children value promises by adults differently from their own promises, and their understanding and expectation of their own performance and obligations may be different from their expectations of adults. For example Gräfenhain and colleagues (2009) report that the reaction and behaviour of three to four year-old children at the termination of play with an adult can differ depending on whether it was the adult who invited them to play together or it was the child who had invited the adult to play.

The above highlight the differences in expectation and meaning-making on the part of children, and the importance of age-appropriate and developmentally appropriate communication with them. We will discuss examples of age-appropriate and effective communication with children later in this chapter.

Touch and vicarious or secondary trauma

CASE STUDY

Three months later Children and Families Services receive a police notification. Teresa's ex-partner (William Allen) contacted the police to report Teresa standing outside of his office and later watching him through the window of the bar he was in.

The following month the police are called to Children and Families Services by Teresa as she had made an accusation of aggression against the duty social worker (Lucy Wong). Teresa accused Lucy of pulling Shane by his arm out of the room and using undue force. The duty social worker highlights the incident:

This is the first time I have encountered such a situation. I have reflected upon how I could have reacted to the situation differently. Ms Williams came into the office requesting to speak with Laura, however, Laura was on annual leave. I therefore went out to see her and she requested money. I provided her with ten pounds and this angered her. She started screaming. I noticed that Shane was becoming upset and therefore, I invited him to wait in the playroom while I spoke with Mummy and led him out of the room by his hand to give Teresa a chance to calm down. This seemed to anger Teresa with her stating: 'you'll be sorry I am calling the police on you touching my boy'.

The police spoke with Teresa, Shane and Lucy separately and no further action was taken by the police.

Reflection

1. *What are your views about touch and its place in social work and social care practice?*

2. *What is vicarious or secondary trauma? And what are some of its effects?*

3. *Can you think of instances of possible aggression toward practitioners? And what are some of the measures that you would take if you had to meet a particularly aggressive individual or family?*

Discussion

Touch and professional boundaries

Examining the above narrative, let's briefly consider the question of touch in social work and social care practice from a psychosocial and relationship-based perspective.

Given the above narrative, it is clear that Lucy was concerned about Shane becoming distressed due to his mother's aggressive gesture and tone and, therefore, led him outside the room and to the playroom. Indeed, research indicates that children and adolescents who witness intimate partner violence (IPV) are at greatly increased risk of experiencing community violence and behavioural and emotional problems (Hughes et al, 2005; Mrug et al, 2008). Furthermore, Ehrensaft et al (2003) found that children who were exposed to parental aggression were more likely to be the perpetrators and/or victims of partner aggression during adulthood than children who were not exposed to aggression.

However, Teresa's reaction is more reflective of her state of frustration and anger. Teresa's unresolved trauma leaves her in a state of anger and constant alert and, as we will see in the next section of this chapter, the fear and feeling of helplessness and other difficulties arising from post-traumatic stress may be expressed as anger either toward self or toward others, as evidenced in Teresa's aggressive tone and behaviour. Teresa is deeply hurt and her aggressive tone and behaviour may be understood as projections of her inner fears and anger. By inflicting pain onto others she is seeking to communicate her pain, and to externalise it, as if to disown the pain and make it of the other. We will explore the difficult dynamic of trauma and its impact later in this chapter. However, for now let us examine the question of touch in practice. Concerned with Shane becoming distressed, Lucy invited him to go with her to the playroom and held his arm to accompany him out of the room and into the playroom and this seemed to anger Teresa who stated: 'You'll be sorry I am calling the police on you touching my boy'.

Appropriate individual, social and professional boundaries are complex, multivariate, multilayered and fluid phenomena that are contextually defined depending on a host of factors including time and place. I have explored the question of professionalism and professional boundaries elsewhere (see Megele, 2015a); however, this statement highlights the importance of maintaining professional boundaries at all times.

Teresa's statement seems to imply that by touching Shane, Lucy has transgressed some boundary, 'You'll be sorry … touching my boy'. Her statement also implies that the boundary in question is socially recognised and, therefore, she is calling the police to report Lucy's presumed transgression: '… I am calling the police …' So let's briefly examine the concept and significance of touch.

Although its meaning and significance has varied and changed considerably over time, touch is one of the most fundamental senses and a deeply powerful sensation. From our childhood we explore the world through touch, in reaching out, pushing, sensing, probing, stroking, hitting or holding the child's hand, soliciting sensory information and learning about the external world. Indeed, as early as eight weeks' gestation in the mother's womb, and after the beginning of the development of the brain and central nervous system, the foetus begins to sense its surroundings and its own body (eg on sonograms, we can see infants in utero sucking their thumb). Therefore, we can assume that from pre-birth, and starting at a very basic level, the unborn infant begins to explore and recognise its own body as *me* and *mine*. Husserl (1989) and Merleau-Ponty (1964, 1968) argue that tactile sensations and their associated perceptions are fundamental to all sensory perception and the ongoing constitution of *my*self as a person and for development of human intersubjectivity (Merleau-Ponty, 1964, 1968).

Touch is one of the most holistic and diversely used senses ranging from gestural touch such as waving your hand to say goodbye, to healing touch. Touch allows us to establish, explore and sense physical boundaries, various shapes and our physical world. While sight and sound are senses that take place from a distance, touch bridges that distance and denotes a sense of connectedness. It has an inherent reciprocity (ie when you touch something that thing touches you in return). Research indicates that the neural networks that are activated during observation of a person acting are also activated when one is touched and this activation carries with it the double experience of touching and being touched (Gallese and Lakoff, 2005). Indeed, touch is also the only sense that is reflexive in its function and sense itself. Your eye can't see or feel itself, your ear can't hear itself, etc; however, your hand can feel itself and the rest of your body.

Frank offers an example of touch in the medical profession and that it reflects

> *how care is enacted in gestures that can console far beyond what they accomplish as practical components of treatment. For touch to console and thus to heal, it must be more than efficient. Touch must be generous, seeking contact with a person as much as it seeks to effect some task. Generosity is the resonance of touch, endowing the act with a capacity to give beyond its practical significance.*
>
> (Frank, 2005, p 6)

Ferguson (2010) speaks of the role of touch and states: '*A walk will take the worker up close to the child, but other movements are necessary if direct contact is to be made: bending down, lifting up, jumping and twisting in play, using the hands and touching.*'

However, while touch is very much a part of certain professions such as medicine, nursing, health and beauty services, physical touch remains controversial in social work, counselling and psychotherapy. I have explored the meaning and significance of tactile and virtual touch and its evolution in time elsewhere (for a detailed description see Megele, 2015b); however, for the purposes of our discussion suffice it to say that although touch remains a contested area of practice, practitioners should be aware of its great impact and power as punishing or an expression of intimacy or compassion and healing potential. '*Touch is more than physical congruity, it blends the perception of quality with the experience of force*' (Jonas, 1966).

Vicarious/secondary trauma

Given the focus of the chapter and the emotional labour associated with relationship-based practice, let's now briefly explore the concept of vicarious, or secondary, trauma.

Vicarious or secondary trauma is the emotional residue of exposure practitioners experience from listening to stories of trauma and witnessing pain, fear, suffering and terror that people with experience of trauma have endured.

We're aware of Teresa's complex and unresolved trauma; however, the continued displays of anger, pain, aggression and conflict and the displacement, transference, projections, projective identifications, etc imply that practitioners are immersed in a sea of emotions and surrounded by fragmented identities, projected pain, splinters of feeling and shrapnel of emotions. In this context, it is important that there is an appropriate recognition and adequate response to secondary trauma that is being experienced, or has been experienced, by practitioners.

As noted in the introduction to this book, social work intervenes in people's lives at a time when they may be overwhelmed by dysphoric emotions and distress and when there is a loss of equilibrium and homeostasis in their lives and they are struggling with issues that are negatively affecting their lived experience. Indeed, practitioners often encounter users of services who are presenting challenges co-occurring with a history of trauma. For example, we're aware of Teresa's complex and unresolved trauma; however, the continued displays of anger, pain, aggression and conflict and the displacement, transference, projection, projective identification, etc imply that Laura and other practitioners experience the projections of Teresa's pain, trauma and turbulent emotions. Therefore, it is important that there is an adequate recognition and appropriate response to secondary trauma that is being experienced, or has been experienced, by practitioners.

The complexity and challenge of interactions with users of services and the graphic disclosures, combined with the containment that is required in relationship-based practice can lead to symptoms of secondary/vicarious trauma, which can produce significant changes in practitioners' world-views, influencing their psychosocial well-being and creating negative professional and personal challenges (Figley, 2002; Pryce et al, 2007).

Symptoms of secondary/vicarious trauma may include: (a) intrusive imagery (unwanted, reoccurring thoughts or images, nightmares); (b) avoidance behaviours (social withdrawal, absenteeism from work, avoiding traumatised users of services, lack of containment and failing to meet the standards of services due to exhaustion, chronic fatigue or as a means of avoiding traumatic disclosures, and other negative coping skills; (c) arousal (hypersensitivity to issues of safety, emotional and/or physical aversion to intimacy); and (d) changes to cognitive schemas (cynicism, pessimistic world-view, low mood and low spirit, negative changes to beliefs) (Pryce et al, 2007).

However, there is continued lack and under-recognition of the challenge of secondary trauma in practice, and although there is greater recognition of the importance of effective supervision, there are still relatively few organisations that offer regular support/debriefing sessions for their social work and social care practitioners.

Consider the situation when a newly qualified worker returns to their office from a home visit feeling emotionally overwhelmed and seeking containment through recounting their experience of the home visit, only to be greeted by the response of 'don't worry, you'll get used to it', or worse 'that's nothing wait till you see ...' Such statements are a negation of the practitioner's identity and discount their experience. Instead, what is needed is a professional with a listening ear and the time and space for the practitioner's narrative. This could be an official debriefing or an informal discussion that can offer the containment that the new practitioner seeks and needs to allow them to unload and unpack the emotional labour and the experience of witnessing trauma. Such a peer support and holding environment serves to reaffirm the practitioner's identity and can nurture their healthy professional development.

Intimidation and the practitioner's anxieties and fear for their personal safety, fears of not being able to cope with the workload, fears of negative outcomes, fears of getting it wrong and fears of being publicly attacked and found wanting by the media present significant challenges and anxiety in practice. Such fears and anxieties can cause substantial stress and can cloud the practitioner's judgement leading to inaction or avoidance strategies that can prove disastrous in the long run. Therefore, it may be helpful to ask one's self: *'Am I able to ask the difficult questions that need to be asked and address the complex issues that need to be addressed?'*

Speaking about practitioners' fears, Smith et al (2003) write:

> One participant envisaged her fears in boxes on shelves. Her concern was that if she got the boxes down to inspect their contents they would then prove too large and difficult to get back on the shelf.

> (p 557)

Fear and anxiety are partly due to the uncertainty associated with one's actions and decisions and inherent in everyday life, and although denial of fear may seem attractive at times, it is a short-sighted strategy that can be gravely damaging. All serious case reviews involving child death have shown that, at some stage, social workers were fearful of negative outcomes or a party involved; however, their fears were not adequately recognised and appropriately addressed.

As mentioned in the introduction to the book, social work operates at the sharp end of society's fears, anxieties and traumas. It is, therefore, crucially important to gain an appreciation of psychosocial and relationship-based dynamics of practice and to acknowledge the emotions, fears, anxieties and traumas experienced in practice, and to be able to navigate the emotional geography of others without losing sense of *self* and self-care.

Therefore, social workers need strong support and containment to enable them to process the effects of the continued secondary/vicarious trauma experienced in their everyday practice, and to acknowledge their fears and raise their concerns in supervision, seeking appropriate help and guidance.

I agree with Smith et al's *'fear audits'* which can bring work-related fears to light. They suggest this would serve a similar function as fire drills, enabling the practitioners to think about threats and fears, and to rehearse strategies for *safe exits* and dealing with potentially dangerous situations and negative outcomes in a relatively calm and thoughtful environment (eg team meeting or training exercise). Precious knowledge gained from such rehearsals can then help practitioners faced with similar situations in their actual practice.

This moves away from the culture of blame and toward establishing and maintaining a culture of learning. Freud (1905, p 224) eloquently encapsulates these ideas in his account of a three-year-old boy afraid of the dark who calls out to his aunt from a darkened room: *'Auntie, speak to me! I'm afraid because it's so dark.'* His aunt answers him: *'What good would that do? You can't see me.' 'That doesn't matter,"* replies the child, *'if anyone speaks, it gets light.'*

Trauma and its intergenerational impact

CASE STUDY

The ongoing private proceedings continue to take their toll on Teresa, Shane and Jefferson, and during the proceedings the court orders that Shane and Jefferson have monthly contact supervised by Children and Families Services.

The supervised visits undertaken go well and Shane really enjoys contact with his father. However, Teresa's emotional and mental health deteriorates. During the first contact supervision, Teresa acts aggressively towards staff at the children's centre where the contact takes place and makes inappropriate comments with sexual undertones. On a number of occasions staff move her away from the proximity of where Jefferson and Shane are playing. However, she continues returning to the same spot.

During the second contact visit a month later, the contact supervisor reports that Teresa was very challenging and did all she could to delay Shane leaving for his contact visit. She also raises concerns about how Shane was dressed as although temperatures were cold and raining Shane was dressed in a t-shirt and jeans, both of which seemed to be too small for him.

Shane's classroom teacher contacts Laura to raise concerns about Shane's emotional well-being. She has seen a drastic change in Shane's behaviour and attitude in the last three months. He has started hitting and biting other children and being very disruptive in school. He often looks very sad and his mother acts aggressively towards staff. The classroom teacher and head teacher don't think that Shane is in immediate danger. However, they are concerned about Teresa's deteriorating mental health and how this is impacting upon her parenting (Greig and Howe, 2001; Howe, 2010). The class teacher also asks whether Shane can be referred for counselling as he seems to be very unhappy and lonely.

Laura tries to refer Shane for counselling; however, Teresa is contrary and does not give consent. A legal planning meeting is convened and it is agreed that supervised contact will end as it is becoming too emotionally distressing for Shane. The local authority will support the father to take up a residency order and if the father is unsuccessful the local authority will initiate care proceedings.

Shane's classroom teacher contacts Laura to raise concerns around Teresa's parenting. Shane tells his teacher: '*it hurts when my mum hits me even when it doesn't bruise*'. Shane is referred to the child abuse investigation team (CAIT) and a strategy meeting is convened.

During the strategy meeting the following course of action is agreed:

1. The situation has become very tense recently due to the supervised contact visits and the ongoing private proceedings.

2. Recent child protection visits have been very difficult and the mother has not allowed the social worker to talk to Shane on his own.

3. There is a historic evidence of the mother *coaching* Shane, and there is concern that a similar instance may occur if a meeting is organised with Shane. Therefore, it is agreed that Laura and a colleague will pay an unannounced visit to Shane's school and will speak with Shane about the allegations of physical chastisement.

4. Teresa continues to refuse mental health support; however, she seems unsettled and there are ongoing concerns for her mental health and well-being.

Reflection

1. *Drawing on previous chapters can you think of any defence mechanisms in the narrative so far?*

2. *What are some of the possible explanations for Shane hitting and biting other children?*

3. *What are some of the intervention approaches to support people experiencing post-traumatic stress?*

Discussion

Trauma and its effects

Merleau-Ponty (1962) drawing on Gestalt theory described the dynamic figure ground structure where perceptions, thoughts and feelings may shift from being in focus to lying at the edge/fringe of the experiential horizon and vice-versa. Indeed, the Gestalt principle posits that in meaning-making what lies at the edge/fringe of our experiential horizon (experience) is as important as what is in focus, and that a change in the horizon may transform the meaning of what is in focus of our consciousness. This means that what is not at the centre of our conscious focus does indeed influence our thoughts, emotions, perceptions and cognitions. While van der Kolk et al (1996) suggest that trauma often violates one's sense of congruence, as reactions may be confusing and misunderstood, and will subsequently shape how one perceives the behaviours of others. Therefore, Teresa's evaluation of others and her perception of their behaviours are shaded and shaped by her past experiences of multiple and complex trauma.

Furthermore, in introducing trauma and its effects we discussed how the present and the future can be overshadowed by the past, and noted how the perceived *impossibility* of developing mastery over one's experience combined with the unpredictability and uncontrollability of traumatic memories can lead to fear. Indeed, the perceived impossibility of resolving the trauma and its recurrence may result in the development of defence mechanisms that further distort and complicate the memory of trauma.

Teresa's experiences of childhood abuse and unresolved trauma of rape by her grandfather represent multiple and complex trauma that have led to a state of anger and emotional pain that is reflected in her threatening and aggressive behaviour toward others.

Teresa's refusal to leave the premises and her loud voice and continued use of aggressive and inappropriate language, often with sexual undertones, are abusive. She is trying to penetrate and dominate the space between Jefferson and Shane during the contact.

Research highlights a link between anger and PTSD (Novaco and Chemtob, 2002). However, anger is a complex construct with multiple dimensions (eg psychosocial, cognitive, behavioural, motivational, physiological, etc). Furthermore, as we have seen, anger can be considered based on the directional nature of its expression as either toward self (anger-in) representing the suppression of the emotion (expressed as depression, withdrawal, isolation, etc), or toward others (anger-out) expressed as aggressive behaviour. However, in their meta-analysis, Olatunji et al (2010) highlight a significantly greater relationship between anger and PTSD than the relationship between anger and any other anxiety disorder.

Novaco and Chemtob (2002) conceptualise anger within PTSD as survival mode functioning in which anger is activated by perceptions of threat, with the survival mode function then taking priority over other cognitive processing. Given the mood-congruent memory facilitating and reinforcing the recall of memories that are in consonance with our mood (Baddeley, 1999), the anger response may bias the individual's cognitive and emotional processing capacity so that threat-consistent information receives priority while inconsistent information is discounted. Furthermore, in time and depending on individual experience, anger can become an automatic behavioural response. Foa et al (1995) suggest that anger is a type of avoidant coping and that individuals may develop a tendency to respond with anger as a strategy for avoiding fear and emotional pain.

The above are not meant as a justification for Teresa's actions and expressions; however, they add further perspective and help us appreciate the relationship between post-traumatic stress and anger. While thinking of Shane, it is clear that he is experiencing a combination of physical, psychological and emotional abuse, as well as relational aggression. Relational aggression can be defined as harming others through purposeful manipulation and damaging (or threatening to damage) relationships and includes acts such as giving someone the *silent treatment*, threatening to end a friendship to get one's own way, using social exclusion as a form of retaliation, or damaging another's feeling of acceptance or friendship (Crick et al, 1999).

Shane's externalising and disruptive behaviour (eg hitting and biting other children) can be understood from a number of perspectives. Firstly, social learning theory suggests that children may learn and adopt their parents' aggressive behaviour through observation and modelling and may imitate these in their interaction with their peers (Bandura, 1973). Therefore, due to Teresa's aggressive behaviour, Shane may have come to view aggressive behaviour as a successful strategy for social interactions (Nelson et al, 2006).

Furthermore, Teresa is Shane's primary caregiver; however, she is also the main source of pain and abuse: in Shane's words, '*It hurts when my mum hits me even when it doesn't bruise*'. Therefore, considering our discussion of attachment in Chapter 1, this superimposition of the punishing figure over the caring figure leaves Shane in a state of '*fright without solution*' (Hesse and Main, 1999, p 484) which may result in ambivalent or disorganised attachment patterns and lead to Shane's externalising behaviour. This in turn may be predictive of Shane's later adjustment in life.

Interventions, support and narrative approaches

As discussed at the beginning of this chapter, the reactivation of traumatic memory can be conceived as incomplete attempts at resolving and integrating the traumatic experience within the individual's internal working model. Therefore, any intervention that can help the individual reorganise and (re)process their traumatic memory can be helpful in restructuring and recalibrating the individual's internal working model to integrate the traumatic memory within the individual's system of value attribution and meaning-making.

People with traumatic experiences have a profound need to find new meaning and to make sense of themselves and their traumatic experiences. However, often the individual cannot find adequate response to the traumatic memory. But, there are a number of therapies and approaches that can help alleviate and resolve trauma and post-traumatic experiences. Some of the therapeutic approaches with high overall effectiveness, safety and acceptability include: narration of trauma memories, emotion-focused or emotion-regulation interventions, cognitive restructuring, education about trauma, anxiety and stress management, and others. Among these modalities, narrative interventions represent a particularly effective approach for supporting users of services experiencing post-traumatic stress. Offering validation and establishing trust, and providing such users of services with the space and the containment to speak about their traumatic stories is one of the most effective coping strategies for dealing with trauma-related distress (Cloitre et al, 2011, 2012).

Telling the trauma story is an excellent strategy that helps the individual organise memories and feelings into a more manageable and understandable psychosocial *baggage* that can eventually be *metabolised* and integrated within the individual's memory and system of values and schemas. Therefore, telling the story, or developing a trauma narrative, is a significant step in the trauma recovery process no matter what array of symptoms is present.

Effective trauma narratives can occur spontaneously in conversation or can be more structured and guided by professional intervention (eg in counselling and psychotherapy). However, it is important to be aware of the appropriate time and place before initiating such narrative conversations. For this reason, a more structured approach, such as a therapy session supported by an appropriately trained professional, may be more effective and less disruptive to people's lives. Nonetheless, practitioners can support positive change and the resolution of traumatic experience by offering a trauma-informed psychosocial and relationship-based practice.

Narrative approaches vary from verbal storytelling to written descriptions, and are supported by a host of creative techniques such as drawing, painting, collage-making, drama therapy and role-playing, creative writing, etc. Practitioners can use these and other techniques in their communication with adults and children to facilitate and support the individual's journey to recovery. We will discuss narrative approaches in the next chapter.

Although we have explored the challenges and dynamics of trauma and post-traumatic stress from the individual's perspective, it is important not to pathologise the individual. Trauma and traumatic experiences are multidimensional phenomena, and often their gravity and challenges are perpetuated and intensified by the ongoing *social trauma* of discrimination, poverty, deprivation and social exclusion. We will explore this topic further together with appropriate communication with children in the next section.

Children's voices – communicating with children in a developmentally appropriate manner

CASE STUDY

Laura and her colleague make arrangements to visit Shane first thing in the morning. Shane is happy to see Laura and responds well to her and her colleague. Laura asks Shane what happens if he has done something wrong; he tells Laura that he sits on the naughty step or he is sent to his room without dinner. Laura asks him if anything else happens and he tells her that he is also hit by his mother. Laura asks Shane whether his mother hits him with anything and he responds by saying that she hits him with a shoe or a belt.

He also tells Laura that sometimes he gets a smack for nothing and this upsets him and this upsets him more than if he gets a bruise. Shane tells Laura that he wishes his mother would stop hitting him because it really upsets him.

The social workers inform the police about the outcome of the visit, and police advise that they will take no further action stating that Children and Families Services should take the lead given Teresa's vulnerable mental health.

Reflection

1. *What are some of points to consider and some of the approaches that you may use for developmentally appropriate communication with children?*

2. *What is the role and significance of play and role play for children?*

3. *What are the consequences of physical chastisement for the child's sense of self?*

Discussion

Listening to the voices of children requires the ability for age-appropriate communication. For example, Laura and her colleague used role play to engage Shane in their investigation of possible physical abuse by Teresa. Therefore, let us explore the value and use of play, drawing and role play in communicating with children. Freud states:

> *A child's play is determined by wishes: in point of fact by a single wish – one that helps in his upbringing – the wish to be big and grown up. He is always playing at being 'grown up' and in his games he imitates what he knows about the lives of his elders.*

> (1908, p 146)

The above suggests that Laura and her colleague's approach in engaging Shane in role play is an effective and developmentally appropriate communication strategy. Indeed, when listening to the voices of children, although the words may come from the child's mouth and the thoughts from their mind, Brenkman (1999) argues that we must pay attention to discern who is really speaking.

Mannoni suggests that to enable each child to 'refind the play space of childhood' (Mannoni, 1999, p 47) we should create a space as free of demand as possible, a space where the child may, perhaps for the first time, experience the possibility of their own desire, a process that is initiated through the experience of being seen in some deep existential way (Cyrulnik, 2005).

In keeping with Winnicott's (1971) injunction against excessive interpretation, it is important that we allow the child to teach us by the ways in which they would prefer to communicate. Mannoni expressed the importance of minimising interpretation even in therapy with children:

> Giving small children the opportunity to paint, to invent a world of their own making is all the more important ... The important thing is that the loneliness, the unhappiness, ... can find expression and can do so without an adult immediately seeking to supply meaning.
>
> (1999, p 85)

It is, therefore, important that we can join the child in the child's animated space of desire and discovery rather than externally interpreting the child's experiences. This animated space is Winnicott's potential space, a place free from demand, duty or rebellious resistance, a place that attends to 'the nonsense of desire' (Mannoni, 1999, p 99). Nurturing and meeting the child in that potential space is essential for communicating with all children. This is even more important when speaking with children with experiences of trauma and abuse. Children's expressions are conditioned by social norms and the values and modes of communication they have learnt from their parents and society. Indeed, it is important to recognise that the child's capacity to say the unsayable (Rogers, 2007) or name the 'unthought knowns' of their experience (Bollas, 1987; O'Loughlin, 2006) is complicated by the presence of ancestral traumas that may be unwittingly present in the lives of children and their parents.

In a society that privileges performativity and often creates intense pressure for children at schools and in families with continued demands and a focus on achievement instead of self-actualisation and demand over desire, play offers a blank canvas that allows embodied engagement with Winnicott's potential space, or the Lacanian space for desire.

My point here is not to describe an intervention or interactional technique, it is rather about a disposition, a way of being and listening mindfully that seeks to understand the human challenges and vulnerabilities that are inherent in children's journey of growing up. Indeed, growing up is perhaps the most challenging and rewarding thing in life.

An example of such unrestricted creativity is Winnicott's (1968) Squiggle Game. There are different versions and derivations of the Squiggle Game. However, one recorded version involved Winnicott drawing a doodle onto a piece of paper which was then given to the child, inviting the child to '*make it into anything*'. Then the roles were reversed with the child drawing a doodle and handing it to Winnicott asking him to make it into anything. Winnicott would draw aimlessly without his pencil leaving the paper and, like looking at cloud formations, the child would make the image come alive by joining up the squiggle into a shape. This process was accompanied by Winnicott engaging the child to converse about the meaning of the drawing and the different representations. In Winnicott's words the objective of the game was to allow the child's '*communication of significance*' and to capture the child's relationships, thoughts and feelings in a visual form (Winnicott, 1968, p 302). Squiggle was Winnicott's '*game without rules*' allowing for maximum freedom of expression. Winnicott describes the game's characteristic features in a way that reserved space for the unprecedented '*... so that any modification may be accepted if appropriate*' (p 303).

Children often carry psychological baggage that does not belong to them, ghost traumas, fears, thoughts, and ways of being that are not theirs, but are often projected onto them and into their lives by parents, caregivers, other adults, past generations and society. Indeed, there is much that the children witness; however, they may lack the necessary language abilities or the psychological capability to tell the untellable and this is further regulated by the socio-cultural norms and values, and acceptable/permissible expressions and modes of communication. Play, role play, drawings and squiggles, and other unstructured engagements that allow expression of children's desires are excellent avenues for children to find their voice and to be heard. Children's drawings are a projection of their psyche and state of mind. Indeed, Winnicott turned to drawing as a means to symbolise a relation to the child's internal and external realm. Drawings and play are an invitation to Winnicott's '*game without rules*' that allows the child to connect with their potential space and to give it expression and to tell the untellable.

Games and role play offer another important and effective avenue for communicating with children. Therefore, Laura and her colleague engaged in role play with Shane as an age-appropriate and effective mode of communication. Indeed, '*the game is a distorted (but recognizable) mirror of reality, just as reality is a distorted mirror of fantasy*' (Fine, 2002, p 153). Role-playing games offer players opportunities to revisit events and to re-examine and work on their self-concept as well as personal and social identities in a reflexive manner.

Play integrates interactive, personal and social dimensions. Children experiment in the social world through play and interactions with others and in relation to their developing sense of identity. Play is a powerful metaphor for the social world that offers a dramaturgical stage for children to enact and experiment with different identities/personas, and to understand and assimilate them into their self-concept. In this sense, children use play and its '*symbolic representation to reorganise their experiences in order to feel secure and in control, and to manage their unmanageable thoughts, emotions and "realities"*' (Landreth, 2012). The make-believe world of play and its dramaturgical aspects offer children the possibility to distance self from their experience and in that distancing to create a temporary space, a potential space, to express their thoughts, feelings and difficult experiences that may otherwise be too intimidating or painful to recall or express. Through the medium of play practitioners can invite the *total child* to engage in creative expressions unburdened by duties and social norms in Winnicott's (1971) '*game without rules*'.

Moving on with the baggage of the past

CASE STUDY

Laura contacts Teresa to talk with her about the visit; however, she refuses to speak with Laura and shouts at her, hanging up the phone. The core group meeting is two days away and Laura is hopeful that Teresa will partake and gain a better perspective on how her behaviour is impacting on Shane. Teresa arrives for the core group meeting; however, she refuses to attend and instead waits outside of the meeting room and continues to peer in through the window. Professionals feel uncomfortable as Teresa peers through the window staring at them.

Laura receives an update from Teresa's GP stating that it continues to be a difficult time for Teresa which means she continues to find it difficult to control and contain her emotions.

A week later the child protection review conference is held and Shane continues to meet the threshold for a child protection plan and a new category of *physical abuse* is added. Hence, Shane is recorded as experiencing emotional and *physical* abuse. Teresa does not attend the child protection conference. However, Jefferson does attend the conference and states that he wants his son to live with him full-time and feels positive that he will be able to obtain residency order from the court.

Three days later Teresa contacts the office and speaks with Laura's manager and informs her that she is moving out of the borough and would like help with securing a moving van. Laura and her manager assist her with finding a moving van and Laura verifies with the housing officer that Teresa is moving from her current location.

Laura transfers the case to the new child protection team in Teresa's new borough. A transfer child protection conference is arranged and is followed by a joint visit to Teresa's new home with the new allocated social worker. The new local authority is concerned and advises Teresa that it may initiate care proceedings if the situation does not improve.

A few weeks later the court grants a residency order to Jefferson and Shane begins to live with his father full-time.

Reflection

1. *Changes of environment can at times help support positive change. Do you think Teresa's move may enable her to initiate positive change in her life?*

2. *What is post-traumatic growth, and what are some of its impacts? Can you identify an example of post-traumatic growth from your own practice experience?*

3. *How will you adopt and apply a trauma-informed psychosocial and relationship-based approach in your practice?*

Discussion

Post-traumatic growth

Following the introduction of the topic of post-traumatic stress disorder (PTSD) by the American Psychiatric Association (1980), the scientific interest in positive changes following adversity was recorded in the late 1980s and early 1990s, when a few studies reported positive changes in people with experience of trauma such as survivors of rape or domestic violence, bereaved adults, heart patients and combat veterans.

'The post-traumatic growth inventory: Measuring the positive legacy of trauma' by Tedeschi and Calhoun (1996) became a point of reference for studies of positive change after experience of trauma. Tedeschi and Calhoun (2004) define post-traumatic growth as '*positive psychological change experienced as a result of the struggle with highly challenging life circumstances*' (p 1).

Joseph et al (2012) suggest, within contemporary literature, post-traumatic growth refers to psychological well-being (PWB), defined as high levels of autonomy, environmental mastery, positive relations with others, openness to personal growth, purpose in life and self-acceptance.

Post-traumatic growth is a wide-ranging concept that is in development, although it has a central focus for positive psychologists (Seligman, 2011).

Tedeschi and Calhoun (1996) suggest that post-traumatic growth involves three main domains of positive change as described by people who have experienced it, namely:

1. Enhancement of *relationships* – they come to value human relations and friends and family and experience greater compassion for others.

2. Changed view of *self-concept* – they experience greater self-acceptance and acceptance of their vulnerabilities and, therefore, a greater sense of wisdom, strength and resilience.

3. Change in *life philosophy* – they value each day as a new beginning and re-evaluating and reprioritising their value attribution and their sense of what really matters in life.

Notwithstanding the challenges in measurement of growth, research indicates that

> greater post-traumatic growth is associated with personality factors such as emotional stability, extraversion, openness to experience, optimism and self-esteem; ways of coping such as acceptance, positive reframing, seeking social support, turning to religion and problem solving; and social support factors.
>
> (Joseph et al, 2012, p 319)

The effects of trauma can be devastating and Teresa is clearly suffering from complex trauma; however, the above evidence indicates that her situation is not without hope. Nonetheless, her continued resistance to engage with a psychiatrist or psychotherapist is the major obstacle preventing her from receiving the support that she needs. She does prefer consultations with her GP, since the GP does not challenge Teresa's behaviour/narrative, and Teresa interprets the lack of challenge from her GP as a sign of acquiescence and a reaffirmation of the accuracy of her interpretation and narrative about others and the events in her life.

One of the greatest challenges for those with experience of trauma is their desire to restore and complete their pre-trauma life-hopes and life-goals, when post-traumatic growth is about *'rebuilding one's shattered assumptive world'* (Joseph, 2012, p 817). To demonstrate the difference, I'll draw on Joseph's (2012) metaphor of a treasured vase. Imagine that you possess a precious flower vase and one day accidentally the vase is knocked over and breaks into tiny pieces. What will you do in such a situation? Will you sweep up the shattered pieces of the vase and throw them away? Or will you try to put the vase back together as it was? The first strategy will result in definite loss of the vase and its total value and will lead to grief, which may be potentially overcome after a period of mourning. The second situation represents an impossible task, as you can never restore the treasured vase to its previous state before it was shattered and, therefore, every attempt at trying to restore the vase to its previous phase will meet with failure. This leads to a never-ending cycle of aborted attempts followed by a feeling of helplessness, frustration and anger. A more resilient option, however, could be to take the beautiful coloured pieces of the vase to make something new, such as a colourful and precious mosaic. Stephen Joseph (2012) states:

> When adversity strikes, people often feel that at least some part of them – be it their views of the world, their sense of themselves, their relationships – has been smashed. Those who try to put their lives back together exactly as they were remain fractured and vulnerable. But those who accept the breakage and build themselves anew become more resilient and open to new ways of living.
>
> (p 817)

Teresa's move may be yet another attempt for a fresh start and a new narrative. The people we know and our relationships with them as well as our social surrounding are an integral part of our social identity and interlinked with our relational concept of self. Indeed, Goffman (1959, 1981) states that we *wear* different identities depending on our social context. Therefore, it may be thought that Teresa is hoping that by changing her social surrounding she may be able to find a new life and a new positive hope. Indeed, often a changed and positive surrounding can offer a new beginning and allow individuals to pursue positive life-goals (eg as we saw in the previous chapter, Jack's placement with Alma allowed him to pursue a positive and healthier growth). However, this should be accompanied with appropriate containment and support that allow the individual to process and make sense of their experiences and find self-acceptance. Indeed, such a transition is a two-way process where the social environment offers the possibility for a *new self-concept*. However, this should be accompanied with effective support and empowerment to initiate positive change. Such an interlinked positive personal and social dynamic will then enable the individual to pursue positive life-goals. However, as described earlier in this chapter, broken or incomplete narratives and what remains as unresolved and unintegrated/unprocessed experiences and memories, either as part of the unconscious or at the *fringe* of consciousness, cast a long shadow over one's present and future. Therefore, it is sad to think that in all likelihood, Teresa's new relationships and social environment will be darkened by the shadow of the past, and in this sense, Teresa's move may not offer an escape from her past and painful memories. Teresa's challenges and uncontained hurt and pain will continue to overflow into her new relation-ships and colour every new encounter with the paint of the past, and in all likelihood, she will once again find herself surrounded by the memories and the hurt and pain that she wished to leave behind. This dynamic will only reinforce Teresa's feelings of frustration, anger and hopelessness and her perception of the impossibility of finding a positive closure or healing for her traumatic experiences (Rubin, 2014). This is an important issue in everyday practice and in the next chapters we will examine some specific approaches (eg transactional ana-lysis and narrative approaches, family and systemic approaches, and motivational interview-ing) for better interventions and support in such situations, while the next section highlights the importance of trauma-informed practice.

Trauma-informed psychosocial and relationship-based practice

We have examined trauma from an interdisciplinary evidence-informed and relationship-based psychosocial perspective. It is important to once again emphasise that trauma or post-traumatic stress are not something that one *has*, they are rather challenges that one experiences. In other words, such challenges are not part of one's identity, character or way of being and are not inherent in individuals. These challenges are what one experiences as a result of one's lived experiences and social environment. We will examine this import-ant distinction further in the next chapter when we discuss narrative therapy. Therefore, it is important to emphasise that relationships are embedded within social contexts and are regulated by cultural values and social norms. Indeed, power imbalances, discrimination and social inequalities are so deep-rooted that they are often taken for granted and become invisible to our consciousness. Poverty, deprivation and social inequality, racism and vari-ous types of discrimination, social exclusion and socio-cultural and other forms of prejudice, social stereotypes and value attribution based on a marketised culture and society, pose significant challenges in our everyday lives and relationships. Such inequities compound the impact of direct and indirect as well as personal and social trauma and perpetuate oppres-sion of peoples and their communities. This is insidious trauma that is normalised through repetition and widespread impact to the point that it is repressed from our personal and social consciousness. Due to this normalisation many of the damaging events and much of the everyday trauma of poverty, deprivation, discrimination and other everyday challenges are not encoded as declarative knowledge but are inscribed in our minds, bodies and psyche and encoded in our culture and social relationship including our professional roles, prac-tices, organisations, legal and political systems, and various policies. Individual events and experiences are part of this larger social formation and historical continuum that have pro-found effects for all individuals, communities, societies and cultures.

Early research in post-traumatic growth focused on growth following typically traumatic events, such as rape, assault, war, etc. However, Tedeschi et al (2007) clarify that post-trau-matic growth 'follows a challenge to and re-examination of core beliefs, not every bad experi-ence' (p 396). Indeed, Aldwin and Levenson (2004) argue that growth is not just restricted to traumatic experiences, but life events, such as childbirth, can also promote growth. Research has, therefore, increasingly examined growth following events such as illness, bereavement and work-related stress (eg Koenig et al, 1998; Paton, 2005; Znoj, 2006), which are challen-ging but not necessarily traumatic.

Psychosocial analysis and reconnecting with our self through critical reflection and with a positive regard, are important factors in our healthy development. However, human development is intimately linked to holistic and harmonious connection between mind, body, spirit, culture and society. Indeed, our experiences take place in Winnicott's potential space in-between self and the Other, personal and social, inter-psychic and interpersonal, individual and societal, and corporeal and virtual, and in-between time and place. It is through the nurturing and development of this potential in-between and in-betwixt space that one may find the promise of a healthy and holistic human growth and a more equitable society.

From its inception, social work has dealt with trauma and supporting individuals in their journey of recovery. However, drawing on the above and recognising the complex, multilayered, psychosocial and personal nature of trauma offer us a broader appreciation of trauma and highlight the importance of a trauma-informed psychosocial and relationship-based practice.

References

Aldwin, C and Levenson, M (2004) Post-traumatic Growth: A Developmental Perspective. *Psychological Inquiry*, 15: 19–22.

American Psychiatric Association Committee on Nomenclature and Statistics (1980) *Diagnostic and Statistical Manual of Mental Disorders* (3rd edn). Washington, DC: American Psychiatric Association.

Astington, J, Harris, P and Olson, D (1988) *Developing Theories of Mind*. Cambridge: Cambridge University Press.

Baddeley, A D (1999) *Essentials of Human Memory*. Hove: Psychology Press.

Bandura, A (1973) *Aggression: A Social Learning Approach*. Englewood Cliffs, NJ: Prentice Hall.

Basoglu, M and Mineka, S (1992) Role of Uncontrollability and Unpredictability of Stress in the Development of Post-torture Stress Symptoms, in Basoglu, M (ed) *Torture and its Consequences: Current Treatment Approaches*. Cambridge: Cambridge University Press.

Bollas, C (1987) *The Shadow of the Object: Psychoanalysis of the Unthought Known*. New York: Colombia University Press.

Brenkman, J (1999) Introduction, in Mannoni, M (ed) *Separation and Creativity: Refinding the Lost Language of Childhood*. New York: Other Press.

Brewin, C (2014) Episodic Memory, Perceptual Memory, and Their Interaction: Foundations for a Theory of Posttraumatic Stress Disorder. *Psychological Bulletin*, 140(1): 69–97.

Calhoun, L G and Tedeschi, R G (2004) The Foundations of Posttraumatic Growth. *Psychological Inquiry*, 15: 93–102.

Ceci, S J and Bruck, M (1995) *Jeopardy in the Courtroom: A Scientific Analysis of Children's Testimony*. Washington, DC: American Psychological Association.

Cloitre M, Courtois C A, Charuvastra A, Carapezza R, Stolbach B C, Green B L (2011) Treatment of Complex PTSD: Results of the ISTSS Expert Clinician Survey on Best Practices. *Journal of Trauma Stress*, 24: 615–27.

Cloitre, M, Courtois, C A, Ford, J D et al (2012) *The ISTSS Expert Consensus Treatment Guidelines for Complex PTSD in Adults*. [online] Available at: www.istss.org/ (accessed 17 December 2014).

Crick, N R, Casas, J F and Ku, H C (1999) Relational and Physical Forms of Peer Victimization in Preschool. *Developmental Psychology*, 35(2): 376–85.

Cyrulnik, B (2005) *The Whispering of Ghosts: Trauma and Resilience*. New York: Other Press.

Ehrensaft, M K, Cohen, P, Brown, J, Smailes, E, Chen, H and Johnson, J G (2003) Intergenerational Transmission of Partner Violence: A 20-year Prospective Study. *Journal of Consulting and Clinical Psychology*, 71: 741–53.

Ferguson, H (2010) Walks, Home Visits and Atmospheres: Risk and the Everyday Practices and Mobilities of Social Work and Child Protection. *British Journal of Social Work*, 40: 1100–17.

Figley, C R (ed) (2002) *Treating Compassion Fatigue*. New York: Routledge.

Fine, G A (2002) *Shared Fantasy Role Playing Games as Social Worlds*. New York: University of Chicago Press.

Fischer, G and Riedesser, P (1999) *Lehrbuch der Psychotraumatologie* (Textbook of Psycho-traumathology). München: Ernst Reinhardt Verlag.

Foa, E B, Riggs, D S, Massie, E D and Yarczower, M (1995) The Impact of Fear Activation and Anger on the Efficacy of Exposure Treatment for Posttraumatic Stress Disorder. *Behavior Therapy*, 26: 487–99.

Frank, A W (2005) *The Renewal of Generosity: Illness, Medicine, and How to Live*. Chicago: University of Chicago Press.

Freud, S (1905) *Three Essays on the Theory of Sexuality*. SE7 (pp 125–245). London: Hogarth.

Freud, S (1908) *Creative Writers and Day-Dreaming: The Complete Psychological Works of Sigmund Freud* (Strachey, J, trans). Vol. 9 SE9 (pp 143–53). London: Hogarth.

Fritzley, V H and Lee, K (2003) Do Young Children Always Say Yes to Yes-No Questions? A Metadevelopmental Study of the Affirmation Bias. *Child Development*, 74(5): 1297–313.

Gallese, V and Lakoff, G (2005) The Brain's Concepts: The Role of the Sensory-Motor System in Conceptual Knowledge. *Cognitive Neuropsychology*, 21: 455–79.

Goffman, E (1959) *The Presentation of Self in Everyday Life*. Garden City, NY: Doubleday.

Goffman, E (1981) *Forms of Talk*. Oxford: Blackwell.

Gräfenhain, M, Behnea, T, Carpenter, M and Tomasello, M (2009) One-Year-Olds' Understanding of Nonverbal Gestures Directed to a Third Person. *Cognitive Development*, 24: 23–33.

Greig, A and Howe, D (2001) Social Understanding, Attachment Security of Preschool Children and Maternal Mental Health. *British Journal of Developmental Psychology*, 19: 381–93.

Hammond, N R and Fivush, R (1991) Memories of Mickey Mouse: Young Children Recount Their Trip to Disneyworld. *Cognitive Development*, 6: 433–48.

Heidegger, M (1962) *Being and Time*, Macquarrie, J and Robinson, E (trans). New York: Harper & Row.

Herman, J (1992) *Trauma and Recovery: From Domestic Violence to Political Terrorism*. New York: Basic Books.

Hesse, E and Main, M (1999) Second-Generation Effects of Unresolved Trauma in Nonmaltreating Parents: Dissociated, Frightened, and Threatening Parental Behaviour. *Psychoanalytic Inquiry*, 19(4): 481–540.

Hiskeya, S, Luckiea, M, Daviesa, S and Brewin, C R (2008) The Phenomenology of Reactivated Trauma Memories in Older Adults: A Preliminary Study. *Aging & Mental Health*, 12(4): 494–8.

Howe, D (2010) The Safety of Children and the Parent-Worker Relationship in Cases of Child Abuse and Neglect. *Child Abuse Review*, 19: 330–41.

Hughes, H M, Humphrey, N N and Weaver, T L (2005) Advances in Violence and Trauma: Toward Comprehensive Ecological Models. *Journal of Interpersonal Violence*, 20: 31–8.

Husserl, E (1989) *Ideas Pertaining to a Pure Phenomenology and to a Phenomenological Philosophy: Second Book Studies in the Phenomenology of Constitution*. Dordrecht: Kluwer Academic Publishers.

Jonas, H (1966) *The Phenomenon of Life: Toward a Philosophical Biology*. Chicago: University of Chicago Press.

Joseph, S (2012) What Doesn't Kill Us…, The Psychologist, *The British Psychological Society*, 25(11): 816–19.

Joseph, S, Murphy, D and Regel, S (2012) An Affective–Cognitive Processing Model of Post-Traumatic Growth. *Clinical Psychology and Psychotherapy*, 19: 316–25.

Koenig, H G, Pargament, K I and Nielsen, J (1998) Religious Coping and Health Status in Medically Ill Hospitalized Older Adults. *Journal of Nervous and Mental Disease*, 186(9): 513–21.

Landreth, G (2012) *Play Therapy: The Art of the Relations*. London: Routledge.

Levine, P A (1997) *Waking the Tiger: Healing Trauma*. Berkeley, CA: North Atlantic Books.

Malloy, L C and Quas, J A (2009) Children's Suggestibility: Areas of Consensus and Controversy, in Kuehnle, K and Connell, M (eds) *The Evaluation of Child Sexual Abuse Allegations* (pp 267–97). Hoboken, NJ: John Wiley & Sons, Inc.

Mannoni, M (1999) *Separation and Creativity: Refinding the Lost Language of Childhood*. New York: Other Press.

Megele, C (2015a) *Professionalism, Ethics and Boundaries in Social Media: The Age of Post-Liquid Fusion* (forthcoming).

Megele, C (2015b) Touché (forthcoming).

Merleau-Ponty, M (1962) *Phenomenology of Perception*. New York: The Humanities Press, Routledge & Kegan Paul.

Merleau-Ponty, M (1964) *Signs*. Chicago: Northwestern University Press.

Merleau-Ponty, M (1968) *The Visible and the Invisible*. Evanston, IL: Northwestern University Press.

Mrug, S, Loosier, P S and Windle, M (2008) Violence Exposure Across Multiple Contexts: Individual and Joint Effects on Adjustment. *American Journal of Orthopsychiatry*, 78: 70–84.

Nelson, D A, Hart, C H, Yang, C, Olson, J A and Jin, S (2006) Aversive Parenting in China: Associations with Child Physical and Relational Aggression. *Child Development*, 77(3): 554–72.

Novaco, R W and Chemtob, C M (2002) Anger and Combat-related Posttraumatic Stress Disorder. *Journal of Traumatic Stress*, 15: 123–32.

Olatunji, B O, Ciesielski, B and Tolin, D (2010) Fear and Loathing: A Meta-analytic Review of the Specificity of Anger in PTSD. *Behavior Therapy*, 41: 93–105.

O'Loughlin, M (2006) On Knowing and Desiring Children: The Significance of the Unthought Known, in Boldt, G and Salvio, P (eds) *Love's Return: Psychoanalytic Essays on Childhood Teaching and Learning*. New York: Routledge.

Paton, D (2005) Posttraumatic Growth in Protective Services Professionals: Individual, Cognitive and Organizational Influences. *Traumatology. Special Issue: Posttraumatic Growth*, 11: 335–46.

Pryce, J G, Shackelford, K K and Pryce, H P (2007) *Secondary Traumatic Stress and the Child Welfare Professional*. Chicago: Lyceum.

Quas, J A, Davis, E L, Goodman, G S and Myers, J E B (2007) Repeated Questions, Deception, and Children's True and False Reports of Body Touch. *Child Maltreatment*, 12: 60–7.

Rogers, A G (2007) *The Unsayable: The Hidden Language of Trauma*. New York: Random House.

Rotenberg, K J (1980) A Promise Kept, a Promise Broken: Developmental Bases of Trust. *Child Development*, 51: 614–17.

Rubin, D (2014) Schema-Driven Construction of Future Autobiographical Traumatic Events: The Future Is Much More Troubling Than the Past. *Journal of Experimental Psychology*, 143(2): 612–30.

Seligman, M E P (2011) *Flourish*. New York: Free Press.

Smith, M, McMahon, L and Nursten, J (2003) Social Workers' Experience of Fear. *British Journal of Social Work*, 33(5): 659–71.

Stern, D N (2004) *The Present Moment in Psychotherapy and Everyday Life*. New York: Norton Company.

Tedeschi, R G and Calhoun, L G (1996) The Posttraumatic Growth Inventory: Measuring the Positive Legacy of Trauma. *Journal of Traumatic Stress*, 9: 455–71.

Tedeschi, R G and Calhoun, L G (2004) Posttraumatic Growth: Conceptual Foundations and Empirical Evidence. *Psychological Inquiry*, 15(1): 1–18.

Tedeschi, R G, Calhoun, L G and Cann, A (2007) Evaluating Resource Gain: Understanding and Misunderstanding Posttraumatic Growth. *Applied Psychology: An International Review*, 56(3): 396–406.

Van der Kolk, B (1994) The Body Keeps the Score: Memory and the Evolving Psychobiology of Posttraumatic Stress. *Harvard Review of Psychiatry*, 1(5): 253–65.

Van der Kolk, B, Pelcovitz, D, Roth, S, Mandel, F S, McFarlane, A and Herman, J L (1996) Dissociation, Somatization, and Affect Dysregulation: The Complexity of Adaptation of Trauma. *American Journal of Psychiatry*, 153(7 Suppl): 83–93.

Winnicott, D W (1968) The Squiggle Game, in Winnicott, C, Shepherd, R and Davis, M (eds) *Psychoanalytic Explorations* (pp 299–317). London: Karnac Books.

Winnicott, D W (1971) *Playing and Reality*. London: Tavistock Publications.

Znoj, H (2006) Bereavement and Posttraumatic Growth, in Calhoun, L G and Tedeschi, R G (eds) *Handbook of Posttraumatic Growth: Research & Practice* (pp 176–96). Mahwah, NJ: Lawrence Erlbaum Associates Publishers.

6 A broken narrative

Transactional analysis and narrative approaches

Chapter summary

This chapter introduces narrative approaches and transactional analysis. Specifically, the chapter begins by introducing the person-centred approach of reflecting back and externalisation of *problems*. This is followed by an example of re-authoring narratives and shifting to the person's preferred narratives.

The chapter then introduces transactional analysis and how it can be used to reflect upon our own thoughts, emotions and behaviour, and to support our users of services.

The chapter concludes with a discussion of loss and grief and by introducing re-membering conversations as an effective narrative intervention that relocates a significant figure in the life of the person and allows continuity of the bonds between them.

Chapter objectives

1. Introduce the importance of narratives and narrative interventions.

2. Introduce the concept and process of externalising problems and re-authoring conversations.

3. Introduce transactional analysis and some of its applications in practice.

4. Introduce loss and grief and re-membering as a narrative intervention for loss and grief.

Exploring trauma and its effects

CASE STUDY

Nicolas was two years old when Ms Bello brought him to the accident and emergency department (A&E) raising concerns about marks she noticed on his bottom. She requested for him to be examined as he had also told her that a man had hurt his bottom. Nicolas was examined by the doctor and nothing of concern was noted or identified. Given the nature of the claim a referral was made to Children and Families Services and an assessment undertaken. Medical and health professionals described Ms Bello as 'manic at times' and 'highly anxious'. However, it was found that Ms Bello provided very good care for her son and, therefore, no further action was recommended. The report, though, suggested that Ms Bello may like to avail herself of counselling.

There was no further contact between Children and Families Services and the family until four years later when Nicolas was six years old and Ms Bello was diagnosed with bowel cancer. Ms Bello started treatment and could no longer work as a freelance photographer. This started impacting upon her financial situation and self-confidence. During this time medical professionals noticed that Nicolas seemed anxious and concerned, wanting to know where his mother was at all times.

Ms Bello underwent a successful operation and was released from the hospital. There was no further involvement from Children and Families Services until six years later when Ms Bello was readmitted to undergo further treatment for cancer, but could not identify any family member or close friend to care for Nicolas during her hospital stay. Therefore, Nicolas (aged 12) was admitted to the children's ward for social reasons while his mother was in the hospital. During his stay he mentioned to staff that sometimes he did not eat dinner, and nurses noticed that he presented as small in stature for his age. He was well-behaved, polite and a kind young person and staff highlighted that he seemed embarrassed at needing to be admitted for social reasons.

The following year Ms Bello presents at A&E intoxicated complaining that her leg is excruciatingly painful. She explains that she tripped over a pot plant and thinks she may have broken her leg. Nicolas was with her and called a taxi to take her to the hospital. Ms Bello became aggressive during her brief visit to A&E and staff at the hospital noticed that Nicolas seemed embarrassed by his mother's actions as he asked her on a number of occasions to stop shouting and asked her to calm down. The consultant who sees Ms Bello is concerned about her alcohol consumption and her ability to care for Nicolas when intoxicated. The consultant was also concerned that she may mix her painkillers with alcohol and refers Ms Bello to Children and Families Services.

During the duty allocation meeting the team manager assigns the assessment to Juliana Macnee. Juliana phones Ms Bello to arrange a home visit:

Juliana: *Good morning Ms Bello, my name is Juliana Macnee and I am a social worker in Children and Families Services. Is this a convenient time to talk?*

Ms Bello: *Hello, I have been expecting your call. Dr Finn told me that he would be referring me to your service as I need additional help and support around the house due to my broken leg.*

Juliana: *It will give us an opportunity to discuss that as well as some concerns around your alcohol consumption.*

Ms Bello: *If you want to talk about that it's fine, but I don't have any kind of problem relating to alcohol. What I would really appreciate is some help around the house. Will you be able to help me with that?*

Juliana: *As part of the assessment I will certainly have a look at that and how you are managing and possible impacts and effects on Nicolas.*

Juliana arranges a home visit to see Ms Bello the following day at 2pm. Juliana rings the bell and Ms Bello asks her to go up to the third floor. Juliana makes her way up to the third floor of a stylish apartment block and is greeted by a tall slim woman with long dark hair, blue eyes and a strong smell of alcohol. Ms Bello greets Juliana with slurred speech and is wobbly on her crutches. She turns and asks Juliana to follow her. Fearful that she might fall Juliana asks Ms Bello if she needs any help. However, she declines Juliana's offer and says she can make it back to the lounge area just fine, and invites Juliana to take a seat opposite her.

Juliana: *Thank you for agreeing to see me today Ms Bello. How are you feeling today?*

Ms Bello: *I am doing really well, and I will be up and about on my feet in no time. I am really looking forward to our summer break. If you really want to help please get me some help for around the house, I can barely move with these things [motioning to the crutches].*

Juliana: *Ok, would you like to tell me a little bit more about the accident and what happened and what you would need help with.*

Ms Bello: *I was rushing around the house and ended up tripping over a pot plant. Nicolas called a cab and we went to A&E where they told me that I broke my leg and that's it really ... that is really it.*

Juliana: *The referring doctor mentioned that you were intoxicated when you arrived at the hospital and he is concerned that you may find it difficult to manage your alcohol intake.*

Ms Bello (irritated tone): *How many times do I need to tell you, the whole thing is being blown out of proportion? I had one glass of wine and it didn't agree with the antihistamines I'm taking.*

Juliana: *So it was a mixture of the antihistamines and one glass of wine. I can't help but notice that you are struggling with your speech today and I wondered whether you are feeling ok today?*

Ms Bello (very irritated tone): *I am fine ... how many times do I need to tell you that I am fine. I don't need to listen to this ... I don't want any help from you. You are all the same, no one really cares. Do you know I am in remission? I had terminal bowel cancer and no one thought I would survive, not the doctors, not my family, no one but Nicolas. I have been through hell and back and you want to talk to me about having a few glasses of wine. I kept on fighting even when I wanted to give up, but I didn't because of Nicolas.*

Juliana: *It sounds like it was a very difficult time for you.*

Ms Bello (crying): *It was very difficult and I am still recovering. I was very scared as I didn't know what would happen to Nicolas. I don't have any family in England, they all live in Paris or Milan and I am not close to my family. It's funny, I always felt a distance between us and then when I was diagnosed my mother told me that I was adopted at seven months. She kept it a secret my whole life. I knew there was something different but I just couldn't put my finger on it.*

Juliana: *That must have been quite a shock for you and also at a vulnerable time for you because of your diagnosis.*

Ms Bello: *It was a very difficult time and Nicolas' father [Jonathan] could not be much support because his wife dislikes me. So he couldn't visit or help with Nicolas although he is the father. I think she's scared that I want him back or that he may leave her again. I met Nicolas' father when he separated from Mia [his wife] and three daughters. We were in a relationship for about six months and then I fell pregnant with Nicolas. We were together until Nicolas was two years old and then he returned to his wife. She resents me because Jonathan is still in my life and will always be a part of my life because we share a child.*

Juliana: *Where is Nicolas today?*

Ms Bello: *I sent him to the movies with his friends. I wanted us to have some time to speak privately and confidentially.*

They continue to talk and Ms Bello admits to having a 'drinking problem' and becomes very forthcoming about her misuse of alcohol.

Reflection

Drawing on what we have discussed in the previous chapters reflect upon the following questions:

1. *Thinking about your own experience, have you encountered similar situations? What did you do and how did you proceed?*

2. *Consider the dynamics of the family and some of their challenges as well as the above conversation, would you do anything differently? And why?*

3. *Why did Ms Bello want to meet privately with Juliana? And why did she become irritated with her?*

Discussion

Let us begin by considering the conversation between Ms Bello and Juliana. Although the conversation started positively, it took a difficult turn after Juliana's reference to the doctor's report that Ms Bello was intoxicated, and Ms Bello eventually responding in an irritated tone that she was fine:

Ms Bello (very irritated tone): *I am fine … how many times do I need to tell you that I am fine. I don't need to listen to this … I don't want any help from you. You are all the same, no one really cares …*

It is always essential to respect and acknowledge the experiences of users of services.

As described in Chapter 2, validation is the first step in building trust and developing a relationship-based intervention. In the above conversation Juliana validates Ms Bello's experience in a non-judgemental manner. It is important to note that she doesn't tell Ms Bello '*I understand …*', or '*I know …*', etc; instead, she simply states: '*It sounds like it was a very difficult time for you.*' This is important as Juliana's reply acknowledges that it must have been very difficult for Ms Bello but, at the same time, honours the uniqueness of Ms Bello's experience. This offers Ms Bello a non-judgemental opportunity to share her feelings, in response to which Juliana continues with the same reserve and containment stating: '*That must have been quite a shock for you and also at a vulnerable time for you because of your diagnosis*', acknowledging and honouring her experience in a non-judgemental and open-ended manner. This non-judgemental conversation allows Ms Bello to acknowledge that she has a '*drinking problem*' and become forthcoming about her misuse of alcohol.

Juliana's stance is in line with person-centred approaches that place the individual at the heart of the intervention. Furthermore, this mode of restating feeling and reflecting back provide an opportunity for the practitioner to check their perception/understanding in an empathic manner with the user of services. While enhancing accuracy of understanding, this process also encourages the user of services to enter more deeply into their personal experiences (Rogers, 1959).

Vanerschot (1993) suggests that such empathy works in three ways. Firstly, an empathic climate created by the practitioner serves to foster self-acceptance and trust by the user of services through the experience of being understood and accepted by another and counters the person's lack of positive self-regard which enables individuals to initiate positive change. Secondly, the concrete empathic responses by the practitioner facilitate the user of services delving deeper into experiences that may be at the edge of their consciousness/awareness (poorly defined or distorted) (Gendlin, 1981). Such responses are also termed *deep* or *advanced* empathy (Mearns and Thorne, 1988) to denote the way that they relate to an aspect of the user of services' experiencing that is not directly being addressed or acknowledged until that point.

Thirdly, all empathic responses to a user of services have a cognitive effect, assisting them to reorganise the meanings of the experiences being processed. This helps focus attention on particular experiences, to recall information relating to an experience or to organise information in a more differentiated and elaborative manner, facilitating a process of cognitive reorganisation and restructuring.

The above is also in line with narrative approaches which move away from pathologising narratives and aim to externalise the difficulties and *problems* as separate from people's identities.

Externalising the problem

A non-judgemental approach does not mean ignoring the challenges and issues or their effects that were the reason for the social work interventions in the first place. To the contrary, it is important to acknowledge the difficulties experienced by users of services and to recognise their damaging effects. However, a non-judgemental approach is about externalising the problem or difficulties as separate from people's identities and as something experienced by the person rather than something that is a character trait or inherent to the individual.

Expressions such as '*John is mentally ill*' or '*Angie has mental illness*' are stigmatising and totalise the identities of individuals. The first statement defines John by his mental health difficulties while the second assumes that *mental illness* is something like a trait that people possess and is part of their identity. Such statements pathologise the individual, and fail to recognise that mental health and illness lie on a continuum and their definitions are influenced by culture and society. Therefore, they are much more fluid than most people appreciate. This leads to stigma which is fundamentally a projection of society's fears and unresolved issues/notions.

Therefore, the appropriate term may be that John or Angie are '*experiencing mental health difficulties*'. Such a definition recognises the challenges faced by John and Angie; however, it also externalises mental ill-health, as something that an individual may experience, and not as something that *they are*. This separates the individuals and their identity from the challenges that they may be experiencing and is fundamental to an empowering conversation.

In social work, we usually enter people's lives at a time when they are experiencing particularly difficult challenges and need some help and support to enable them to restore balance and homeostasis in their lives. Separating issues, problems, difficulties or challenges from people's identities highlights the fact that although they may be experiencing certain problems and/or difficulties, they are not defined by them and such challenges are not part of their identity or *character* or a trait that they possess or that defines their lives or is inherent to them.

Through externalising conversations we can support others to begin re-authoring their often socially-imposed totalising narratives to an alternative and preferred storyline that celebrates individuals' uniqueness, and highlights their strengths and possibilities, based on the individual's preferred identity narrative.

Narrative approaches centre people as the experts of their own lives and view problems as separate from people; this offers a powerful method for effective and empowering interventions.

In the next section, we will examine how Juliana applies narrative approaches in her conversation with Ms Bello.

A psychological crutch

Ms Bello and Juliana continue to talk and Ms Bello admits to having a *'drinking problem'* and becomes very forthcoming about her misuse of alcohol.

Referring to Ms Bello's acknowledgement of having a *'drinking problem'*, Juliana asks how she would characterise her drinking and what it feels like? She adds: '... *if you were to give it a name that described your feeling and experiences, how would you call it?'*

Ms Bello: *You don't feel the pain as much. It numbs your feelings and you don't care anymore. You become like a different person, kind of like being an observer instead of being yourself. But, it also works like a psychological crutch. Yes, if I were to give it a name I would call it 'the crutch'.*

Juliana: *Can you tell me some more about 'the crutch'?*

Ms Bello continues to describe how she feels depressed and her love and anger for Nicolas' dad who does not want her anymore, and that nobody cares about how she feels. She acknowledges that she drinks 4–5 glasses a day of wine and that this is a regular occurrence. Juliana speaks of the *'psychological crutch'* as something that was separate from Ms Bello's identity while recognising the effects of *'the crutch'*.

Juliana: *I was just curious about whether 'the crutch' has any impact on your life or your relationships?*

Ms Bello explains that it helps her when she is down but she also adds that she frequently skips meals and is often invited to places where there is a lot of alcohol freely available. She describes how she has lost some of her old friends because of the effects of *'the crutch'* and that she would like to give up drinking but sometimes feels that she can't handle the situation without *'the crutch'*.

Juliana asks whether *'the crutch'* had any impact on Nicolas or her relationship with him or the way she cared for him?

Ms Bello states that Nicolas is a sensitive boy, and that they love each other very much. She cries and acknowledges that when she drinks (uses *'the crutch'*) she seems to become unable to respond to Nicolas the way she would want to, and this hurts her very much as she doesn't want to be like her mother. She explains how Nicolas is everything in her life and she wants the best for him.

Juliana asks Ms Bello how she thinks Nicolas is feeling about *'the crutch'* and its effects and how she would judge the effects of *'the crutch'*? Are they good or bad, or a bit of both?

Ms Bello explains that *'the crutch'* makes her forget some of the pain. However, although she initially thought she could shield Nicolas from it, she realises that he knows about it and that she thinks the effects of *'the crutch'* are mostly negative. She adds that it has made her lose many of her friends and alienated Nicolas' father even more. She describes how she is worried that it may negatively affect Nicolas and that it makes Nicolas worry about her, and that she wants Nicolas to have a good childhood and not to worry about her.

Based on Ms Bello's description, Juliana and Ms Bello then explore what she values and the things she considers as important in her life. In the course of discussion, Juliana asks Ms Bello why does she think that the effects of 'the crutch' are mostly negative, and Ms Bello explains that she values relationships and 'the crutch' has resulted in her losing most of her friends. It becomes evident that Ms Bello loves and values Nicolas above all, and would like to restore her relationship with her friends who had distanced themselves from her due to alcohol misuse. Juliana then discusses different treatment plans and options for alcohol and substance misuse and Ms Bello agrees to attend a drug and alcohol detox programme and would like this to coincide with Nicolas going to boarding school which is in a month's time. Ms Bello explains that Nicolas has received a full scholarship to attend a boarding school and it's a great opportunity for him to nurture his talent. Juliana explains that she will also need to meet Nicolas and have a conversation with him and Ms Bello raises objections explaining that she doesn't want Nicolas to become aware of her substance misuse as she is scared he may view her as a failure. Juliana provides reassurance and explains that she will ask Nicolas about his school, his health and his relationships with different family members. After Juliana's explanation Ms Bello consents.

Reflection

1. *At the beginning of their conversation, Ms Bello was quite irritated with Juliana; however, she is very forthcoming in the above conversation. What changed and how?*

2. *Drawing on the previous chapters, what is your reflection and analysis of the above conversation?*

3. *How can Juliana build on this positive start, and what are the next steps she needs to consider?*

Discussion

We have discussed the importance of externalising conversations which is a central principle in narrative approaches, and the above conversation offers a good example of narrative intervention. Therefore, let us briefly examine the components and the process of narrative intervention as outlined by White (2005) and applied by Juliana in her intervention with Ms Bello.

1. Describing the problem – *negotiation of an experience-near definition of problem*

After Ms Bello's acknowledgement of having a 'drinking problem', Juliana ask how she would characterise her drinking and what it feels like? She adds: '... *if you were to give it a name that described your experience, how would you call it?'*

By asking Ms Bello to describe her experiences with alcohol, rather than making assumptions about Ms Bello's experience, Juliana demonstrates her appreciation for the uniqueness of Ms Bello's experiences, allowing her to describe and define them in her own terms. By asking Ms Bello to choose a name that is descriptive of her experiences Juliana is enabling Ms Bello to separate the problem from her identity and to externalise it as '*the crutch*' or her psychological crutch. Such a descriptive name highlights how Ms Bello views her drinking and enables Juliana to address the *problem/issue* in terms that are meaningful and relevant to Ms Bello.

Juliana's approach involves what White describes as '*experience-near definition of the problem*', since it begins the process of having the person describe the specifics of their own lives and experiences.

Narrative work is also a strength-based approach and therefore involves building on people's strengths and resilience. Therefore, Juliana could also explore and identify times when Ms Bello did not use '*the crutch*'. This is important to lessen the effect of the *problem* narrative and facilitate identification and adoption of an alternative and preferred narrative.

2. Mapping/describing the effects of the problem

Noting that Ms Bello is feeling comfortable to speak about her drinking ('*the crutch*'), Juliana asks: '*I was just curious about whether "the crutch" has any impact on your life or your relationships?*'

This question enables Ms Bello to consider and describe the consequences and effects of '*the crutch*' in her life and on her relationships. Describing narrative approaches in a sequence of steps highlights a practical approach to their application in our interventions. However, at times it is necessary to move back in the process and to explore and consolidate an earlier step before we can move forward again. For example, if the user of services begins to find it difficult to engage or answer questions, you should be ready to move back to the first step and ask them to describe their challenges and experiences in more detail.

This allows Ms Bello to describe the *problem* from her own perspective and in her own words, and enables her to acknowledge the *problem* (alcohol misuse) and its effects. This is also in line with the person-centred approach. Indeed, Rogers states:

> *It seems to me that only when a gut-level experience is fully accepted and accurately labelled in awareness, can it be completed ... It is the sensitive empathic climate that helps to move experiencing forward to its conclusion ...*
>
> (1980, p 158)

Here the '*labelled in awareness*' is equivalent to the psychoanalytic idea of bringing the unconscious into one's consciousness and the concept that only those experiences that match the self-concept are admitted into awareness, while others are repressed into the subconscious/unconscious or are perceived in a distorted form. By externalising Ms Bello's alcohol misuse, the *problem* is no longer an all-consuming and totalising experience. This combined with an emphasis on the other positive aspects of Ms Bello's identity can allow for a re-authoring of her identity narrative based on her strengths and the positive aspects of her life. This is at the heart of the strength-based approach. We will re-examine the strength-based approach and the re-authoring of identity narratives later in the book.

3.   *Evaluating the effects of the* problem

Having described the effect of the *problem* it is important to ask the user of services how they evaluate the effects of the problem. This question may sound redundant or one may think that it is *obvious* that the effects of alcohol misuse are negative. However, we need to remember that different people may experience the same phenomenon differently, and that it is important to value the other person's views, way of thinking and preferences over our own, and to respect their lived experience, perspective, values and expertise by allowing them to define, describe and evaluate their experiences of the *problem* and its effects. This is empowering for the user of services while enabling the practitioner to learn about the other person's preferences and what they value. Therefore, Juliana asks Ms Bello how she would judge the effects of '*the crutch*' and whether they are good or bad, or a bit of both?

This is empowering for Ms Bello and enables her to describe the effect of the problem from her own perspective, while allowing Juliana to see the effect of the *problem* from Ms Bello's perspective. This is a novel experience for Ms Bello as most of the time this question is answered by others in her life (eg friends telling her, or other people assuming, that her drinking is a problem). This also enables Juliana to learn about what Ms Bello values and the relationships that are important to her.

4.   *Justifying the evaluation*

In the final stage of applying a narrative approach in her intervention, Juliana prompts Ms Bello to reflect on her evaluation of the impact of the *problem* and to *justify* her evaluation. This is the fourth step of externalising and re-authoring conversation as applied by Juliana in her intervention. By thinking about her evaluation of the effects of '*the crutch*' (alcohol misuse) Ms Bello is able to reflect upon and identify what she values and is important to her based on her own judgements. It is important to note that by asking Ms Bello to justify her evaluation of the effects of '*the crutch*', Ms Bello has a chance to explicitly verbalise and acknowledge that its effects are '*mostly negative*', and that relationships are important to her. This in turn offers Juliana the opportunity to discuss different treatment options for alcohol and substance misuse with Ms Bello agreeing to attend a drug and alcohol detox.

By asking questions in relation to the landscape of identity, practitioners can help users of services develop a thicker description of the subordinate storyline and bring it out of the past and into the future (White, 2005). Steps in re-authoring conversations alternate between:

A.   *Exploring the present situation of the problem with fine detail (the landscape of action);*

B.   *Exploring what this meant to the client/user of services, why they did the actions above, etc and what this says about them (landscape of identity).*

Once the person's values and preferences have been discussed, clarified and made explicit, it is possible to begin a conversation about change and alternative visions and to consider how the person's life could be different if they were to prioritise the values that they had identified as important to them.

The positive manner in which Juliana was able to turn the conversation from a confrontational situation to a coproductive and constructive dialogue, demonstrates the powerful nature of narrative interventions.

We will discuss another example of narrative intervention when we discuss systemic family approaches/interventions.

Meeting with Nicolas

CASE STUDY

Juliana saw Nicolas at the end of the week and explained that she was there to help him and his mother as she was aware that his mother was going through a difficult time. Nicolas was polite and seemed shy and quiet but happy to talk about his skateboarding, surfing and photography. He was nervous about starting school and being away from home but also excited. He hinted at family difficulties and having concerns for his mother.

Juliana: *Is anything worrying you at the moment?*

Nicolas: *No, everything is fine*

Juliana: *Are you worried about your parents?*

Nicolas: *No, there's nothing to worry about.*

Juliana: *Are you worried about your dad?*

Nicolas: *No, he has lots of money and can take care of himself but my mum doesn't have any money and she's worried about it …*

Juliana: *Sounds like you are a bit worried about your mum.*

Nicolas: *No, she's fine …*

Juliana: *Your mum is having some difficulty with her leg at the moment because she hurt it and I know you helped her to get to the hospital, were you a bit worried about that?*

Nicolas: *A bit … she gets like that but she'll be ok … my dad has a big house and lots of things and I wish he would help my mum more.*

Juliana: *Like what do you mean?*

Nicolas: *I don't know like if my mum was also allowed to come to my dad's house things would be better. I think she would feel better.*

Juliana and Nicolas continue their conversation and Juliana is able to reassure Nicolas that she is there to support him and his mother.

Inter-agency checks

Ms Bello provides consent for all agencies to be checked apart from the school. Ms Bello is fearful that Nicolas may be stigmatised when social workers contact the school, therefore, it was agreed that Ms Bello could provide a letter of correspondence from the school verifying Nicolas' place at the school as well as school reports and emails from the school.

Julianna contacted Ms Bello's GP and Nicolas' GP and both report that Nicolas is in good health. Ms Bello's GP informs her that Ms Bello is currently under treatment with the community mental health team for post-traumatic stress disorder and has monthly appointments with a psychiatrist.

Ms Bello starts and completes her detox programme and her aftercare programme successfully. Information and letters were sent to Children and Families Services confirming that Nicolas attends boarding school and is doing well. Given that the family are managing well the case is closed with no further action needed. All agencies involved were informed of the case closure and asked to contact the service if any concerns arise.

Reflection

1. *What are your thoughts about the conversation between Nicolas and Juliana? How can Juliana better engage Nicolas?*

2. *What are your thoughts about the situation so far? Do you have any concerns at this time for the family? Please explain.*

3. *Can Juliana apply the same re-authoring approach in her conversation with Nicolas? Please explain why and how.*

Discussion

What is transactional analysis?

Have you found yourself in a situation with someone where you seem to repeat the same pattern of uncomfortable or damaging behaviour every time you meet them? For example, there may be someone who you would like to impress positively but your nerves get the better of you every time you meet them and you end up fumbling and making the opposite impression, or it may be that you feel you are never able to say no to someone, or someone in your life seems to always put you on the defensive, or perhaps someone always discounts what you are saying and relegates you to the role of listener. In such encounters, each time we may think '*Never again. Next time I will be different*'. But, it never is and next time you meet them the same pattern repeats itself. Transactional analysis suggests that one of the main factors in perpetuating such patterns of behaviour or thoughts is our own state of mind rather than the other person's behaviour.

Transactional analysis (TA) is the method for studying of interactions/transactions between individuals. Berne defines a transaction as the fundamental unit of social intercourse/inter-action, while a stroke is the fundamental unit of social action or a unit of recognition (ie when one person recognises another person verbally (eg by saying hello) or non-verbally (eg by waving or a nod)) (Berne, 1964).

Drawing on the work of Spitz, Berne suggested that adults need attention (strokes) like infants; however, they have learnt to substitute their need for strokes with other forms of recognition (eg smile, handshake and other hand gestures, wink, etc) instead of physical stimulation; Berne refers to this as the recognition hunger. For example, you may greet a colleague and the person may greet you back. This is an example of a positive stroke. Your colleague could also frown at you and say nothing. This is an example of a negative stroke. Berne suggests that both of these strokes (positive or negative) are better than no stroke at all which is if your colleague completely ignored you.

TA uses the metaphorical groupings of thoughts, emotions and behaviour to identify three main ego states or states of mind, namely Parent, Adult and Child. Berne defined an ego state as *'a consistent pattern of feeling and experience directly related to a corresponding consistent pattern of behaviour'* (Berne, 1961, p 13).

In Parent state we think, feel and act based on how our parents or other authority figures in our lives may have acted. Berne suggests that the Parent ego state represents our psycho-logical recording of external events experienced/perceived in early years (approximately the first five years) of childhood. The Parent ego state can be divided into two functions, namely controlling parent or a nurturing parent. The controlling side of the Parent ego state contains our prejudged thoughts, feelings, beliefs and value judgements that we learned from our parents or authority figures. The controlling Parent ego state is usually judgemental and wants to take charge/control of the situation, while the nurturing side of the Parent ego state is gentle, loving and permissive. Some of the notions and messages held by the Parent ego state can be helpful for living while other Parent ego state messages may not be.

In contrast to the Parent ego state, the Child represents the recordings of internal events associated with external events that the child perceives; this is the collection of emotions and feelings that accompanied the external events experienced in childhood (approximately the first five years of our lives), these include feelings and associations such as *'The clown at the birthday party was funny'* or *'The spider in the garden was scary'*. In the Child ego state, we think, feel and behave as we did in our childhood. The Child state has two functions: adapted and free. The adapted Child state responds to the controlling Parent state and is the state where the child adapted herself/himself to the demands of their parents, caregivers or authority figures in their life. Feelings of guilt or shame are associated with this state. The free Child state is the child who just does what s/he likes.

Unlike the Parent or Child states the Adult state is balanced and integrated and, therefore, it does not have different functions. Berne describes the Adult as being *'principally concerned with transforming stimuli into pieces of information, and processing and filing that informa-tion on the basis of previous experience'* (1961, p 15). In other words, the Adult ego state enables us to consider the information from three sources: the Parent ego state, the Child ego state, and the information which the person has gathered and is gathering from a given situation/context. The Adult state enables us to think, feel and behave in response to here-and-now and taking into account the current situation and drawing on our full-life experience. Therefore, this state offers a more *realistic* appraisal of our experiences. It can be said that the goal of TA interventions is to strengthen the Adult state within the individual.

It is important to note that *'Parent, Adult, and Child are not concepts, like Superego, Ego, and Id, or the Jungian constructs, but phenomenological realities'* (Berne, 1961, p 4) and that TA is different from psychoanalysis or most approaches to psychotherapy. For example, whereas in psychoanalysis and psychotherapeutic approaches the practitioner asks the client/user of services about themselves, TA is based on observing clients/users of services' communication (words, body language, facial expressions, etc). Therefore, instead of asking the client questions, Berne frequently observed his clients in a group setting, noting every transaction between his client and others in the group.

Ego states are not static, indeed we change our ego states depending on the situation and in response to different people and the thoughts and feelings we experience. For example, consider the following situation.

Frank is Jenny's boss and Jenny arrives late in the office missing an important meeting. Frank seeing Jenny arrive late gets angry and in controlling Parent state tells Jenny: *'You are of no use'*. Jenny in response to Frank's anger and his Parent state shifts to the adapted Child state and feels ashamed and bad and apologises: *'I know. I am sorry'*. This is a complementary interaction or a *transaction* representing a reciprocal pattern that could be perpetuated as long as both parties maintain their given ego states in their transactions (see Figure 6.1, Pattern A).

However, not all transactions are complementary. Indeed, the conversation between Frank and Jenny could have gone quite differently if Jenny had adopted a different ego state. For example, in response to Frank's *'You are of no use'* Jenny might have felt offended and expressed her outrage by assuming a Parent state: *'You can't talk to me like that'*. This represents a crossed transaction (see Figure 6.1, Pattern B) and in contrast to complementary transactions that are stable, crossed transactions are highly unstable. In crossed transactions, either there will be a shift of ego state in one of the parties to create a new and stable complementary transaction or the transaction will stop between the parties involved. For example:

FRANK: *You are of no use.*

JENNY: *You can't talk to me like that.*

FRANK: *You didn't attend the meeting.*

JENNY: *I had an emergency, and in any case you can't talk to people like that.*

FRANK: *Ok, I am sorry. But, you should have been there.*

JENNY: *I can report you to HR for harassment.*

FRANK: *I am really sorry. I didn't mean it in that way.*

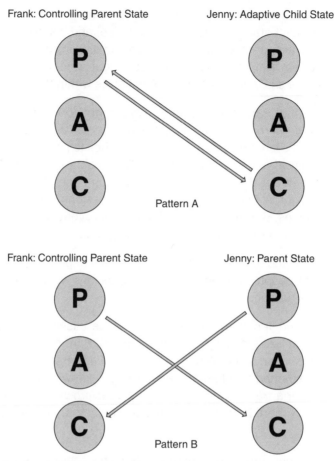

Figure 6.1 Example of complementary and crossed transactions

Although the conversation started with Frank trying to put Jenny in a Child state, it resulted in Frank being put in the Child state. Since Frank is Jenny's boss this may not be a comfortable position for him, but because it is a complementary transaction it is a psychologically stable transaction between Frank and Jenny and, therefore, can be repeated. For example, Frank may become very cautious in dealing with Jenny in the future, to avoid upsetting her, while Jenny may assume a more open or critical/assertive tone in her future communication with Frank. This will generate a complementary and self-sustaining cycle of transactions between the two.

Looking at Ms Bello's and Nicolas' interactions, when Ms Bello broke her leg, Nicolas called a taxi and took his mother to hospital. Here Nicolas was the nurturing Parent while Ms Bello was in adapted Child state. However, later in the hospital when Ms Bello, in her free Child state, became aggressive in A&E, Nicolas seemed embarrassed by his mother's actions, shifting to adapted Child state toward the A&E staff, while assuming a controlling Parent state with his mum asking her to stop shouting and to calm down.

In the conversation between Juliana and Nicolas, Juliana shifts between the nurturing Parent state (showing concern and care for Nicolas and his mother) and the Adult state (inviting Nicolas to think about the situation and share how he feels), while Nicolas shifts between adapted Child state (feeling embarrassed), and the nurturing Parent state toward his mum (becoming concerned and protective of his mum and not sharing information).

For Juliana to establish an effective relationship with Ms Bello and Nicolas, she needs to strengthen Ms Bello's and Nicolas' Adult states so they can evaluate the situation based on the information from here-and-now.

Thinking about the examples of the repeated cycles, let us consider some other uncomfortable but psychologically stable situations that we mentioned earlier. For example, constantly being spoken over by someone in your life. TA suggests that you may feel overwhelmed or dominated by the other person, or you may feel you are somehow less entitled, or perhaps as a child you were taught to listen when others were talking. It is useful to consider how you may be experiencing the other person. For example, you may experience the other person as more important, or feel concerned about the prospect of their anger or disapproval. If this is the case, then you have a Child–Parent relationship with the other person. Although neither of you may be saying any child- or parent-like words, you are relating to the other person as a psychological child. This does not happen in the Adult state since unlike in the Child state where you may feel inferior or entitled to less, in the Adult state you feel equal and see yourself as equal. Instead of using the Child ego state strategies such as listening when others are talking, in Adult state you act spontaneously and in a contextually appropriate manner. As an Adult you don't see others as bigger or more entitled, you see them as equals and relate to them in an Adult way, and if they are unable to reciprocate your ego state, you realise that it is because of their own difficulties and not yours. Therefore, the Adult ego state's response to criticism or disapproval by others is not fear or guilt/shame or aversion but a careful appraisal of the situation and one's own response/behaviour.

We often observe repeated cycles of behaviour or situations in our own lives and the lives of others that may have a negative outcome for us or others. TA offers an approach to understanding the nature of such situations based on participants' interactions/transactions, and provides some possible ways to strengthen our own and their Adult ego state to enable positive change. More importantly, TA offers a methodology for better understanding our own state of mind and for reflecting upon our own actions and interactions/transactions and how they impact our users of services.

Can you think about any unhelpful or uncomfortable patterns of interaction (transaction) with your users of services? How can the knowledge of TA help in understanding and modifying those patterns of interaction?

When grief strikes home

CASE STUDY

Eight months later, it is Saturday morning and Nicolas is at home with Ms Bello and looking forward to the day. It is his birthday and his parents have agreed to give him the gift he had asked for. They have agreed to meet at a restaurant and have lunch together with Nicolas, and in the evening some of his best friends are coming to Ms Bello's place to celebrate his birthday.

Nicolas and Ms Bello arrive at the restaurant a few minutes before noon and sit at the table next to a large window looking onto the street. Nicolas is excited and expectantly looking onto the road to see any sign of his father's car, however, he is late. It is 12:15 and he has not yet arrived. Nicolas tells Ms Bello that *'He is most probably stuck in traffic and will be arriving soon'*. A couple of minutes later, he receives a call from his father saying he is five minutes away and sorry for the delay. Nicolas' eyes light up as he tells Ms Bello that his father is just five minutes away.

His father arrives and parks across the street, and Nicolas tell Ms Bello: *'I'll go get him'* and runs out of the restaurant and toward his father. All he can see is his father and the thought of them spending some time together as a family. In his excitement he doesn't see the approaching car that hits him from his right. Nicolas falls onto the road hitting his head against the pavement. His father and Ms Bello run to him while the restaurant calls for an ambulance. Ms Bello holds Nicolas and crying notices the blood coming out from his ear and shouts *'Oh God. Please don't take him from me'*.

It is heart-breaking and deeply traumatic for the family as Nicolas passes away before the arrival of the ambulance.

Ms Bello finds it very difficult to deal with the pain and starts drinking again.

Reflection

1. Reflecting on loss and grief from a psychosocial and relationship-based perspective, what are your thoughts about the family and the support they need?

2. What are your thoughts about Ms Bello and the impact of the traumatic passing of Nicolas? How about Juliana and her experience of secondary trauma (is this an example of disenfranchised grief)?

3. Reflect upon your own feelings at this moment. How has this case impacted upon your own feelings? Does this case remind you of anything or evoke any specific emotions? What are the implications of what you feel for your personal and professional self? Ask an appropriately experienced peer to read this chapter and to explore these questions together.

Discussion

Loss and grief

The passing of Nicolas was clearly a traumatic shock to the family and especially Ms Bello and his father. Indeed, the death of a significant other is the most irretrievable loss, and is often the only loss that is validated as legitimate grief experience (Miller and Omarzu, 1998). The first-person experience of watching Nicolas being hit by a car and the subsequent events have significant implications for parents. Especially Ms Bello, whose world and life narrative were built around Nicolas, and who is now alone with no support network and facing serious financial difficulties. This is further complicated by the fact that Nicolas' father is married and his family have strong feelings toward Ms Bello. Indeed, Doka (2002) defines disenfranchised grief as *'the grief that persons experience when they incur a loss that is not or cannot be openly acknowledged, publicly mourned or socially supported'* (p 4). However, loss is pervasive and there are many other forms of loss that generate grief response. For example, loss can be physical (eg death of a loved one or loss of a body part) or psychosocial, involving intangible and symbolic loss (eg unemployment, isolation and loss of social network, loss of sense of self, etc). Take a moment to reflect about who else may be touched by the traumatic passing of Nicolas. How about his friends, or others who were present at the scene? How about Juliana? How do you think she may have felt and how does this influence her?

Grief is interlinked with a variety of other emotions including: guilt, aggression, yearning, anxiety, fear (Archer, 1999), anger and rage, although some of these feelings are inadmissible and ignored in Western cultures (Rosaldo, 1989).

Therefore, let us first consider what is grief. Traditionally, there are four terms that are used in bereavement research: (a) bereavement, (b) coping, (c) grief and (d) mourning (Valentine, 2008).

Bereavement refers to the situation of having lost something or someone significant. Grief is *'the subjective emotional response to loss with mental, physical, and social manifestations'* (Charmaz and Milligan, 2006, p 518), while mourning refers to the expressions of, and practices associated with, grief in a given society and culture. Hence, grief is about what is felt while mourning is what is done and the acts that are expressive of grief. Coping refers to processes or strategies for managing the experiences, emotions and consequences of loss and grief.

It is important to note that bereavement, grief, mourning and coping are interlinked. For example, mourning practices are influenced by experiences of grief and vice-versa, and both of these influence the coping processes. These terms are indicative and do not reflect how many individuals may experience the loss of a loved one.

Grief presupposes a self-concept and mental representations of a lost significant figure, and represents a multifaceted and complex experience that involves and encompasses cognitive, affective, behavioural, social and cultural dimensions.

From Freud to Kubler-Ross and subsequent explanations, there is a wealth of literature and research about loss and grief. Freud's (1957) paper on 'Mourning and melancholia' examined melancholia and argued that in order to resolve grief the person needed to withdraw their feelings and attachment from the lost significant figure and reinvest this energy into another person or object. This withdrawal of feelings and attachment had to be complete to lead to *normal* grief otherwise it would lead to *pathological* grief. Freud later modified his view acknowledging that complete withdrawal and reinvestment of the person's feelings and attachment was not possible.

Extending his studies of attachment and separation response in children, to the grief response in adults experiencing death, Bowlby (1969) described grief as a form of separation anxiety in the process of breaking the emotional bonds of attachment. Bowlby emphasised the relationship between the person experiencing the loss and a significant figure/relationship, and identified four phases in the process of *healthy* grief: (1) numbing; (2) yearning and search-ing; (3) disorganisation and despair; and (4) reorganisation.

Kubler-Ross (1970) in her book, *On Death and Dying*, described her five stages/phases of grief and loss, namely, denial and isolation, anger, bargaining, depression and acceptance. She subsequently added an additional stage of hope to her explanation.

However, the dominant theoretical perspectives on grief are based on the medical model (Charmaz and Milligan, 2006; Walter, 2000) in which grief is categorised and resembles an illness that requires recovery (Bradbury, 1999; Charmaz and Milligan, 2006; Cochran and Claspell, 1987; Valentine, 2008). This approach separates the experience of grief from its social, cultural and intergenerational/historical dimensions (Charmaz and Milligan, 2006, p 527).

A psychosocial understanding of grief offers a shift away from the medical model, and con-siders the complex, multifaceted and multidimensional nature of grief. From this perspec-tive, as long as there are social and interpersonal relationships, friendship, attachment and love, there is grief. Indeed, loss and grief are integral parts of living, with all changes in life entailing loss and all losses in life leading to change (Neimeyer, 1999).

'*The pain of grief ... is, perhaps, the price we pay for love, the cost of commitment*' (Parkes, 1972, p. 5), and an integral part of life. From a sociological perspective, grief is a social emo-tion and a process that is structured and expressed through and in relation to relationships, attachments, commitment and expectations (Charmaz and Milligan, 2006).

Although in a medicalised sense grief is often classified as either *normal* or *pathological* (Walter, 2005), psychologists recognise the personalised nature and cultural diversity and the personal/individualised nature of grief and coping (Klass, 1999; Klass and Walter, 2007; Nadeau, 2007).

Contrary to the Freudian idea that bereavement and grief is about disconnecting from the lost significant figure and relocating our attention and affect, the psychosocial and rela-tionship-based perspective focuses on continuing bonds (Klass et al, 1996; Walter, 1996) and the continued relationship with the significant figure that remembers and relocates the significant figure in the life of the person, restoring a sense of meaning and continuity (Valentine, 2008, p 5). This is in consonance with the narrative perspective which enables a re-authoring of an individual's narrative and (auto)biography and re-calibrating of their sense of self and relational identity.

Narrative interventions and re-membering conversations

White (2007) draws on Myerhoff's (1986) work to apply her concept of re-membering in nar-rative therapy. Myerhoff in White (2007) defines re-membering as '*a purposive, significant unification*' (p 136) while White suggests:

> definition of Re-membering evokes an image of a person's life and identity as
> a membered association or club. The membership of this association of life is

composed of the significant figures of the person's history, and those figures of the person's contemporary circumstances of life whose voices are influential in regard to matters of the person's identity. Re-membering provides an opportunity for persons to engage in a revision of the membership of their association of life.

(White, 2000)

Therefore, re-membering in this context is not about remembering (recalling details), but rather about reorganising *memberships*. By thinking of people's involvement in our lives as membership in our *association of life*, and by examining the effect of their involvement (membership), we can adjust their involvement and influence in our lives by adjusting their membership. For example, by highlighting the positive about one person's involvement (membership) we can raise their position relative to others and consequently diminish the role of others. It can be potentially empowering for people who have experienced trauma, abuse or violence to note that by raising the positive impact of some significant relationships in their lives, they can diminish the effect of the perpetrator in their lives. However, considering that re-membering can only raise a significant figure's position in the person's *association of life*, it cannot be applied to situations where there is a need to directly diminish a significant figure's negative impact/effect in the person's life.

There are four steps to re-membering conversations in response to loss and grief (White, 2000). Therefore, let us examine how this approach can be applied to support Ms Bello. The main objective is to re-member Nicolas in Ms Bello's life and identity narrative by recognising the reciprocal nature of their relationship and how they both contributed to each other's lives. Rather than forgetting, such a conversation is about recalling and re-membering how the person is keeping the significant figure's presence in her life.

Step 1: Recounting of what the significant figure contributed to the person's life

Recounting Nicolas' contribution to Ms Bello's life involves asking Ms Bello to recall and recount the what, where and when relating to their time together and how it impacted her life. In this process it is important to ask Ms Bello to share her thoughts about Nicolas' contribution to her life in concrete ways. This means asking questions like: What was Nicolas like? What did he like to do? How did you share your time together? What were some of the things you enjoyed together? How did these things impact your life? What difference did it make and how did you feel? How did Nicolas contribute to your life? This part of the conversation focuses attention on how their relationship and the time they shared together made a difference for Ms Bello.

Step 2: Person's identity through the eyes of the significant figure

The second step is about recognising how the significant figure contributed to the person's sense of self and shaped their identity and what their life is about. This allows the person (Ms Bello) to reflect on her identity narrative and how the significant figure (Nicolas) contributed in shaping her sense of self. This step involves questions such as: How did Nicolas' birth change your life and your identity? How do you think he felt about you? Thinking about yourself from Nicolas' perspective what do you think he valued most about you? How did this influence you and your life? How did it contribute to your sense of self and shape your identity?

The above enable Ms Bello to consider how she is different because of Nicolas' contributions to her life and identity. Such a conversation reminds the person (Ms Bello) that the passing of the significant figure (Nicolas) is not the end of their relationship, instead the person (Ms Bello) continues to maintain their connection and relationship with the significant figure (Nicolas) and maintain the significant figure's (Nicolas') contributions, legacy and presence in her life.

Step 3: Recounting of what the person contributed to the life of the significant figure

The third step explores Ms Bello's contributions to Nicolas' life and to highlight the reciprocity of the relationship and how they enriched each other's lives. This refocuses the conversation from a discussion of identity to actions and stories of the times they shared together. This involves asking Ms Bello questions such as: What are some of the things you did for Nicolas and how did these shape his life? How did you show your love/care/interest in Nicolas' life? What did you do together that contributed to Nicolas' life?

Some people may find it difficult to talk about themselves and their own achievement or abilities. Therefore, it is important to be sensitive and supportive of the individual as they explore their experiences and re-member their relationship and reconsider/re-author their narrative. This process highlights the reciprocity of the relationship between the person (Ms Bello) and the significant figure (Nicolas).

Step 4: Implications of the person's contribution for the significant figure's sense of identity

The fourth step is asking Ms Bello to reflect on how she contributed to and shaped Nicolas' identity. This returns the conversation to the landscape of identity and is about considering how the person's (Ms Bello's) involvement and actions have contributed to shaping the significant figure's (Nicolas') life and identity. This involves questions such as: How do you think you influenced Nicolas? or How do you think your presence and contributions influenced Nicolas' life and identity? or What difference do you think your presence made to Nicolas, his life and his identity?

Such questions can evoke strong emotions, moving experiences and powerful and intense reactions, as the person considers how they made a lasting positive difference in the life of a significant person in their life. Here the person attempts *'to enter the consciousness of this figure on matters of this figure's identity, initiating a rich description of the ways in which this connection shaped/had the potential to shape this figure's sense of who they were and what their life was about'* (White, 2005).

It is important to note that the above steps and questions apply to the situation where grief is due to the death of a significant person in the life of the survivor. Therefore, the above questions need to be adjusted appropriately if they need to be applied to separation from a person who is alive. Furthermore, the above process/steps are not rigid and linear, they rather represent different focus areas for the conversation. However, the response from the person involved may vary and, at times, may shift from one area to another. For example, while speaking about how Ms Bello contributed to Nicolas' life and identity, she may also talk about how Nicolas enriched her life and how they both made each other's lives happier and more rewarding.

Grief is a personal/individualised experience and, therefore, depending on the person's sense of self and an array of other emotions and circumstances, its expression and processes may vary from one person to another.

It is important to conclude the above steps by reconnecting the past with the present and the future to generate recognition of the continuity of the relationship and allow for re-membering of the continued presence of the significant figure in the person's life. This enables a re-authoring of the person's narrative with a focus on a tale of continuity and enduring bonds rather than disjuncture and broken narratives.

References

Archer, J (1999) *The Nature of Grief: The Evolution and Psychology Reactions to Loss*. London and New York: Routledge.

Berne, E (1961) *Transactional Analysis in Psychotherapy*. New York: Grove Press, Inc.

Berne, E (1964) *Games People Play*. New York: Grove Press, Inc.

Bowlby, J (1969) *Attachment and Loss*. New York: Basic Books.

Bradbury, M (1999) *Representations of Death: A Social Psychological Perspective*. London and New York: Routledge.

Charmaz, K and Milligan, M J (2006) Grief, in Stets, J E and Turner, J H (eds) *Handbook of the Sociology of Emotions* (pp 516–38). New York: Springer.

Cochran, L and Claspell, E (1987) *The Meaning of Grief: A Dramaturgical Approach to Understanding Emotion*. Westport, CT: Greenwood Press.

Doka, K J (ed) (2002) *Disenfranchised Grief*. Champaign, IL: Research Press.

Freud, S (1957) Mourning and Melancholia, in Rickman, J (ed) *A General Selection from the Works of Sigmund Freud*. New York: Doubleday.

Gendlin, E T (1981) *Focusing* (2nd edn). New York: Bantam Books.

Klass, D (1999) Developing a Cross-Cultural Model of Grief: The State of the Field. *Omega*, 39: 153–78.

Klass, D and Walter, T (2007) Processes of Grief: How Bonds Are Continued, in Stroebe, M S, Hansson, R O, Stroebe, W and Schut, H (eds) *Handbook of Bereavement Research: Consequences, Coping, and Care* (pp 431–48). Washington, DC: American Psychological Association.

Klass, D, Silverman, P R and Nickman, S L (eds) (1996) *Continuing Bonds*. Washington, DC: Taylor & Francis.

Kubler-Ross, E (1970) *On Death and Dying*. London: Tavistock.

Mearns, D and Thorne, B (1988) *Person-Centred Counselling in Action*. London: Sage.

Miller, E and Omarzu, J (1998) New Directions in Loss Research, in Harvey, J (ed) *Perspectives on Loss: A Sourcebook*. Philadelphia: Brunner/Mazel.

Myerhoff, B (1986) Life Not Death in Venice: Its Second Life, in Turner, V and Bruner, E (eds) *The Anthropology of Experience*. Chicago: University of Illinois Press.

Nadeau, J W (2007) Meaning Making in Family Bereavement: A Family Systems Approach, in Stroebe, M S, Hansson, R O, Stroebe, W and Schut, H (eds) *Handbook of Bereavement Research: Consequences, Coping, and Care* (pp 329–47). Washington, DC: American Psychological Association.

Neimeyer, R A (1999) *Lessons in Loss: A Guide to Coping*. New York: McGraw-Hill.

Rogers, C R (1959) A Theory of Therapy, Personality, and Interpersonal Relationships as Developed in the Client-Centred Framework, in Koch, S (ed) *Psychology: Study of a Science: Vol 3: Formulation of the Person and the Social Context* (pp 184–256). New York: McGraw-Hill.

Rogers, C R (1980) *A Way of Being*. Boston, MA: Houghton Mifflin.

Rosaldo, R (1989) Introduction: Grief and the Headhunter's Rage, in Rosaldo, R (ed) *Culture and Truth: The Remaking of Social Analysis* (pp 1–21). Boston, MA: Beacon Press.

Seale, C (1998) *Constructing Death: The Sociology of Death and Dying*. Cambridge, UK: Cambridge University Press.

Shuchter, S R and Zisook, S (2006) The Course of Normal Grief, in Stroebe, M S, Stroebe, W and Hansson, R O (eds) *Handbook of Bereavement: Theory, Research, and Intervention* (8th edn, pp 23–43). Cambridge, UK: Cambridge University Press.

Valentine, C (2008) *Bereavement Narratives: Continuing Bonds in the 21st Century*. London and New York: Routledge.

Vanerschot, G (1993) Empathy as Releasing Several Microprocesses in the Client, in Brazier, D (ed) *Beyond Carl Rogers*. London: Constable.

Walter, T (1996) A New Model of Grief: Bereavement and Biography. *Mortality*, 1: 7–25.

Walter, T (2000) Grief Narratives: The Role of Medicine in the Policing of Grief. *Anthropology & Medicine*, 7: 97–114.

Walter, T (2005) What Is Complicated Grief? A Social Constructionist Perspective. *Omega*, 52: 71–9.

White, M (2000) Reflecting-team Work as Definitional Ceremony Revisited. [online] Available at: www.narrativetherapylibrary.com/media/downloadable/files/links/R/O/RONP4White_2.pdf (accessed 27 July 2014).

White, M (2005) Michael White Workshop Notes. [online] Available at: www.dulwichcentre.com.au/michael-white-workshop-notes.pdf (accessed 27 July 2014).

White, M (2007) *Maps of Narrative Practice*. New York: W W Norton.

7 Searching for love in all the wrong places (Part 1)

Family therapy and systemic approaches

Chapter summary

This chapter offers an introduction to systemic family interventions.

The chapter begins with a brief reflection on domestic violence followed by a discussion of systemic thinking and systemic family approaches. This includes:

*   structural family interventions, examining family organisation/hierarchies and relationships;

*   strategic family interventions, brief solution-focused interventions; and

*   family life cycle model.

The above intervention approaches enable practitioners to work collaboratively with the family, agree the definition of the family, and to visualise its boundaries and the type and quality of relationships between its members. By modifying relationship boundaries practitioners can support families to effect change in behaviour that can address the family's concerns/*problems*/difficulties.

The chapter concludes with a discussion of the use of *outsider witness* and *definitional ceremonies* to support users of services in initiating and sustaining positive change. This is an especially powerful approach to enabling users of services to adopt a new narrative and to address *problems*/challenges.

Chapter objectives

1.   Introduce the concept of systemic thinking/approaches.

2.   Introduce the concept and some of the ideas relating to systemic family interventions.

3.   Introduce structural family model/interventions.

4. Introduce strategic family model/interventions.

5. Introduce the family life cycle model.

6. Introduce the concept of outsider witness and its application in practice.

7. Introduce the concept of definitional ceremony and its application.

Self-referral – can you help ... we're becoming desperate

CASE STUDY

On Monday morning the duty social worker (Mark Rivers) receives a call from a distressed parent (Nick LaFar) asking for parenting advice and help. He explains that his 12-year-old daughter (Kate) is *'out of control'*.

Nick: *Kate is impossible to manage, completely out of control, shouting, spitting, refusing to go to bed, trying to climb out of her bedroom window at night. She won't listen to reason and she doesn't respond to punishment. I've had to physically restrain her because she was hell-bent on going to meet up with her mates at 11pm on a Sunday night. She hit her younger sister [Brenda] who's only seven until she had bruises.*

Mark: *You say that your daughter is 12 years old and she's unmanageable at the moment.*

Nick: *Yes that's right.*

Mark: *When you say she doesn't respond to punishment what do you mean?*

Nick: *I threaten to take away her mobile phone, I threaten to ground her. I tell her she won't get any allowance and then I dock her allowance. But she doesn't listen, she just does as she pleases.*

Mark: *When did this behaviour start?*

Nick: *About 12 months ago ... and she has been on a downward spiral ever since then. It's as if she's no longer my daughter ... I don't recognise her anymore ... her eyes are always bloodshot with dark rings. She constantly has bruises on her arms, she smells of alcohol, drugs and sex when she comes back from school ... I am pretty sure she's sexually active, she carries condoms in her school bag and she can't be away from her phone even for a minute. She's always receiving texts on her phone but all these friends are a mystery ... we are never allowed to meet them.*

Mark: *The situation seems very serious and escalating. Have you had social services involvement in the past?*

Nick: *To be honest I didn't really want to contact you. I thought we would be able to deal with this problem as a family ... the last thing I want is a social worker in our lives but we are desperate and we have called everyone including the police, you're our last hope.*

We've tried to put firmer and stricter rules in place but Kate just laughs at us. I think she's being influenced by her so-called friends and they seem to be part of a gang.

Mark: *Does Kate stay with you and are you the main carer for Kate? Does she have contact with her mother and does Kate have any siblings?*

Nick: *I have two girls [Kate and Brenda] and they both stay with me and my new girlfriend during the week. My ex-partner [Helen] lives with her mother so the girls stay with Helen and her mother every other weekend.*

Mark: *Have you discussed the situation with Helen? What are her views?*

Nick: *Helen has a small baby and that's about all that she can manage ... but that's Helen.*

Mark: *Do you know where Kate's trying to get to at night when she tries to leave through the window?*

Nick: *I'm not sure ... I don't know ... I think London but I'm not sure. Can you help ... we are becoming desperate.*

The duty social worker takes further information including more specific information about Kate's behaviour, the family composition, wider family information, race and ethnicity of the family, school information, health information, living arrangements, parental responsibility and contact details for both parents and partners.

Family composition

Name: Kate LaFar	(Subject)	Age: 12	Ethnicity: White British
Name: Brenda LaFar	(Sister)	Age: 7	Ethnicity: White British
Name: Helen Brookes	(Mother)	Age: 30	Ethnicity: White British
Name: Nick LaFar	(Father)	Age: 31	Ethnicity: White British
Name: Missy Harper	(Step-sister)	Age: 1 month	Ethnicity: White British
Name: Lucy Scallion	(Step-sister)	Age: pre-birth	Ethnicity: White British
Name: Lee Harper	(Mother's partner)	Age: 33	Ethnicity: White British
Name: Mia Scallion	(Father's partner)	Age: 38	Ethnicity: White British

Mark checks the system to ascertain whether the family is known. The ICS system shows that the family are known to services. Two police reports for domestic violence dating back to when Brenda (Kate's younger sister) was first born are noted.

The first police report notes that there were verbal arguments between the couple and neighbours contacted the police. Kate was five years old and Brenda was a few months old at the time. The case was closed with no further action as the couple explained that they had an argument and denied any domestic violence. The police reports indicate a second incident of domestic violence when neighbours reported hearing loud arguments and shouting. Kate was six years old and Brenda one year of age. Once again the couple explained that they just had an argument and denied any domestic violence. However, after that incident, Helen left the home and stayed in a woman's hostel. At the time her key worker was under the impression that Nick was behaving in an inappropriate manner and when she discussed this with Helen, Helen denied it.

Reflection

1. *Drawing on what we have discussed in the previous six chapters, what are some of your thoughts and reflections about this case so far?*

2. *Based on the above information, can you produce a family genogram for this family?*

3. *Reflecting on the above narrative, what defence mechanisms can you identity? What are some of the dynamics (types and quality) of the relationships within this family?*

Discussion

Thinking about domestic violence

Domestic violence is a hideous and complex crime, therefore, let us briefly consider the meaning and implications of domestic violence in general and in this case in particular.

Let us first consider what constitutes domestic violence. The UK Government's new definition of domestic violence as of March 2013 states that domestic violence and abuse is:

> *Any incident or pattern of incidents of controlling, coercive or threatening behaviour, violence or abuse between those aged 16 or over who are or have been intimate partners or family members regardless of gender or sexuality. This can encompass, but is not limited to, the following types of abuse:*

> * *psychological*
> * *physical*
> * *sexual*
> * *financial*
> * *emotional.*

> *Controlling behaviour is: a range of acts designed to make a person subordinate and/or dependent by isolating them from sources of support, exploiting their resources and capacities for personal gain, depriving them of the means needed for independence, resistance and escape and regulating their everyday behaviour.*

Coercive behaviour is: 'an act or a pattern of acts of assault, threats, humiliation and intimidation or other abuse that is used to harm, punish, or frighten their victim'.

The Government definition, which is not a legal definition, includes so-called 'honour' based violence, female genital mutilation (FGM) and forced marriage, and is clear that victims are not confined to one gender or ethnic group.

(Home Office, 2013)

It is important to highlight that the above is an expression of the government policy rather than a statutory definition of domestic violence. Nonetheless, based on the above definition the two reported incidents between Nick and Helen constitute domestic violence. However, part of the complexity of domestic violence is due to its hidden nature since it often casts its darkest shadow in the *privacy of personal relationships*. Power dynamics, coercion and domination are at the heart of domestic violence, and systematic alienation and isolation of the person by the perpetrator lay the foundation for other forms of abuse. The *web of control* is often reinforced by multiple barriers and *walls of exclusion* represented by a combination of psychological, social, economic, physical, cultural and other obstacles that present *formidable* barriers, escape from which seems extremely difficult if not impossible.

Domestic violence occurs throughout all social groups, irrespective of class, race, age, disability, sexuality and lifestyle (Dodd, 2009). The British Psychological Society (2007) states that children exposed to domestic violence have suffered psychological abuse.

Domestic violence negatively affects the quality of the parent-child relationship and parental capacity (Mullender et al, 2002), and hinders maternal control and discipline (Holt et al, 2008), yet women are expected to cope with children with heightened needs while simultaneously trying to maintain their own physical and emotional survival (Humphreys and Stanley, 2006).

Domestic violence negatively affects the development of infants' and children's mentalisation and attachment (Gerhardt, 2004; Winnicott, 1989) and generates anxiety and fear. Children with a history of domestic violence may experience low self-esteem, high anxiety, depression and emotional difficulties including post-traumatic stress (Carlson, 2000).

Reflecting on our case study, the two incidents of domestic violence occurred when Kate was five and Brenda was just a few months old. From a developmental and attachment perspective, child-bearing and the initial stages of motherhood are particularly important times in women's lives. During this period, the woman goes through a liminal period in which her body and mind 'make room for the child-to-be' and for her new self-as-mother (Leckman et al, 2007; Stern, 1995; Winnicott, 1965). This period of transition is usually accompanied by psychological openness that allows mental representations and internalisation of her new self, baby, and family. However, this openness also exposes the mother to greater vulnerability to psychological harm from her partner and other significant relationships. Maternal representations, which develop during early motherhood, lay the foundation for, and are part of, the mother's caregiving system. However, experience of domestic violence and abuse can disrupt or distort this process and, therefore, could have influenced Helen's internal working model of caregiving (Dayton et al, 2010; Huth-Bocks et al, 2004). Furthermore, considering the complementary nature of the mother-child relationship (composed of two complementary systems, namely: the mother's caregiving system and the child's attachment system), this could have influenced Kate and Brenda. George and Solomon (2008) suggest that domestic violence can result in women *abdicating* their caregiving role.

Children need to be held in the arms and the minds of their parents and caregivers and through a *holding environment* (Winnicott, 1960) in order to explore and develop their potential space (Winnicott, 1989[1967]) and secure attachment bonds. The mother's mentalisation capacity has a significant impact on children's mentalisation, attachment bonds and emotional development (Fonagy et al, 1991).

A detailed discussion of domestic violence is beyond the scope of this chapter, however, it is important to note that any reflection or analysis of domestic violence should acknowledge the hegemonic and patriarchal roots of domestic violence. Lapierre (2008) captures this eloquently and states that a *'general move away from an analysis that centralizes issues of gender and power'* combined with a *'deficit model of mothering'* have constituted the principal trend within domestic violence discourses (p 455). The absence of this power analysis has resulted in scrutinising and blaming of women and their capabilities as mothers:

> *Women have been relegated to the periphery, to be solely considered in relation to their children, and there appears to be no commitment to the development of a holistic understanding of abused women's complex experiences as mothers ... A crucial issue in locating the problem primarily with women and their mothering is that it shifts the attention away from men's violent behaviours and their consequences for both women and children.*
>
> (p 456)

Domestic violence discourses and analysis have been dominated by patriarchal models of male dominance and female liability, and this in itself represents a psychosocial and cultural violence toward women. Therefore, it is crucial to maintain an intentional focus, and think about and recognise, the intricacy of the parenting/mothering role and the centrality of the perpetrator's behaviour, role and responsibility.

Systemic thinking and approaches

Thinking about the above scenario, there are many factors that can contribute to Kate's feelings and behaviour. Therefore, it is crucially important to adopt a holistic approach that can address the different, and seemingly competing needs of the family and its members. Systemic family interventions offer an integrated and holistic approach to complex situations and interventions with families. Hence, let us examine some possible systemic family approaches.

What is systemic thinking/approach?

As the name implies systemic family approaches apply systemic thinking within the context of the family. This definition seems broad, however, it offers much flexibility for practitioners to think creatively and apply systemic thinking in their practice. Indeed, Kaur et al (2009) state that there is no one single definition of systemic family therapy.

Systemic thinking is different from analytical thinking, systematic thinking or synthetic thinking. Analytical thinking is about understanding the parts of a system and/or problem. It is about breaking down the whole into its parts/components and thinking about how each part/component works. On the other hand, synthetic thinking is about looking at the whole and thinking about how the parts work together. Systematic thinking refers to thinking methodologically (ie having a clear approach to thinking, problem-solving, or doing something. For example, starting from smaller problems, or smaller components of the problem, and working your way through to solution/resolving the bigger problem).

Systemic thinking is a holistic approach that considers the components of a system as inseparable and integral parts of the whole and with reciprocal relationships with each other. This approach combines both analytic and synthetic thinking and offers a situation-wide view and an enhanced insight into complex situations and problems.

Social workers have played a key role in the development of systemic thinking and its application in social care. This is unsurprising, as systemic theories provide an excellent approach to thinking about and appreciating the experience of users of services and the complexities of intervention and everyday practice.

Instead of a narrow focus on the individual, systemic thinking/approaches emphasise communication, patterns of interaction and relationships with others.

Systemic family approaches

Systemic approaches assert that the family is an organic whole with its own identity and dynamics that is more than the sum of its parts, and individuals are best understood within the context of their relationships and through assessing their interactions with their entire family.

Systemic family approaches suggest that *problems*/difficulties are created by the interactions between family members, and are not *in the person* but *between persons*, with some patterns of behaviour having passed across generations (Baum, 2006). Therefore, systemic practitioners are interested in what happens between family members, how they communicate and how they express their feelings.

There are a range of approaches under the umbrella of family therapy that use systemic thinking. These include: Adlerian Family Therapy, Experiential/Symbolic Family Therapy, Human Validation Process Model, Milan Systemic Family Therapy, Multi-Generational Family Therapy, Strategic Family Therapy, Structural Family Therapy, and others. Indeed, systemic thinking can be used as a *metaframework* and applied as an overlay to almost any theoretical orientation and almost any approach, enhancing almost any intervention.

The recursive and cyclical reciprocity of systemic approaches may raise questions in relation to their applicability to social work practice, specifically in the context of statutory social work practice. In other words, how can practitioners reconcile the timed and target-driven framework of statutory practice with the recursive complexity and the openness and flexibility of systemic approaches? Lang et al's (1990) concept of the domain of explanation and the domain of action can be helpful in this context.

The domain of explanation refers to the open-minded curiosity and the stance of not knowing that enable better appreciation/understanding of the complexities of practice and the lived experience of users of services. This allows for diversity of ideas and multiplicity of narratives and plausible explanations. The domain of production, sometimes referred to as the domain of action, is where practitioners apply their understanding, professional experience and expertise as well as knowledge and theory to make decisions, judgement, assessments and formulations.

Lang et al (1990) explain that the practitioners must decide regarding the relevance and applicability of each domain in their practice *conscious of the ethical dimension of their activities*.

Systemic approaches suggest that we are in a constant feedback loop with the people in our lives (ie *cybernetic loops* or *synchronous feedback*). This offers a shift away from linear explanations/reasoning/causality to circular explanations/reasoning/causality. Linear causality/explanations try to locate *problems* within a source (ie person who is at fault or to blame), while circular causality/explanations try to understand the role of each person in sustaining the problem and what can be done to change the situation (ie problems involve series and series of feedback loops). For example, a linear explanation for Kate's behaviour is that she has difficulties in managing herself and her emotions and, therefore, reacts with anger and aggression (the problem is *in Kate*). While a circular explanation for Kate's behaviour may be that Kate gets angry and acts aggressively → this upsets Nick who shouts and threatens punishment (eg take her phone away, or withhold her allowance, etc) → Nick stereotypes Kate as the *bad child* → Kate feels frustrated and depressed → Kate gets angry and acts aggressively. This is a loop that will continue and escalates until one of the participants stops the feedback loop.

In systemic family approaches, the family is defined based on significant relationship networks/systems to which someone belongs. This definition has great flexibility and takes into account the many different forms of family and relationships including: birth family, single parent family, extended family, family of choice, and others, and can also include a network of friends or helping professionals.

Given the flexibility of the above definition, it is important to identify and agree the definition of the family in consultation with users of services and based on significant relationships in the family system. Genograms offer a helpful tool that allows practitioners to collaboratively develop and define the family boundaries, and this is one of the initial steps in systemic family interventions.

The genogram offers a visualisation of the family and its different relationships over time. This can help highlight some of the structural and relational factors in the family system that may be contributing to the family's difficulties/*problems*. Furthermore, genograms and other relationship maps can be extended to include other support networks including any professionals supporting the family.

Like all psychosocial and relationship-based interventions, reflective practice is central to systemic family interventions. This includes reflection and careful consideration of personal and professional selves as well as resources and constraints and any factors/dynamics that can help or hinder the systemic work with the family. Systemic approaches value diversity of perspectives and recognise the validity of multiple perceptions and narratives. However, although all of the different systemic approaches share a systemic perspective, they vary in their emphasis and their way of thinking about change. Therefore, it is important to use the approach that offers the best *fit* for the family and their specific difficulties and circumstances.

Systemic family interventions have an added complexity as practitioners must interact with multiple individuals during their interventions, and carefully observe the interactions between the different members of the family to identify patterns of behaviour and small verbal or non-verbal cues that may offer an indication of the family dynamic or the relationship between two or more participants while maintaining a position of curiosity, *respectful and safe uncertainty*. It is important to ensure a balanced approach and neutrality as any alliance with one member can influence the entire family system.

Narrative interventions discussed in the previous chapter are an example of systemic approaches, and we will discuss further applications of systemic approaches in this chapter.

Family history and speaking with Nick

CASE STUDY

Historic notes highlight that after the second reported incident of domestic violence, Helen left the home with Kate and Brenda and stayed in a women's hostel. At the time her key worker was under the impression that Nick was behaving in an inappropriate manner and when she discussed this with Helen, Helen denied it.

The key worker contacts Children's Services to report her concerns: *I am worried that he is threatening her. She seems very rattled and nervous most of the time like she's waiting for something terrible to happen. She jumps for the slightest noise and I think he [Nick LaFar] is calling her and telling her that he is going to take the children away. She receives calls on her mobile almost daily and she's always very upset and distressed after the call. We can hear that there's a man on the other end of the phone talking very loudly to her – shouting at her really – but she doesn't say anything back.*

As part of our one-to-one I have asked her if there were any incidents of domestic violence but she has always denied it.

She's very insecure and finds it difficult to make decisions. She's always second-guessing herself and changing her mind. She often asks me what I think and what would I do if I were her. I told her that I can't make those decisions for her and only she can make those decisions. Managing the girls is very difficult for her and she finds it difficult to calm them when they are upset.

Shortly after the key worker's conversation with the social worker, Helen leaves the women's hostel and returns to Nick.

A few weeks later Helen leaves Nick but this time she also leaves Brenda and Kate with Nick. At the time she tells the social worker that the girls are better off with Nick. During supervision the allocated social worker raises concerns about the reports of domestic violence.

Kate and Brenda continue to live with Nick and he becomes the sole parent for the girls. Contact arrangements are drawn up via solicitors and it is agreed that the girls will see Helen two weekends a month.

The case is assigned to Nancy Hassleback and Mark passes the above information to Nancy, and mentions that Nick seems very keen on receiving support as in his words they are '*becoming desperate*' and have no one else to turn to.

Nancy makes contact with Nick to arrange a home visit and explains to Nick the importance of seeing the whole family. However, Nick seems irritated and upset.

Part of the exchange between Nick and Nancy is captured below:

Nick: *Look, I am not sure why my partner [Mia] needs to be involved in this. Kate's my problem … anyway it's not even possible for us to meet this week, I am very busy. Wednesday we're watching Brenda in her school play and on Thursday she has a softball match after school and we've promised to watch her game. We can't be letting Brenda down because of Kate. We can see you on Saturday afternoon at about 4pm.*

Nancy: *Can we arrange a meeting on Friday as our office is closed on weekends?*

Nick: *That's not possible. I have promised Mia an evening away from the children … we have a reservation at a restaurant.*

Nancy: *Can I suggest that I speak with Kate at school this week to gain a better understanding of the situation and I can meet with you and Kate's mother later to discuss the situation further.*

Nancy couldn't reconcile Nick's reaction with the information she received from Mark mentioning that the family were really seeking urgent advice and support. Nancy's assessment of the situation was that Nick seemed ambivalent about her and the service. Nancy was pleased that she had managed to secure a date to visit Kate at school, but was frustrated that she had not secured a home visit to speak with Nick and his partner.

Reflection

1. *Why is Nick so ambivalent about the service? How do you reconcile Nick's conversation with Mark, asking for social work interventions, and his conversation with Nancy?*

2. *What are your thoughts and reflections about domestic violence in general, and the two police reports and risks of domestic violence in this case?*

3. *Consider the genogram that you developed earlier for this family. Do you see any emerging patterns of behaviours and relationships within the family? How will you modify the genogram to reflect this new information?*

4. *Do you see any emerging patterns from the above? What are some of the systemic issues that you can identity?*

Discussion

Systemic family intervention models

Careful observation is essential in systemic family interventions. It is important to observe interactions carefully and to consider subtle verbal or non-verbal communications that may be indicative of people's feelings and the quality of relationships between them. Through careful observation practitioners may be able to identify patterns of behaviour and to pay attention to both content and process. For example, in his conversation with Mark, Nick seeks social work interventions stating that the family is becoming desperate (content). However, when speaking with Nancy he seems hesitant and does not make himself available so the family can meet with Nancy to discuss appropriate support for Kate and the family (process). Such differences between content and process are an important source of conflict and difficulty in many situations and for many individuals and families.

Furthermore, in his conversation with Nancy, Nick states: '... *We can't be letting Brenda down because of Kate*'. This offers an important point for reflection about how the children's identity narratives are constructed within the family.

Language and narratives construct and constrain our identities and lived experience, and as Shotter (1993, p 20) suggests, through language and narratives, we '*unknowingly "shape" or "construct" between ourselves ... not only a sense of our identities, but also a sense of our "social worlds"* '. If Nick and the family construct Brenda as the *good child* and Kate as the *bad child* these identity narratives can condition Kate and Brenda's thinking and behaviour. Therefore, drawing on our discussions in the previous chapter, there seems to be a need for re-authoring of Kate's narrative and identity, and re-membering Kate within the family. How will you go about helping the family to re-author its narrative and re-member Kate?

The involvement of families and carers in decision-making and interventions is well recognised in social work. However, involvement of family is a fundamental requirement for systemic family interventions.

In systemic approaches, the practitioner enters the world of the family through attentive observation of verbal and non-verbal behaviours, and tries to understand the language, perceptions, beliefs and values of users of services in order to find motivation for change.

Prior to meeting users of services, it is important to reflect on self and any factors that may impact our work with the family and to ensure an empathic and effective relationship-based approach in all our interventions. In this process it is important to move from *safe certainty* to *safe uncertainty* and assume a position of *not knowing* and *respectful curiosity*, aiming to understand and identify any safeguarding issues or issues relating to an empowering anti-oppressive and anti-discriminatory practice (eg gender, age, race, ethnicity, culture, education, physical or mental difficulties, and others).

The practitioner reframes the *problem*/situation so that the motives, values and beliefs of the users of services will allow them to accept the change (using the belief system and the social context to disrupt patterns of behaviour). We have seen an example in the previous chapter when Juliana helped Ms Bello re-author her identity narrative and find the motivation to attend a drug and alcohol detox programme. Another example is the following attempt in reframing anxiety:

Practitioner: *Anxiety has an important protective function. It is your body's signal that something is wrong. It is a protective signal. What do you need to do to answer the signal?*

Systemic theories provide an enriching and excellent approach to appreciating and thinking about the experiences of users of services and the complexities of everyday practice and interventions. Therefore, let us examine some examples of systemic family intervention strategies that may be relevant in this case.

Structural family interventions

Minuchin (1974) developed the structural model for understanding families based on their structural hierarchies/organisation and quality of relationships (rigid/diffused). Minuchin states:

> In all cultures, the family imprints its members with selfhood. Human experience of identity has two elements; a sense of belonging and a sense of being separate. The laboratory in which these ingredients are mixed and dispensed is the family, the matrix of identity.

(p 47)

This above offers a language for describing the dimensions of family life based on closeness and distance of relationships and the quality of boundaries (rigid/diffused).

In this model, the family is considered as a basic human system and is divided into subsystems that encompass various categories such as household, parental, siblings or extended.

The quality of relationships is defined by boundaries. Boundaries are the emotional barriers that protect and enhance the integrity of individuals, subsystems and families. Rigid boundaries reflect a transactional relationship that is disengaged. Rigid boundaries may limit families' adaptability and prevent them from changing when it is required while diffused boundaries reflect a transactional relationship that is enmeshed. Diffuse boundaries may lead to chaos and lack of security (Minuchin, 1974).

Some of the observational signs for diffused/enmeshed boundaries include: excessive togetherness, lack of privacy, tendency of the members to speak for one another, etc. In cases of diffused/weak boundaries it is suggested that the perception of oneself as distinguished from the other family members is poorly differentiated. Families with diffused/

enmeshed boundaries may give great importance to *family loyalty* and this may mean that asserting one's point of view, if different from that of the family's, could be seen as a threat for family well-being.

Clear and healthy boundaries lie at the mid-point between rigid and diffused, and represent a balanced combination of the two.

For example, the relationship between Nick and Helen's mother may be disengaged, a rigid boundary. Can you think of an example of a diffused/enmeshed boundary?

There are criticisms of this model, since it may sometimes lead to normative ideas of family that do not offer sufficient diversity. However, this model can provide a purposeful and structured approach for interventions.

For example, this model can be helpful in gaining a better understanding of the structure and quality of relationships within the family, and enabling the practitioner to better support the family. By collaboratively developing a genogram of the family in consultation with the members, Nancy can capture the structure of the family, visualising the type and quality of different relationships. The family can then discuss and reflect upon these relationships, aiming to modify the boundaries and hierarchies between them. For example, perhaps a re-authoring of Kate's narrative from that of *troubled child* to an alternative and preferred narrative can help modify her behaviour. Also, perhaps Nick's realisation of the discrepancy between content and process in his communication, as described earlier, can result in modifying his behaviour and allowing a greater recognition of others and their views. This can lead to a healthier and a more integrated family system with clearer and more balanced relationships and boundaries. These in turn change the family system and result in new behaviours and new possibilities that may address the family's difficulties and concerns. Furthermore, by modifying rigid boundaries, the family, or its members, may be able to draw on relationships that have not been considered before. This can expand the family's, or the person's, support network and enhance their social capital.

Strategic family interventions

Strategic family interventions aim to transform affect to create change opportunities and facilitate appropriate connections between family members. Strategic family interventions focus on changing process and not the content of family systems. Examples of content include: family members, friends, Kate leaving home to go to see friends in London, etc while examples of process include: conflict, connection, behaviour control, etc.

Strategic family interventions are concerned with family rules, and the process of interaction among family members determines the rules by which the family is governed (this includes both overt and covert rules). This is the family's level of cohesion, its adaptability, and its communication style. These interactions work together to serve individual members and collective family needs.

Family function is the output of the interactional system. Utilising resources available through its structure (input), the family interacts to produce responses that fulfil its needs.

Strategic interventions are generally problem-focused and pragmatic and aim to create change in behaviour rather than change in *understanding*. Being problem-focused, strategic family interventions are usually short-term with a clear ending point (ie when the family meets its behavioural change objectives which are agreed at the beginning of the intervention). Therefore, in this discussion we will focus mainly on Brief Strategic Family Intervention (BSFI).

This approach suggests that families tend to remain in the same state of functioning unless challenged to change. Change may disturb the family homeostasis which then the family as a system will seek to restore. It is suggested that the reciprocity/circularity in family relationships results in a quid pro quo approach where members tend to treat others the way they are treated.

All family communication/messages are considered either as reports or commands. In reports, the content of the message conveys information (eg Nancy spoke with Kate, Kate is trying to climb out of her bedroom window), while commands solicit a response/action, asking someone to do something (eg do something, or stop trying to climb out of the window). Commands can be either implicit (non-verbal) or explicit (verbal). BSFI suggests that in families, command messages are patterned as rules (Jackson, 1965).

BSFI posits that families have a limited repertoire of behaviours and interactions that are replayed over and over again, and that families attempt to solve *problems* through various means. However, if the problem persists, the families tend to do more of the same attempted solution, and this escalates the problem, creating a feedback loop that creates a cycle that is often self-reinforcing (eg patterns of conflict that escalate and are repeated).

There are two types of relationships in strategic family interventions: symmetrical and complementary. Symmetrical relationships have a lot of similarity and equality; they share common ground and are comfortable with one another. Complementary relationships are based on differences and opposite attraction; they do not have much common ground, and are very dynamic.

The strategic approach considers triangles/triangular relationships as one of the main sources of family *problems*. Triangles form when a person seeks out a substitute for relating to another person with whom they have difficulties. An example of triangle is the cross-generational coalitions between one parent and a child against the other parent.

In understanding the situation, the practitioner assumes that any behaviour has a function and is protecting either the system or a person in the system, then attempts to rewrite the story.

Family life cycle model

The family life cycle introduces the element of change into the family system and assumes that families go through stages in their lives. These stages include: unattached young adult; newly married couple; family with young children; family with adolescents; leaving home and starting a new family; family in later years.

As the family moves through time, developmental (eg changes and events associated with different stages of family life cycle) and non-developmental changes (eg unexpected events that affect the family functioning) alter the family structure and/or the family's needs. These, in turn, produce change in the way the family interacts. This means that families have to continually change their behaviours, values, beliefs and relationships to meet their evolving needs and in response to internal and external changes/demands. Every family is faced with the test of allowing growth and change while maintaining integrity of the system; however, family stability should be balanced by openness to change.

At times social workers may encounter resistance in families; however, conversations about how the family has changed in the past and how families have to change over time may be helpful to reduce resistance to change. Furthermore, exploring common experiences of family members can provide a platform for relating to and understanding others. For example, conversations with parents about their own childhood and expectations for their family and children can be helpful to highlight similarities and connect the parent with experiences of their children. When children are involved or when there are any communication difficulties/disabilities, it is important to consider age and developmentally or contextually appropriate communication. For example, children drawing pictures of their family and how they would like their family to be, can help capture their views and can serve as a powerful communication and motivational medium.

We will discuss other examples of cognitive and behavioural approaches/interventions in the next chapter.

Meeting Kate

CASE STUDY

Two days later Kate is reported missing after not making it home from school and is located 48 hours later by the police. When Kate returns to school Nancy undertakes a school visit to meet with Kate. Kate attends one of the new academies in the borough. The building is modern with large windows and an airy reception area. The vice-principle comes to meet Nancy and explains that she has booked a room for Nancy and Kate to use and that another member of staff has gone to collect Kate.

Vice-principle: *We are really pleased that Kate and her family are receiving support from your services. We've been worried about Kate for some time and her latest incident of running away is just one of her many attempts at communicating that something is seriously not ok. She's a lovely girl but as you'll soon find out with Kate you're never sure where you stand. One minute she's up and smiling and happy and the next she's in a mood wanting to fight, aggressive, spitting and shouting.*

Nancy is led into a small room which looks like it could be a counselling room.

Vice-principle: *Anyway here we are ... it's a private room and she will be able to speak with you in confidence ... sorry I need to dash off. I am teaching a class in five minutes. Will you keep us updated?*

And with that the vice-principle is off. A few minutes later and Kate arrives.

Kate is tall and slim in appearance, her hair is cut unevenly and very short in some parts and long in other areas resulting in her hair poking out in different directions. She wears heavy eyeliner around both eyes and both of her cheeks are pierced.

Nancy finds it difficult to engage Kate in conversation as Kate makes no eye contact with her at all. Kate eventually looks up to tell Nancy: '*I am bored ... you are boring ... has anyone ever told you that you have a really ugly face? ... do I have to be here ... I am not sure what you want from me ...*'

Nancy: *I am here because your parents are very worried about you ...*

Kate: *Really, they've got a funny way of showing it by sending you here ... You don't really care ... you're paid to be here ... my dad said you wouldn't come out to visit on Saturday and that's why you've come to see me now. It's just a job for you so you can stop pretending.*

Nancy: *I have something for you ...*

Nancy removes a small matching notebook and pen and hands it to Kate.

Nancy: *It can be difficult to talk and sometimes it's easier to write about what you're thinking or feeling. It's up to you, how you want to use it.*

Kate is quiet for a minute and then shrugs her shoulders.

Kate: *.... I don't really care ... I don't really need it ...*

Nancy asks Kate how she finds school, and who among her teachers she likes the most, and why? Kate mentions Surita (her maths teacher) because she is good at maths and so Surita thinks of her as a good student.

The conversation ends by Nancy telling Kate that she'll come back again soon so they can talk some more about the situation, and Kate responding: '*Don't bother*'.

Nancy can't help but reflect upon how vulnerable Kate comes across. Her physical appearance seems older than her age and her appearance is dishevelled. There are some bald patches on her head that Nancy noticed. Behaviourally and emotionally Nancy felt that Kate's actions, answers and demeanour were at times aggressive and at other times child-like.

During the conversation Kate found it difficult to concentrate on one topic and jumped from one topic to another and from one emotion to another.

A few days later the school informs Nancy that Kate has threatened another student and has been sent home due to the incident.

Nancy arranges to go to the school the following day to speak with Kate; however, this time she also calls Surita (Kate's maths teacher) introducing herself and asking her about Kate.

Nancy: *I know that Kate may be challenging at times, and that many of the teachers may see her as a 'troubled' young girl. However, Kate thinks that you may be one of the few people who may think differently about her. Is that right? What have you noticed about Kate? And how come you maintain a different opinion of Kate?*

Surita explains that she thinks Kate is an intelligent young woman who is very vulnerable at the moment, and needs support. Nancy asks if Surita would be willing to join her conversation with Kate, and explains the structure of discussion with Kate and the role of Surita in the meeting as an *outsider witness*. Surita agrees to help and to support Kate after the meeting during their interactions in the school.

Reflection

1. *What are some of your reflections about the conversation between Kate and Nancy? Consider appearance, language, defence mechanism, etc.*

2. *Why is Nancy inviting Surita to join her as an outsider witness in meeting with Kate?*

3. *Have you used outsider witness(es) in your practice? If yes, what were the outcomes, and what do you think about it? And if no, do you think you may use outsider witnesses in a similar situation? Please explain.*

Discussion

Most people who need social work interventions have their life narratives dominated by stories of dominant *problematic* accounts. Narrative practitioners aim to make visible the ways that people would prefer to see themselves and be seen by others. Indeed, narrative interventions/therapy is often referred to as a therapy of acknowledgement. Myerhoff states:

Unless we exist in the eyes of others, we may come to doubt even our own existence. Being is a social and psychological construct; it is something that is made, not given.

(2007, p 31)

For example, Kate may be seen as aggressive and uncooperative or a *troublemaker* by those around her – parents, teachers and others. However, although there may be occasions when Kate may have acted, or may act, in an aggressive or threatening manner, there are also many actions that Kate does and can do that do not fit this *troubled* description. Therefore, to encourage and initiate positive change Nancy and Kate can discuss and think about these actions to explore an alternative and more positive identity narrative for Kate. Indeed, further exploration of Kate's motivations for these actions may reveal motivations that do not fit the *troubled* description. By asking about and highlighting these occasions, Nancy can validate and explicitly witness these preferred narratives.

Thinking about the relational aspects of identity, and the idea that identity is achieved through social interactions (Goffman, 1959; Mead, 1967), acknowledgement by others (eg parents, teachers and Kate's other significant relationships), especially public acknowledgement of Kate's positive identity narrative can help Kate experience this alternative narrative as authentic and credible, which in turn makes it more important and influential in shaping her life.

As part of growing up, young people experiment with different identities, and responses affirmative of positive identity narratives can help to acknowledge the young person's alternative ideas of their preferred narrative and what is important to them. Such an acknowledgement opens up the possibility for Kate to see her preferred identity claim as one that is possible and authentic while externalising the *problem* (see previous chapter) reinforces hope and positive change, and is empowering.

Therefore, depending on the situation it may be helpful to use *outsider witnesses* in order to create a relational context that is authenticating of the person's preferred narrative. Outsider witnesses may be anyone who has a significant relationship with the person and is able to offer acknowledging reaffirmation of the person's preferred or alternative narrative/identity. This could be a friend, or a person of authority in the person's life, a colleague, etc.

Surita as Kate's teacher makes a good outsider witness as she is in a position of power and status in Kate's life, and can help support Kate and respond in a supportive manner to Kate in their everyday interactions.

Public acknowledgement does not only have a supportive function, but can also counter the *problem* narrative held by others about Kate while generating social commitment on her part.

Nancy in her initial meeting/conversation with Kate asked about the school aiming to learn more about Kate's experiences and to identify possible outsider witnesses.

In preparation of her second meeting with Kate, Nancy has decided to use Surita as an outsider witness. Therefore, Nancy's conversation with Surita is in preparation of what Myerhoff refers to as *definitional ceremony*. Myerhoff (1982) suggests that sometimes an outsider witness '*may be hard to find. Natural occasions may not be offered and then they must be artificially invented. I have called such performances Definitional Ceremonies*' (p 105) and adds that:

> Definitional ceremonies deal with the problems of invisibility and marginality; they are strategies that provide opportunities for being seen and in one's own terms, garnering witnesses to one's worth, vitality, and being.
>
> (1982, p 267)

Nancy's aim is to contribute to Kate's sense of self-worth, vitality and well-being and to help Kate identify an alternative narrative. During the meeting Surita (outsider witness) will be asked to offer responses to Kate's account that can enrich the description of Kate's preferred/positive identity narrative. We will explore this case further in the next chapter.

References

Baum, S (2006) Evaluating the Impact of Family Therapy for Adults with Learning Disabilities and Their Families. *Learning Disability Review*, 11: 8–18.

British Psychological Society (BPS) (2007) *Child Protection Position Paper*. Leicester: BPS.

Carlson, B E (2000) Children Exposed to Intimate Partner Violence. *Trauma, Violence and Abuse*, 1(4): 321–42.

Dayton, C J, Levendosky, A A, Davidson, W S and Bogat, G A (2010) The Child as Held in the Mind of the Mother: The Influence of Prenatal Maternal Representations on Parenting Behaviors. *Infant Mental Health Journal*, 31: 220–41.

Dodd, L W (2009) Therapeutic Groupwork with Young Children and Mothers Who Have Experienced Domestic Abuse. *Educational Psychology in Practice*, 25(1): 21–36.

Fonagy, P, Steele, H and Steele, M (1991) Maternal Representations of Attachment During Pregnancy Predict the Organization of Infant-Mother Attachment at One Year of Age. *Child Development*, 62: 891–905.

George, C and Solomon, J (2008) The Caregiving System: A Behavioral Systems Approach to Parenting, in Cassidy, J and Shaver, P R (eds) *Handbook of Attachment: Theory, Research, and Clinical Applications* (pp 833–56). New York: Guilford Press.

Gerhardt, S (2004) *Why Love Matters*. London. Routledge.

Goffman, E (1959) *The Presentation of Self in Everyday Life*. Garden City, NY: Doubleday.

Holt, S, Buckley, H and Whelan, S (2008) The Impact of Exposure to Domestic Violence on Children and Young People: A Review of the Literature. *Child Abuse and Neglect*, 32: 797–810.

Home Office (2013) Information for Local Areas on the Change to the Definition of Domestic Violence and Abuse. [online] Available at: www.gov.uk/government/uploads/system/uploads/attachment_data/file/142701/guide-on-definition-of-dv.pdf (accessed 5 May 2014).

Humphreys, C and Stanley, N (eds) (2006) *Domestic Violence and Child Protection Directions for Good Practice*. London: Jessica Kingsley.

Huth-Bocks, A C, Levendosky, A A, Bogat, G A and von Eye, A (2004) Infant-Mother Attachment: The Impact of Prenatal Maternal Representations and Social Support in a High Risk Sample. *Child Development*, 75: 480–96.

Kaur, G, Scior, K and Wilson, S (2009) Systemic Working in Learning Disability Services: A UK Wide Survey. *British Journal of Learning Disabilities*, 37: 213–20.

Jackson, D D (1965) Family Rules: Marital Quid Pro Quo. *Archives of General Psychiatry*, 12: 589–94.

Lang, W P, Little, M and Cronen, V (1990) The Systemic Professional: Domains of Action and the Question of Neutrality. *Human Systems*, 1(1): 39–56.

Lapierre, S (2008) Mothering in the Context of Domestic Violence: The Pervasiveness of the Deficit Model of Mothering. *Child and Family Social Work*, 13: 454–63.

Leckman, J F, Feldman, R, Swain, J E and Mayes, L C (2007) Primary Parental Preoccupation: Revisited, in Mayes, L, Fonagy, P and Target, M (eds) *Developmental Science and Psychoanalysis: Integration and Innovation* (pp 89–108). London: Karnac.

Mead, G (1967) *Mind, Self, and Society*. Chicago: University of Chicago Press.

Minuchin, S (1974) *Family & Family Therapy*. Cambridge, MA: Harvard University Press.

Mullender, A, Hague, G, Iman, U, Kelly, L, Mallos, E and Regan, L (2002) *Children's Perspectives on Domestic Violence*. London: Sage.

Myerhoff, B (1982) Life History Among the Elderly: Performance, Visibility, and Remembering, in Ruby, J (ed) *A Crack in the Mirror: Reflexive Perspective in Anthropology*. Philadelphia: University of Pennsylvania Press.

Myerhoff, B (2007) *Stories as Equipment for Living*. Michigan: The University of Michigan Press.

Shotter, J (1993) *Conversational Realities: Constructing Life Through Language*. London: Sage.

Stern, D (1995) *The Motherhood Constellation: A Unified View of Parent-Infant Psychotherapy*. New York: Basic Books.

Winnicott, D W (1960) The Theory of the Parent-Infant Relationship. *International Journal of Psychoanalysis*, 41: 585–95.

Winnicott, D W (1965) *The Maturational Process and the Facilitating Environment*. New York: International Universities Press.

Winnicott, D W (1989[1967]) The Location of Cultural Experience, in *Playing and Reality*. New York: Brunner-Routledge.

8 Searching for love in all the wrong places (Part 2)

That's the way I feel about myself: motivational interviewing, cognitive and behavioural approaches

Chapter summary

This chapter begins with a brief note about gangs and gang membership followed by a discussion of rape and multiple perpetrator rape. The chapter then continues with a brief note on self-harm, before introducing motivational interviewing and demonstrating its application in practice.

The chapter will then introduce cognitive and behavioural interventions and approaches.

The concluding section offers a discussion of unresolved trauma and its impact. This section offers an example of unresolved trauma and its transmission through projective identification between father and child. The chapter concludes by emphasising the importance of identifying and assessing such dynamics in practice.

Chapter objectives

1. Briefly discuss gangs and multiple perpetrator rape.

2. Briefly discuss self-harm.

3. Introduce motivational interviewing and its application.

4. Introduce cognitive and behavioural interventions.

5. Introduce an example of interplay between unresolved trauma and projective identification, and the intergenerational transmission of trauma.

Multi-perpetrator rape

CASE STUDY

Three days later the duty desk receive a police notification reporting that Kate has been sexually assaulted. Her parents are aware of this, since Nick contacted the police to report that Kate disclosed to him that she was forced to perform oral sex on older males. Kate had skipped school to hang out with her friend Ruby in London. They had a fight and she left Ruby's house.

Feeling as though she had nowhere to go Kate walked to the off-license and sat outside on the pavement smoking cigarettes. She was approached by five older males. They chatted for a while and asked her if she wanted to hang out with them. They took her to an old derelict building in London and forced her to perform oral sex on them. They didn't allow her to leave the building and it was only when she promised to buy vodka and cigarettes for everyone that they let her go. She ran to the closest petrol station where the shop assistant helped her to phone her parents. Kate phoned Nick who picked her up and took her to the closest police station. Upon arrival at the police station Kate refused to speak with the police.

Nick tells the police that he fears this is part of some gang initiation and he is fearful that these males have her personal details and may seek her out. He also adds that a social worker is involved and refers to the social worker as '*absolutely useless*'.

Strategy meeting

Children and Families Services convene a strategy meeting for the following day. The police, social worker, school and school nurse attend.

The school reports that Kate is a very vulnerable young person and is easily influenced by her peers. The school are concerned that one of the drivers of Kate's behaviour is her wanting and/or seeking out attention from her peers. The school notes that Kate will often do things to attract attention of older males, often placing herself in a vulnerable position. The school also reports that Kate has a preoccupation with gangs and gang culture and she has told other pupils that gang members will '*beat the crap out of you if you diss me in any way*'. Kate seems to think that such an association gives her a higher status within the school and her peer group.

Teaching staff report that Kate acts very aggressively towards younger pupils or pupils who are deemed '*weaker*' or '*vulnerable*' and actively tries to intimidate other pupils.

The police report that she is not a member of any gang and at this stage she is aspiring to be part of a gang. The police are concerned that she will be sexually exploited by gangs if her behaviour continues. Their investigation into her sexual assault is particularly difficult as she does not want to provide any statements or identify the perpetrators.

Given the risk factors it is agreed that an initial child protection conference should be convened.

Reflection

1. *Drawing on the previous chapters, critically reflect upon the above narrative. What are some of your thoughts, reflections and analyses so far? Discuss your views with a colleague or in small groups and seek feedback from your peers.*

2. *What is the meaning and significance of Kate's risk-taking behaviour? How does this relate to the question of belonging, power difference and potential space?*

3. *Is there a difference between multiple perpetrator rape and lone perpetrator rape? Is there a relationship between the history of domestic violence between Nick and Helen and Kate's emotions and behaviour and experience? Can you think of any connection between Kate's family structure and relationships, and her sense of self, sexuality and meaning of family?*

Discussion

Young people who do not experience a sense of belongingness to their families will often find some other group of individuals with whom to identify; one possibility is a gang (Le and Stockdale, 2008). As mentioned in Chapter 1, such young people may be seeking a point of hold and anchoring, and a sense of connectedness and belonging, and in that sense they may feel that it is better to be part of something, whether good or bad, than to be part of nothing and be alone. Blomquist (2001) suggests that young people do this in an effort to lose their identity in a group as a way to gain an identity, which otherwise they feel they lack. This puts them at risk of getting involved in harmful activities just to be part of the group. Indeed, often young people join gangs to find a sense of belonging and as a substitute for family. For such children and young people, gangs, like families, offer a unit of security in a *world of exclusions* that is *too dangerous for individuals alone*. In a *hostile world*, gangs, like families, provide individuals with a role model and an anchoring point, structure and routine, and a much-needed sense of identity and belonging.

Gangs often require new members to commit crimes before accepting them as part of the gang. Kate has aspired to be part of a gang and has been subject to Multiple Perpetrator Rape (MPR). This is a significant factor as suggested by De La Rue and Espelage (2014). In regression analysis of their data on family and abuse characteristics of gang-involved, pressured-to-join and non-gang-involved girls, De La Rue and Espelage (2014) found that physical abuse was not a significant predictor for joining gangs, and instead sexual abuse distinguished gang-involved girls from the non-involvement group and the pressured-group. These data highlight the importance of considering how victimisation influences gang involvement among young people.

Research suggests that there are different motives and dynamics in MPR from Lone Perpetrator Rape (LPR). Whereas LPR is hypothesised to be rooted in perpetrator *pathology* (Bijleveld and Hendricks, 2003), explanations of MPR focus on social processes and MPR offences and are correlated with the person's social status within the group.

There are many stereotypes about rape and some people try to distinguish between *real rape* involving sexual intercourse, and oral sex. Indeed, there are many misconceptions surrounding rape, and these include *real rape*: happens between strangers, involves forceful sexual intercourse, involves physical violence, happens out of home, survivors demonstrate active resistance, rapist(s) use or threaten the use of force (Estrich, 1987). Therefore, survivors of rape whose experiences do not match these stereotypes are sometimes discounted and treated as less credible even in police interviews and emergency medical services (Maier, 2008).

However, it is important to note that the very expression *real rape* is a misconceived and misguided stereotype that perpetuates hegemonic patriarchal ideas and values. Survivors of rape come from all sorts of backgrounds in terms of race, age, gender, economic and social class, culture, etc. Furthermore, many perpetrator(s) know their target. In fact, in a sample of multiple perpetrator sex offences the perpetrators tended to know their victims (Bijleveld et al, 2007) and in 43 per cent of cases from a sample of 251 MPR of varying ages, at least one perpetrator knew the survivor (Porter and Alison, 2006). These data negate the *stranger* assumption about rape. Furthermore, MPR offences offer the perpetrators the opportunity to create a consistent account (Bijleveld et al, 2007), making the survivor(s) appear inconsistent and less reliable/credible. Kelly et al's (2005) study of *Attrition in Reported Rape Cases* in England found that only 3 per cent of reported MPR led to convictions (compared to 8 per cent for overall reported rape cases) and no cases with more than three perpetrators resulted in conviction. This suggests that survivors of MPR are even less likely to receive justice.

There are many reasons for which children and young people may or may not disclose their experience of sexual abuse. Examining 191 forensic interviews of child sexual abuse with survivors between 3 and 18 years old, Shaefer et al (2011) identified five categories of barriers to disclosure: (1) threats by the perpetrator(s) (eg the child was told they would get in trouble if they disclosed); (2) fears (eg the child was afraid something bad would happen if they disclosed); (3) lack of opportunity (eg the child felt the opportunity for disclosure never presented); (4) lack of understanding (eg the child failed to recognise abusive behaviour as unacceptable); and (5) relationship with the perpetrator (eg the child thought the perpetrator was a friend). This is an important point and reflects the dominance of patriarchal stereotypes and the stigma experienced by many survivors of rape and sexual abuse, as well as the need for greater awareness and education.

Thinking in psychosocial terms and drawing on a relational psychoanalytic perspective, we can conceive of the sense of guilt or shame experienced by the survivors of rape and other sexual abuses as an expression of repressed anger. Survivors of rape and sexual abuse understandably experience anger and grief in relation to the abuse. However, the dominance of patriarchal values does not offer adequate recognition and the space for acceptance and appropriate expression of survivors' grief and the processing of their traumatic experiences. This results in repression of such feelings out of the societal and into the personal realm. Hence, the anger and hurt that is redirected toward the self is then expressed as feelings of guilt and shame, a de facto double jeopardy for the survivors.

Youth who engage in greater levels of delinquent behaviours have been shown to be more likely to join gangs (Esbensen et al, 2001), and gangs have been shown to facilitate delinquent behaviours (Curry et al, 2002), and without clear intervention and support policies, these can form a vicious, escalating and self-reinforcing cycle.

Moving to a PRU, and mental health assessment

CASE STUDY

Two days later Kate is arrested for taking a knife to school, and given the historical concerns including Kate being abusive and physically violent to staff and peers, frequent absences, wearing excessive make-up and smoking on school property, the school informs Helen and Nick that Kate will be permanently excluded from school. Upon hearing that she's excluded Kate threatens staff: *'You'll be sorry. You'll see, you will be very sorry that you even thought about messing with me. You'll see, my crew will mess you ugly bitches up.'*

That night Kate makes three large cuts on her upper right arm. Nick is furious and phones Nancy the next morning telling her that it's her fault for not doing more for Kate. Nick tells Nancy that if she does not find a school for Kate before midday he will personally sue her for negligence.

Nancy feels shaken after the phone call with Nick. Nancy has noticed that in meetings and conferences Nick often talks over her or blatantly ignores her, while when dealing with his male colleagues he always seems to act in an appropriate manner. Nancy reflects upon her observations and feels that Nick has a tendency to display aggressive behaviour towards women.

Nancy makes arrangements for Kate to attend a Pupil Referral Unit (PRU).

CAMHS report and in-patient unit

A week later and the initial child protection conference (ICPC) is convened and Kate is made subject to a child protection plan under the category of neglect. An extensive package of support is put in place for the family including a two-day in-patient assessment with CAMHS (Child and Adolescent Mental Health Services) and the psychiatric unit at the hospital. The psychiatrist's assessment concludes that Kate has behavioural problems as opposed to psychiatric problems.

Mental health

The psychiatrist provides the following assessment in relation to Kate's mental health:

Kate does suffer from depressed mood and behavioural problems. She finds it difficult to contain her emotions and adults around her also find it difficult to provide a containing environment for her. There have been suicidal gestures and risk-taking behaviour such as internet conversations with unknown males and running away.

... Kate holds strong beliefs about her physical looks. She believes that her nose and lips are too big and that her body is too large for her head. She has a preoccupation and concern with her perceived defects and this causes her distress and impairment in functioning. These beliefs fulfil some of the criteria for Body Dismorphic Disorder.

The psychiatrist recommends in-patient care and not a specialist foster placement.

The mental health assessment is shared with the parents and Nancy speaks with Helen and Nick who are both unsure and hesitate about the in-patient admission.

Nick: *It's like saying that I'm giving up on her ... I am not having it ...*

Reflection

1.   *What are your thoughts and reflections about self-harm and suicide in general, and Kate's self-harm in particular?*

2.   *What is the significance of Kate's threats to the school staff? And what would you do if you were in Nancy's shoes?*

3.   *What is the significance and meaning of Nick's statement: 'It's like saying that I'm giving up on her ... I am not having it ...'. What are some of your thoughts and reflections about this statement?*

Discussion

Thinking about self-harm

Young people who self-harm usually do so without suicidal intent and because they find it helps relieve distressing feelings and helps them cope with problems in their lives. Cutting is perhaps the most common form of self-harm and is sometimes accompanied with other self-injuries such as skin-burning, hair-pulling and anorexia.

After her exclusion from school, Kate made three cuts on her arms. Although this may not be a suicide attempt or intended to inflict long-term self-harm, it is a reflection of underlying mental and emotional distress. Self-harm is one of the strongest predictors of eventual death by suicide in adolescence, increasing the risk of suicide up to ten-fold (Hawton and Harriss, 2007).

There are many factors, triggers and life stresses that contribute to self-harm, including: academic pressures; family problems such as parental separation or divorce; exclusion or feeling isolated; suicide or self-harm by a significant person in the young person's life; being bullied; low self-esteem; and others.

However, despite its high prevalence, there is no agreement about the definition of self-harm. Hawton et al (2003) defined (deliberate) self-harm as intentional self-injury or self-poisoning, irrespective of type of motivation or degree of suicidal intent.

Many European researchers use this definition of self-harm; however, many American researchers subdivide self-harm into two main categories, suicidal acts with intent to die and suicide-related behaviour with no intent to die (Silverman et al, 2007). Non-suicidal self-injury is included in section 3 (conditions for further study) of the Diagnostic and Statistical Manual (DSM 5).

Nancy may use motivational interviewing skills to help Nick resolve his ambivalence and decide about Kate being placed in an in-patient therapeutic community. Therefore, let us briefly examine motivational interviewing.

Motivational interviewing

Based on his work with people who misuse alcohol, Miller (1983, 1985) developed the Motivational Interview (MI) model. This was more fully developed through the collaboration between Miller and Rollnick who defined MI as a person-centred *'directive approach for enhancing intrinsic motivation to change by exploring and resolving ambivalence'* (Miller and Rollnick, 2002, p 25). Some Rogerian and person-centred practitioners may consider the *person-centred* and *directive* approaches as incompatible. However, MI offers a practical motivational approach to behaviour change.

One of the most powerful aspects of MI is that instead of the *deficit model* of focusing on the *problem* and *putting something into* the person and pathologising them (eg by characterising people as lazy, stubborn, oppositional, in denial, addict, and others), MI is designed to build on the person's strengths and to draw the person's own motivation, desires, hopes and aspirations out of them and to build on their strengths in order to achieve positive behavioural change.

MI is grounded in the Transtheoretical Model (TM) (Prochaska and DiClemente, 1982) which considers behaviour change as a process with different stages/phases. These phases run along a continuum of motivational readiness and include: precontemplation, contemplation, preparation, action, maintenance and relapse.

Precontemplation is the phase in which the person is not yet considering the possibility of change.

Contemplation phase is marked by ambivalence and in this phase the person is weighing the pros and cons of the change. People can get stuck in the contemplation stage and this is sometimes misunderstood as resistance. Miller suggests that ambivalence in people who misuse substances is often pathologised.

Preparation phase is characterised by an intention to change in the immediate future (usually within a month or so).

Action phase is when the person takes action in order to achieve a behaviour change.

Maintenance phase involves the person's effort to maintain and integrate the new behaviour that has been successfully started/changed.

Relapse represents the phase when the individual re-engages with the previous undesired behaviour.

The spirit of MI involves: collaboration, evocation and autonomy.

Collaboration/partnership – the practitioner and user of services work collaboratively to establish a shared understanding and agreement about the intervention, the process and its outcome.

Evocation – direct persuasion is not an effective method for resolving ambivalence, instead it is important to elicit the person's motivation in a person-centred manner while remaining directive in helping the user of services to examine and resolve ambivalence. Indeed, the best ideas about change come from the person and these are the ideas that they can most readily act upon.

Autonomy – the practitioner affirms the user of services' right and capacity for self-direction and facilitates informed choice. Autonomy is in contrast with authority and is an important element of empowerment and an anti-discriminatory and anti-oppressive practice. The delicate balance between autonomy and authority is at the heart of good and effective social work practice.

Aside from the above, some also add acceptance and compassion to the spirit of MI:

Acceptance – honouring the lived experiences, expertise preferences and autonomy of users of services while pursuing and achieving mutually-agreed objectives.

Compassion – focusing on the interest of the users of services with empathic understanding.

The four basic principles of MI are: express empathy, support self-efficacy, roll with resistance, develop discrepancy.

Express empathy – this involves congruity and connection with users of services on an emotional level and the ability to relate to their perspective and to appreciate their lived experiences. This demonstrates genuine interest and care, and provides the basis for ensuring that the users of services are heard and understood, and helps build trust which supports positive change.

Support self-efficacy – MI is a strength-based approach that draws on the person's own motivations, capabilities and preferences. A person's belief that change is possible (self-efficacy) is needed to build hope about making those difficult changes. Sometimes in spite of efforts the person may not achieve the desired change. MI practitioners would then highlight the previous successes of the person to emphasise strengths and encourage/support self-efficacy.

Roll with resistance – MI focuses more on ambivalence than resistance. However, given the person-centred and yet directive approach of MI, it is important to remember that any discrepancy between the practitioner's views and those of the users of services about the *problem* or the *solution* is a reflection of the person's ambivalence, and should not be escalated to resistance. Therefore, actions of statements that demonstrate reluctance or resistance, especially at the early stages of intervention, are not elevated or confronted, instead it is important to *roll with it* and ask more open questions to uncover possibilities for positive change. This de-escalates the difference and avoids *struggle* and instead refocuses on MI values of allowing users of services to define the *problem* and develop their own solutions which leave little space for *resistance*. In this sense, the MI approach is more of *dancing* rather than *wrestling*.

Develop discrepancy – motivation for change is rooted in a discrepancy between *where we are* and *where we want to be*, and MI practitioners highlight such discrepancies and the cost and advantages/disadvantages associated with current behaviour/circumstances and the person's values and future goals. When the person recognises the discrepancy and conflict between their current behaviour and their values and their achievement of self-identified goals, they experience the need and an increased motivation for change.

The core skills for MI include the use of: (1) open-ended questions, (2) affirmations, (3) reflections, and (4) summaries. These are also referred to as OARS.

Open-ended questions are those that are not easily answered with a *yes/no* or short answer containing only a specific, limited piece of information. Open-ended questions induce elaboration and thinking more deeply about an issue. Although sometimes closed questions can be valuable (eg when collecting specific information in an assessment), open-ended questions create forward momentum and enable users of services to explore the reasons and possibilities for change. For example:

Closed question: *How much alcohol do you drink each day?*

Open-ended question: *What is the role of alcohol in your life?*

Affirmations are positive statements that recognise the strengths of users of services. They help build rapport and help users of services see their strengths and gain confidence and feel that change is possible. However, they must be genuine and congruent to be effective. Affirmations often involve reframing behaviours or concerns as evidence of positive qualities. Affirmations support and enhance the person's self-efficacy. For example:

This is hard work and takes a lot of courage, and you have done very well succeeding in doing it.

You really care about your family.

Reflections or reflective listening is perhaps the most crucial skill in MI. Reflection allows the practitioner to express empathy; by offering careful listening and reflective responses, the users of services can feel that the practitioner understands the situation/issues from their perspective. Reflections emphasise the difficulties/negatives of the status quo and the positives of making change, and guide users of services toward examining and resolving ambivalence. Reflections need to be attuned to the level of motivation and readiness for change of users of services. Reflections can be used in a variety of circumstances and contexts.

Summaries are a special type of longer reflection in which the practitioner recaps the salient points as of that point. Summaries communicate interest and understanding, and can be used to direct attention toward resolution of ambivalence and change. By highlighting both sides of the ambivalence argument and strategically selecting the information that is highlighted and what is minimised, practitioners can produce discrepancy that focuses attention and induces further thinking toward resolving the ambivalence.

There are four steps to MI, namely: engaging, focusing, evoking and planning. These are somewhat sequential processes. You engage the users of services before you can focus on a particular topic/*problem*, and you'll need to focus on a topic/*problem* before you can explore discrepancy and evoke motivation. Finally, you need the motivation before you can do any planning for action.

Engaging involves establishing a trusting and mutually respectful relationship. This requires empathy and a relationship-based approach, in addition to anything that can make the user of services feel welcomed, comfortable, understood and hopeful, helping us to reach mutual goals. Therefore, it is important to start with open questions to allow users of services to talk about their experiences, views and preferences, and to remain aware of power differences that can affect relationship-building.

Focusing is an ongoing process of seeking and maintaining direction. It involves agreeing an agenda by taking into consideration the goals and priorities of the users of services, the practitioner and the agency. The objective is to set a clear direction for resolving ambivalence and developing a change plan. This is achieved through the OARS and reflective listening.

Evoking is defined as eliciting a person's own motivation for change. It requires listening to the person's statement, (change talk) that indicate an inclination/movement in the direction of change (eg I want …, I wish …, I can …, I hope …, the reasons are …, that would solve …, etc). MI practitioners encourage and reinforce change talk by asking questions such as: Why do you want to make a change? What would some of the benefits be in your view?

Planning involves collaboratively developing a change plan in agreement with users of services. Change talk does not only reflect the person's reasons for change, it also often points to ways in which the person could make, or would prefer to make, the change and be successful at achieving and maintaining it. By identifying these details the planning process can then draw and build on them by moving from general concepts to specific actions and behaviours that can effect and support change.

Planning is the last step in the MI process; however, it is important that planning is SMART. This means that plans need to be: Specific, Measurable, Achievable, Relevant and have a clear Timeframe for their completion.

Below is an example of motivational interviewing as used by Nancy to support Nick in resolving his ambivalence. The descriptions enclosed in brackets are meant to offer explanations based on the above discussion of MI and to add clarity about the process taking place.

Motivational interviewing and resolving Nick's ambivalence

CASE STUDY

Nancy goes for a home visit to speak with Nick and try to motivate Nick to agree with placing Kate in an in-patient facility. She uses her motivational interviewing skills to resolve Nick's ambivalence. Below is part of the conversation:

Nancy: *Could we briefly discuss the options available for supporting Kate?*

Nick: *Yes, you're here. So go ahead.*

Nancy: *So, how do you feel about the recommendation for Kate to stay in an in-patient facility?* [asking an open question]

Nick: *As I said it's like saying that I'm giving up on her … I don't want it.* [precontemplation phase – highlighting reason for his reluctance]

Nancy: *You are concerned about Kate and want her to be supported* [affirmation]. *What do you think could be some advantages or disadvantages if she was to stay in an in-patient facility* [asking an open question]?

Nick: *Yes, of course. She could be better supported by doctors, nurses and other workers. They might understand better how to deal with her and they might be able to calm her and stop her behaviour. But, it just feels like we're giving up on her, and accepting that we don't care for her* [contemplation – ambivalence and an opportunity to highlight discrepancy between current situation and desired goals].

Nancy: *So let me see if I understand this right. You feel if she is in an in-patient facility she'll be well supported by doctors, nurses and other workers, and they have the expertise to help her with her anxiety and to change her behaviour. But, you have some reservations about it because of the way it makes you feel. Is that right* [reflecting back]?

Nick: *Yes, that's right. I just need time to think about all this* [contemplation].

Nancy: *On a scale of 0 to 10 with 0 being not at all important and 10 being absolutely urgent and very important, how important is it to you that Kate receives expert support that could help her feel less anxious and change her behaviour* [checking Nick's motivation while helping Nick recognise the urgency of the matter]?

Nick: *Of course it is very important. Definitely a 10.*

Nancy: *Ok. So it is absolutely urgent and very important for you that Kate receives expert support that could help her feel less anxious and change her behaviour. You also believe that if she is in an in-patient facility she'll be well supported by doctors, nurses and other workers, who can offer Kate the expert support she needs. But, if she is in an in-patient facility you feel like you are giving up on her* [summarising and emphasising the positives of change]. *What makes you feel like you might be giving up on her* [open question]?

Nick: *It's just that she should be staying home. Staying with us. But then if she goes to this in-patient thing, it feels like I've failed, or haven't been a good father to her. It makes me feel like a failure.*

Nancy: *What do you think would be best for Kate* [refocusing the conversation on Kate]?

Nick: *She needs the help, and yeah, I can see the advantages of the in-patient facility. She'd probably be better off there and they'll know better how to manage her, calm her and deal with her* [contemplation phase].

Nancy: *So you think she would be better off in an in-patient facility, and they have the expertise to give her the support she needs and to contain her emotion and deal with the situation when she is anxious. What could be some of the reasons you think she shouldn't go to the in-patient facility* [summarising and asking an open question. Probing to reinforce the discrepancy]?

Nick: *It just makes me feel like a failure. But then we can't control her anymore. It is probably better for Kate. But, I need more time to think about it* [contemplation and moving toward resolution of ambivalence].

Nancy: *So you feel it is absolutely urgent and very important that Kate receives specialist support. You also think that the in-patient facility would be able to offer her the specialist support she needs to manage her anxiety and behaviour, and it is quite difficult to manage Kate at home when she is anxious and feels out of control. Is that right?*

Nick: *Yes, that's right. It is difficult to manage her. It's really impossible sometimes to deal with her, and nothing seems to stop her. She has become too dangerous for herself.*

Nancy: *You think she cannot be contained at home and has become dangerous for herself. Let me ask you a hypothetical question just to make sure I understand the situation. Let us say Kate fell and broke her leg, and the doctor asked for her to be hospitalised. Would you agree for her to be hospitalised* [reflecting back and posing a hypothetical question to highlight discrepancy]?

Nick: *Yes, of course. That's obvious.*

Nancy: *Would it make you feel like you are giving up on her* [highlighting discrepancy]?

Nick: *Of course not. I would take her to hospital myself. It is obvious. If she broke her leg she would need whatever is necessary to make sure her leg is ok. I would feel like a failure if I didn't take her to the hospital.*

Nancy: *So if Kate broke her leg you would take Kate to hospital yourself. And if you did not take her to the hospital, you would feel like you have failed to support her* [summarising and highlighting the discrepancy]. *What do you think has more serious consequences, Kate's current anxiety and behaviour or if she broke her leg* [highlighting discrepancy]?

Nick: *I understand. The current situation is much worse. You can fix a broken leg easily, but at the moment it seems Kate is broken inside, and I just don't know how it can be fixed. It is much, much worse. I see your point. Yeah. Perhaps it is better she goes to the in-patient facility* [preparation – acknowledging the discrepancy in reasoning and the need for change].

Nancy: *So, if Kate had a broken leg you would have taken her to the hospital immediately, and you feel Kate's current anxiety and behaviour are much much worse than if she broke her leg* [reflecting back]. *How quickly do you think she needs the specialist help from the in-patient facility* [checking Nick's motivation level]?

Nick: *As soon as possible. I think she needs it immediately. Yeah, I think she should go to the in-patient facility as soon as possible. It is best for everyone* [preparation phase].

Nancy: *I know how much you care for Kate, and I know that you will miss Kate at home. But also, as you have said, she needs the specialist support and this is absolutely urgent and important, and she needs the help that the in-patient facility can offer as soon as possible. Plus she will be coming home every weekend* [summarising]. *What could prevent you from agreeing for Kate to be placed in a therapeutic community* [open question]?

Nick: *No. that's fine. I understand the situation and don't think I will change my mind. I will sign the papers* [action phase].

Nancy: *If you were going to rate how determined you feel about Kate going to the therapeutic community, on a scale of 0 to 10, with 0 being …*

Nick interrupts Nancy, saying: *Ok. I know. I know. The answer is 10. That's fine. I am decided and she is going to go to the in-patient facility* [action phase].

In the next two days, Nick and Helen sign the necessary paperwork and Kate goes to Kingswood.

Reflection

1. Reflect upon and carefully analyse the above conversation between Nick and Nancy, and note down some of the more important points and dynamics. Critically discuss this with a colleague or in a small group.

2. What are some of the points Nancy could have considered in the above conversation?

3. How can you apply motivational interviewing in your own practice? Think about a case and plan how you would approach the situation. Practice this with a peer.

Discussion

The above conversation between Nick and Nancy offers a good example of motivational interviewing, and although it seems self-explanatory, let us briefly examine some of the important features of this conversation.

Firstly, it is important to note that after inviting Nick to speak about Kate ('*Could we briefly discuss the options available for supporting Kate?*') Nancy starts the conversation with an open question allowing an open conversation.

After Nick expresses his reluctance, Nancy begins her response with an affirmation followed by an open question. This is important as the affirmation highlights Nick's concern for Kate's well-being. This acknowledgement of Nick's concern is validating for Nick and helps demonstrate understanding. She then asks another open question rather than enumerating the reasons why Kate would be better off in an in-patient facility. Rather than telling Nick her reasons, this gives Nick the opportunity to uncover the reasons for himself.

After Nick outlines the reasons why the in-patient facility could be good for Kate, Nancy reflects back, helping to reinforce the idea. Reflecting back also allows Nick to hear his own reasoning and have the opportunity to reflect on it as a listener.

Nancy then tries to check the strength of Nick's motivation and recognition of the urgency of Kate's need for specialist support. This also helps highlight the importance and the urgency of Kate receiving specialist support.

After Nick's strongly affirmative response: '*Of course it is very important. Definitely a 10.*' Nancy continues by summarising and reflecting back to reinforce what has been discussed so far, followed by another open question.

Nick's answer is quite revealing as it reflects feelings of guilt; however, with a focus on self rather than Kate and her interest. We'll return to this point in the last section of this chapter. It is important to note Nancy's response: '*What do you think would be best for Kate?*' This is another open question that aims to refocus Nick's attention on Kate and Kate's best interest. Here, Nancy makes a strategic choice of not addressing Nick's self-focus.

This is a non-argumentative, person-centred and yet directive manner of engagement that allows Nick to acknowledge Kate's needs explicitly, and hence, refocusing the discussion on Kate's best interest.

After Nick's acknowledgement of Kate's needs and the positives about the in-patient facility, Nancy reinforces these points by reflecting back. However, she does not rush to a conclusion. Nancy recognises that the act of signing the papers that authorise Kate's placement in the in-patient facility bears significant meaning for Nick, and that Nick is still in the preparation phase. Therefore, Nancy summarises the situation and continues with another open question about possible reasons why Kate should not be placed in an in-patient facility.

Nick's response is a good indication of why Nancy did not rush Nick into a decision, as he recognises the positives of the in-patient facility, and the negatives of Kate being at home; however, he adds that he needs more time to think about it. This shows that if Nancy had rushed Nick to sign the papers for placing Kate in an in-patient facility, she would have most likely received a negative response and jeopardised her motivational interviewing conversation which was heading in the right direction. This is because Nick had not yet reached the action phase.

Nancy continues by summarising the conversation highlighting the discrepancy in Nick's reasoning and allowing Nick to further acknowledge the difficulties in having Kate at home. Then she follows with a further reflection and a hypothetical question, aiming to highlight the discrepancy in Nick's reasoning.

It is important to note that Nancy stays with the conversation and the motivational interviewing process, remaining person-centred and yet gently guiding Nick to note the discrepancy and to commit to change. It is only toward the end of the conversation that Nick enters the action phase and commits to change. Nancy still reflects back and tries to check and at the same time reinforce Nick's commitment to change. The result is a stronger expression of commitment on Nick's part.

Honouring the expertise and experience of users of services, and the importance of self-determination, and having the *good enough* care and empathy to stay with users of services as they navigate their own thoughts and emotions and resolve ambivalence is the most empowering and effective way to initiate, reinforce and maintain positive change.

Experiences in the in-patient unit (Kingswood)

CASE STUDY

Kate is offered a place on a tier 4 in-patient unit for adolescents. She will reside there five days a week, returning home at weekends. She will attend the school attached to the hospital and will receive intensive therapeutic work from a holistic team within the unit, including psychiatrists, mental health workers, social workers and family therapists.

Kingswood stress the importance of the whole family being part of the solution for Kate. Key aspects of the work include family therapy; both parents and their partners are expected to attend weekly meetings and commit to visiting Kate at least once a week, and parents are expected to telephone the child every night. The psychiatrist recommends that Kate stays as an in-patient for 16–18 weeks.

Kate continues to display violent, aggressive and threatening behaviour towards other staff and especially other children, and after two weeks, Kingswood become concerned that they can no longer contain/manage her safely.

A professionals meeting is convened with those working with Kate and it is recommended that Kate is placed in a therapeutic placement for 38–52 weeks and for Nancy to discuss this option with the family. Nancy contacts Nick and Helen and they agree for Kate to be transferred from the in-patient facility to a therapeutic community for 38–52 weeks. With the help of Kingswood, within the next few days Nancy finds a more suitable community for Kate.

Starting a new life in the new therapeutic community

Nancy had hoped that Kingswood could contain and hold Kate enabling her to unpack some of her difficult feelings. However, Kate found it very difficult to talk about her emotions at the in-patient unit. But, she is now in a small therapeutic community that specialises in helping adolescents who have experienced multiple and severe complex trauma. Kate has recently turned 13 and her new therapeutic community houses 12 young people ranging from the ages of 12 to 18 years old. Therefore, she is one of the youngest residents at the community.

Kate is assigned a key worker who will work with her and support her and help her settle into the community. Kate will also receive group counselling daily.

The first few weeks are very difficult for Kate and she tries to run away and self-harm but the staff are able to contain her and talk to her about her feelings.

Kate starts to settle down and begins to adjust to her new life at the therapeutic community. She is also building a good relationship with her key worker. However, Kate's group therapist and key worker feel that she seems reluctant to speak about family problems. There seems to be a fear on Kate's part that she may be betraying her parents and family by speaking about the past. Kate is effectively seeking her parents' permission to talk about the pain and hurt inside.

It is around this time that the clinical staff group at the therapeutic community become increasingly concerned about Nick's engagement with the community. Nick wants daily detailed reports on Kate's progress and wants to know about what Kate is discussing in group and/or individual key worker sessions. Nick also becomes increasingly worried about who receives the information from group and individual work and how it is stored. As the weeks go by Nick insists on more and more detailed reports from the community. He becomes angrier and angrier with clinical services' refusal to provide him with detailed notes of Kate's therapy sessions, since the community provides overview summaries of Kate's overall day and events of note.

The community is the right place for Kate. She is engaging with staff and it is clear that the community is able to contain her and keep her safe. Through a combination of individual and group work as well as structured and personalised support Kate is starting to build trusting relationships with clinical staff.

However, as Kate's mental health and feelings improve, Nick's mental health seems to deteriorate, and after six weeks from Kate's placement in the therapeutic community Nick is admitted into hospital as he is experiencing a *nervous breakdown*. After his discharge Nick is offered Cognitive Behavioural Therapy through the IAPT (Improving Access to Psychological Therapies) team.

Kate feels responsible and blames herself for her father's *nervous breakdown* and hospitalisation, and begins to regress. She seems depressed and hopeless and starts to refuse to eat or to engage in activities. Then a new young person arrives at the community and there is a change in Kate's attitude and demeanour.

Reflection

1. *Drawing on what has been discussed so far in this book, can you hypothesise any reasons or links between Kate's improvement and Nick's deteriorating mental health?*

2. *Given the apparently turbulent relationship between Kate and Nick, what is the significance of Kate feeling responsible and blaming herself for her father's nervous breakdown and hospitalisation?*

3. *Nick is supported by a cognitive behavioural therapist. Can you think of some of the applications of cognitive and/or behavioural skills in your own practice?*

Discussion

In the previous chapter we have discussed the importance of a systemic approach that includes the whole family and, therefore, we can appreciate Kingswood's policy that the whole family needs to be part of the solution for Kate. We will briefly explore Nick's nervous breakdown and hospitalisation in the next section. However, at this point let us examine the idea and principles behind Cognitive Behavioural Therapy (CBT) and Cognitive and Behavioural Interventions (CBI).

Cognitive therapy/cognitive approaches/interventions

Our cognitive processes include our thoughts, ideas, mental representations, beliefs and attitudes. Cognitive interventions are based on the principle that certain ways of thinking can trigger/evoke certain emotions and behaviours as well as health and well-being problems/difficulties (eg anxiety, depression, phobias, and others including physical problems such as headaches, etc). Therefore, cognitive therapy/interventions help us understand our current thought patterns. In particular, they help us identify harmful or unhelpful ideas or thoughts that may trigger or worsen a given challenge/problem/difficulty. Therefore, the aim of cognitive interventions is to change our thought and thought patterns.

Behavioural therapy/behavioural approaches/interventions

These interventions aim to identity and change any behaviours that are harmful or unhelpful. There are a variety of techniques that may be used. For example, a common unhelpful behaviour is to avoid situations that can make us anxious. For some people experiencing phobias this avoidance can become extreme and affect everyday life. In such cases, exposure therapy can be used to gradually expose the person to the feared situation, and by using different coping skills to control anxiety (eg deep breathing and other behavioural techniques).

Cognitive Behavioural Therapy (CBT)/Cognitive Behavioural Approaches/ Interventions (CBI)

Our thoughts affect the way we behave and our behaviour reflects how we think about certain things or situations. Therefore, Cognitive Behavioural Therapy/Interventions (CBT/CBI) combine a combination of cognitive and behavioural skills. CBT looks at how people can change any negative patterns of thinking or behaviour that may be causing difficulties. In turn, this can change our feelings. Indeed, the basic premise of CBT/CBI is that emotions are difficult to change directly, so CBT/CBI targets emotions by changing thoughts and behaviours that are contributing to distressing emotions.

There can be varying emphasis on behavioural and cognitive aspects of the intervention to offer the best *fit* for the situation. For example, we may use more cognitive approaches when dealing with depression, and use more behavioural skills when dealing with obsessive compulsive behaviour. The length of CBI can vary from six weeks to six months, and its focus on thoughts and behaviour make it readily suitable for social work, social care and health care interventions.

CBI focuses on what is going on in the present rather than the past, although CBI may also look at the past and how past experiences may impact on the way the person interprets the world at present.

CBT and CBI may not remove the root of the problems/difficulties, but they can help us deal with the situation in a more positive manner.

CBI recognises that thoughts, feelings, physical sensations and actions are interlinked, and that negative thoughts and feelings can trap people in vicious cycles. Therefore, CBI focuses on breaking these negative cycles by breaking down overwhelming problems into smaller parts and addressing these smaller parts to improve the way people feel.

An important limitation of CBT and CBI is that they focus on the individual's capacity to change their own thoughts and behaviour, and do not address wider systemic and social problems that have significant impact on the individual's health and well-being. Also considering the structured nature of CBT/CBI, they may be of limited suitability for people with more complex mental health needs or learning difficulties. However, because of its structured nature, CBI can be provided in different formats (eg in intervention with groups and families) and can offer practical and helpful skills that can be used by users of services in their everyday lives to cope with various stresses and difficulties/challenges.

It is important to appreciate that *positive* emotions and feelings such as happiness, warmth, admiration, love, trust, serenity, calmness, etc, are as important and useful for our survival as emotions and feelings such as sadness, coldness, disgust, doubt or distrust, anxiety, anger, and others. Each emotion has its function in our system, and based on the CBI perspective, each emotion is triggered by a range of stimuli. Therefore, it is important that we can appreciate each emotion and its significance and are able to use them in a constructive manner.

In CBT/CBI, practitioners draw on a range of strategies and approaches to support users of services which can also be helpful in social work interventions. These include:

Psychoeducation: CBT/CBI incorporate overt use of psychoeducational processes as a core feature of the intervention. Psychoeducational information and material are incorporated into the interventions in a seamless manner to de-emphasise formal *instruction*. One objective, for example, is to enable users of services to recognise their automatic thoughts/reactions and explore how CBI strategies could help modify the meaning of personally significant situations.

Collaborative empiricism: CBI is based on a high level of collaboration between the practitioner and the user of services, and this is also an important area of focus in social work and social care interventions.

Socratic questioning: CBT/CBI practitioners use Socratic questioning and the use of inductive reasoning to identify and modify *distorted* or biased cognitive styles. This empowers users of services and supports mutual collaboration.

Empathic conversation: Establishing an empathic connection with the user of services is the first, and an essential, step in developing a relationship-based intervention in CBT/CBI as well as social work and social care interventions.

Thought recording: This involves users of services self-monitoring their thought patterns, to identify automatic thoughts. This offers a supplementary approach to supporting the development of problem-solving skills as well as self-reflection, and mood regulation.

Role playing and guided imagery: These are applicable when direct questioning does not fully reveal significant fundamental cognitions. These approaches augment the person's emotions, increasing the likelihood of significant change. They can also be used to support users of services for relaxation and mood regulation.

Cognitive rehearsal: This involves users of services imagining difficult situations/experiences in the past, to practice/rehearse dealing with them successfully. The objective is to enable the person to draw on the rehearsed behaviour when faced with the difficult situation/experience in the future.

Cognitive and behavioural reattribution: CBT/CBI state that our emotional reaction to events/experiences in our lives is based on the meaning that we attribute to those events/experiences. Therefore, CBT/CBI incorporate aspects of behaviour modification with cognitive restructuring methods and target emotions through thoughts and behaviour to reattribute meaning to events/experiences that are causing unhelpful emotional states. Therefore, we need to identify the *hot* thought that accompanies the emotion (*hot* thoughts are thoughts that provoke the strongest negative reaction to an external factor). Then we need to work to change the thought or the pattern of thoughts that are unhelpful for the user of services. Some examples of unhelpful patterns of thought include:

All-or-nothing thinking: Viewing situations from one totally positive or totally negative extremes, instead of on a continuum.

Mind reading: Believing you know what others are thinking. *'I didn't get the job, so I know my partner will think I'm a loser.'*

Disqualifying/discounting the positive: *'My boss said that I did a good job yesterday, but I think he was just trying to be nice.'*

Emotional reasoning: Making a judgement or holding a belief based on personal feelings while ignoring/discounting information/evidence to the contrary.

Catastrophising: Predicting exaggerated negative outcomes: *'If I fail this test, my life is destroyed.'*

Labelling: Giving someone/something a label without finding out more about them.

Mental filter/tunnel vision: Seeing only the negative in a situation. *'Jenny failed the exam, and I think she is a loser and will never be anybody.'*

Personalisation: Thinking that negative behaviour of others has something to do with you. *'Jenny and Jack are whispering. I am sure they're talking about me.'*

Should *and* must *statements*: Having prescriptive ideas about life events and experiences.

Structure of Cognitive Behavioural Interventions (CBI)

CBT/CBI approaches are highly structured approaches and below are what takes place in such interventions as applicable to social work and social care context:

Mood check: At the beginning of each CBI (eg home visit) it is important to check how the user of services is feeling at the moment, and to consider any discrepancies (improvements or setbacks) from last intervention (eg last visit). This mood check will help identify any events/issue/problems that may have affected the user of services either positively or negatively. This enables the practitioner first to build/draw on positives and to place negative items on the agenda for discussion during the intervention.

Bridging discussion: It is important to bridge discussion from the previous session with the current session. Bridging sessions enable us to check the strength of our empathic relationship and what and how much the user of services has understood and assimilated from what was discussed in our last intervention. This also reinforces any learning from the last session. In CBT this is done using specific questionnaires; however, in social work and social care interventions this can be done verbally. Some of the points discussed during this phase can become items on the agenda for the current discussion/intervention.

Setting the agenda: Setting the agenda and prioritising items for discussion in current intervention/session are fundamental to the structure of CBI approaches. Clearly you would have your items to be included in the agenda; however, it is important to first ask users of services about their goals/priorities and then you can include your own and the agency's goals/priorities. Social work and social care interventions are more flexible than typical CBT interventions which usually take between 30 and 60 minutes; therefore, the agenda should be able to address most of the issues (ie priorities/goals raised by users of services, the practitioner and the agency).

Review homework: Homework is an important aspect of CBI. Homework enables users of services to apply what they have learnt from the intervention in their daily lives, and empowers them to take responsibility for completing well-defined tasks or behaviours that contribute to the achievement of their own goals and priorities or enhance their well-being. Similar to task-focused approaches, reviewing homework enables the practitioner to reinforce its importance and check the progress or any difficulties for its successful completion. Homework should follow the SMART principles.

Discuss agenda items and set up new homework: Discuss agenda items, starting with the first and most important. However, if you are running short of time, reassure the user of services that you will discuss any remaining items in your next meeting/visit. Set up homework for the period up to the next meeting/visit that is directly connected to what has been discussed in the session. The homework should be SMART and should be agreed collaboratively to ensure it does not overwhelm or feel imposed.

Session summary and feedback: Summarise the current session and ask for feedback. There are two types of summary: (1) a brief summary at the end of each section of the agenda to reinforce what has been discussed; (2) summary of the overall session/visit/meeting. It is more effective to try to use the specific words used by users of services in summarising their thoughts. This shows respect for the person's views and expressions, making it easier for them to identify with the summary. At the end of the meeting/session ask for feedback to check progress and shared understanding and to check if you are on the right track. Close the visit/meeting by offering encouragement to motivate users of service to continue working toward positive change.

Solution focus, task focus, crisis intervention

Given the greater flexibility in the timing and structure of social work and social care interventions than those of CBT, it is possible to apply CBT skills in social work and social care interventions with greater flexibility. For example, pacing the discussion in CBT sessions is a challenge due to the structured nature of intervention and limited time for each CBT session (usually 30–60 minutes); however, this can be managed more flexibly in social work and social care interventions as both the length and eventual number of visits/meetings with users of services may vary as need be. However, maintaining a solution-based focus can help ensure steady progress toward change and the desired goals of users of services. In fact, in setting the agenda for CBT sessions it is important to collaboratively prioritise topics/issues/*problems* to be able to adhere to the allocated time while addressing the most important/pressing topics/issues/*problems*. However, given the flexibility of social work and social care visits/sessions practitioners are able to address the different issues, with variable pace that ensures a co-productive solution-focused approach.

Projected pain – that's the way I feel about myself

CASE STUDY

Lalya turned 12 last month and has just joined the therapeutic community, so she is now the youngest resident. Lalya has long brown hair and dark eyes. She displays sexualised behaviour towards male and female members of staff and other young adults within the therapeutic community. She wears provocative clothing and acts in a manner to draw attention to herself. She wears excessive make-up, swears frequently and has scars on the outside of her arms from self-harming. At times Lalya goes up to Kate and says something to her to provoke a reaction or an answer and on one occasion Kate reacted and physically hurt Lalya, ripping an earring out of her ear. That incident marked a turning point in their relationship, and from that point it was Kate who sought out Lalya and often swore at her, hit her or ridiculed her in front of the other young people.

One evening, Kate finds Lalya alone in her room speaking with another resident (Michael). Kate initially starts to tap Lalya on her head and call her ugly and asks Michael to start filming her on her phone. Michael starts to record Kate and Lalya. Kate then picks up a razor from the bathroom and tells Lalya that if she doesn't look into the camera and tell everyone that she is a dirty ugly whore Kate would cut her with the razor. Lalya feels scared and begins to cry. She is intimidated by Kate and Michael, and looks into the camera and does what Kate tells her to do. Kate then gives her a scissor and tells her to cut off her long hair. She then asks Lalya to say '*sluts like me don't need long hair*'.

She then asks Lalya to hit herself in the face and tell everyone to leave negative comments about her because she deserves it. Kate and Michael load the video onto YouTube and show the YouTube video to other young people and this results in clinical staff finding out about the video. The next morning the matter is discussed in group therapy.

The group sit in silence for almost ten minutes before Jane, one of the older community members, addresses Kate.

Jane: *I am really upset about the video you made of Lalya. What makes you think it's ok to do that to someone else?*

Kate: *Shut up. You don't know anything about what happened.*

Jane: *I know that you bullied someone that looked up to you. You bullied someone that was a lot younger than you. Someone that looked up to you. You completely broke that trust.*

Edward: *It was a cruel thing to do, Kate. I think you were jealous of her because she was pretty.*

Jack: *What gives you the right to put it on YouTube for everyone to see? I am really angry with both of you for doing it.*

Facilitator: *Kate, a lot of people are very upset with you about what happened last night. Can you understand why they are upset with you?*

Kate: *They don't know what it's like to be me. But they are sitting there and judging me telling me what to do and how to be.*

Facilitator: *So why don't you tell us.*

Kate: *Everyone is always attacking me, blaming me ... everything is my fault, it's never someone else's fault. It's always mine ... fuck you all.*

Facilitator: *Who are you really angry with?*

Kate: *I don't know ... maybe myself.*

Facilitator: *When you told Lalya to say those things what made you think of those things and those words?*

Kate: *I don't know ...*

Facilitator: *You told her to say she was a 'dirty ugly whore'. Who were those words for?*

Kate: *[Silence] ... For me ... [Silence] ... that's the way I feel about myself.*

Reflection

1. *What is your analysis and reflection about this case so far? What is the meaning and significance of Kate's behaviour toward Lalya?*

2. *What is the meaning and significance of unresolved trauma? And how does it impact practice? What are your own practice experiences relating to unresolved trauma?*

3. *Reflecting critically on yourself and your own emotions, thoughts and behaviour, can you think of any unresolved trauma that you may have experienced?*

4.   *Reflect upon and analyse Kate's statement:* 'For me ... that's the way I feel about myself.' *What is the significance of this statement, and how does it relate to the rest of the narrative?*

Discussion

Young people's exposure to potentially traumatic events that prompt a range of reactions from survivors (Ogle et al, 2013) has increased in both frequency and intensity over the past several years, and this has been accompanied with a steady rise of multiple victimisation (Finkelhor et al, 2009).

Reflecting on the above narrative, Kate's statement: *'that's the way I feel about myself'* highlights the deep pain and difficulty that she feels inside.

Young people's complex trauma include experiencing acute or chronic trauma such as abuse or neglect, in combination with other traumatic experiences such as: rape, incest or sexual abuse, bullying, violent events, medical trauma (eg cancer, emergency surgery and other critical incidents), and others. However, although such events may lead to post-traumatic stress disorder (PTSD), many young people with experiences of complex trauma do not qualify for a trauma-related diagnosis, and instead are diagnosed with a range of other co-occurring diagnoses that may lead to ineffective or misguided treatment (Courtois and Ford, 2009; van der Kolk and Pynoos, 2009). Therefore, once again this highlights the importance of a trauma-informed psychosocial and relationship-based intervention as discussed in Chapter 5.

Kate was offered daily group therapy sessions and this is a particularly suitable treatment for children and young adults with traumatic experiences including rape and sexual abuse. Adolescence represents a critical period for human growth and development, as young people experiment with, and develop, their sense of self and identity through peer relationships and belonging (Hill, 2005; Khattab and Jones, 2007). Group therapy offers a context within which participants can meet their social bonding needs and form peer groups that can provide both a containing and corrective influence in their lives (Steward et al, 1986). This creates an atmosphere of mutual support that meets children's and young people's dependency and developmental needs *'without the threatening level of intimacy associated with individual treatment'* (Sturkie, 1994, p 814). Such therapy sessions create a supportive and unique peer containment group that enhances feelings of belonging, safety and protection which are violated by/after rape and/or sexual abuse. Furthermore, the group mitigates the feelings of social isolation, stigma, shame, guilt, rejection and differentness in these young people through their shared narratives and experiences of pain and abuse (Frawley-O'Dea, 1997; Hall-Marley and Damon, 1993).

Reflecting on the above narrative it is important to note the relationship between Nick and Kate. Thinking about the situation from a systemic family perspective, every behaviour in the family's repertoire has a function and, therefore, Kate's *bad* behaviour had a distinct function within the family system. Indeed, the relationship between Nick and Kate is a good example of projective identification. Drawing on our discussion about object relations in Chapter 2, we observe Nick's splitting of good and bad objects within the family system where Brenda is the repository of all the good (the *good* object/child) while Kate is repository of all the bad (the *bad* object/child). This splitting may have served an important psychological function for Nick, as Kate served as the object of Nick's projective identification, and the container in which Nick could evacuate his unwanted emotions and unwanted part of self (the split *bad* self). In fact, as Kate's emotions and mental health improved, Nick's mental health deteriorated leading to his hospitalisation due to a *nervous breakdown*. Subsequently Kate felt responsible for her father's hospitalisation and began to regress. This may be a reflection of the psychological co-dependence between the father and daughter, where each fulfilled a role/function within the family system. Kate's continued improvement in the therapeutic community may have disrupted the cycle of projective identification between Nick and Kate, resulting in Nick's inability to evacuate his negative emotions, thus leading to his deteriorating mental health. Nick's increasing anger toward the clinical staff and increasing demand for more and more detailed information about Kate's progress may be understood as transference and a reflection of his displaced anger. However, the insufficiency of these defence mechanisms may have resulted in his eventual hospitalisation. Kate and Nick's behaviours can be understood as a reflection of the hurt/pain and the unresolved trauma that they carry inside. For example, Kate's externalising behaviours represent her attempts at carving a small space in which to be and to grow.

To understand Kate's behaviour toward Lalya, it is important to first understand her behaviour toward herself. Although Kate's self-harm evokes horror and aversion in others, it also evokes concern in her parents. Furthermore, from an object relations perspective, her self-harm could serve a double purpose: on the one hand it allows her to enact the fantasy of revenge against the hated object (the split *bad* self) and experience satisfaction; on the other hand it may solicit some compassion in a *hard and lonely world of isolation and blame*, while watching others' terrified and helpless expressions helps mitigate her feelings of powerlessness. In this sense, her behaviour toward Lalya may be understood as the transference and projection of her own pain and hatred for the *bad* self onto an external object (Lalya) who is a younger version of her own unresolved trauma and her *hated* self.

There are usually two possible responses to unresolved trauma, namely hyperarousal or dissociation. Traumatised individuals 'see *and feel only their trauma, or they see and feel nothing at all; they're fixated on their traumas or they are somehow psychically absent'* (Sykes Wylie, 2004, p 34).

Unresolved trauma can influence individuals and their families in a number of ways. For example, unresolved trauma can influence the attachment between caregiver and the child. When distressed, the child's attachment system is activated and when this is met with consistent and *good enough care* the child is soothed/comforted. However, it seems that for some parents with unresolved trauma the activation of the child's attachment system serves as a trigger/reminder of their own unresolved attachment needs and childhood emotions of fear, anger, distress and abandonment. 'Overwhelmed by his own attachment needs, the parent then fails to provide care and abdicates his position as protector precisely at the moment of the child's greatest need' (West and George, 1999, p 143).

People with unresolved trauma may resort to a number of defence mechanisms that could raise safeguarding issues. These include: substance misuse, dissociation, narrative re-enactment of the trauma and identification with the aggressor.

In Chapter 2, we saw an example of dissociation leading to neglect. It is possible that a parent with unresolved trauma identifies with the abuser/aggressor in their childhood, and this can increase the likelihood of the person treating their own children in the same manner that they were treated in their childhood. Furthermore, unresolved trauma may result in narrative re-enactment where the person unconsciously and repeatedly recreates and re-enacts the traumatic situation(s) and event(s) (Neborsky, 2003).

Some of the features of unresolved trauma include: intrusive thoughts and flashbacks, nightmares, repetitive patterns of behaviour, talking about a dead person as if they were alive and fixation with an event/experience. It is important to carefully check these aspects when trying to identify/assess unresolved trauma. It is especially important to assess the person's ability to provide a coherent life narrative, including an account of any traumatic events in a clear and consistent manner. Incoherence or inconsistency may be indicative of dissociation. Indeed, Ogden et al (2006) suggest:

> PTSD patients experience their traumatic memories as timeless, intrusive, sensory fragments that often cannot be expressed as a narrative, whereas people who have suffered a trauma but do not suffer from PTSD usually recall traumatic memories as an integrated whole that can easily be expressed as a narrative.
>
> (p 156)

Therefore, narrative interventions and the practitioner's ability to engage users of services in revisiting, exploring and re-authoring their narratives is an indispensable element of effective psychosocial and relationship-based interventions.

References

Bijleveld, C and Hendricks, J (2003) Juvenile Sex Offenders: Differences Between Group and Solo Offenders. *Psychology, Crime and Law*, 9: 237–45.

Bijleveld, C C J H, Weerman, F M, Looije, D and Hendriks, J (2007) Group Sex Offending by Juveniles: Coercive Sex as Group Activity. *European Journal of Criminology*, 4: 5–31.

Blomquist, B T (2001) *Insight into Adoption*. Springfield, IL: Charles C Thomas Publisher.

Courtois, C A and Ford, J F (2009) *Treating Complex Traumatic Stress Disorders: An Evidence-based Guide*. New York: Guilford Press.

Curry, G D, Decker, S H and Egley, A, Jr (2002) Gang Involvement and Delinquency in a Middle School Population. *Justice Quarterly*, 19: 275–92.

De La Rue, L and Espelage, D (2014) Family and Abuse Characteristics of Gang-Involved, Pressured-to-Join, and Non–Gang-Involved Girls. *Psychology of Violence*, 4(3): 253–65.

Esbensen, F, Winfree, L T, Jr, He, N and Taylor, T J (2001) Youth Gangs and Definitional Issues: When Is a Gang a Gang, and Why Does it Matter? *Crime & Delinquency*, 47: 105–30.

Estrich, S (1987) *Real Rape: How the Legal System Victimises Women Who Say No*. Boston, MA: Harvard University Press.

Finkelhor, D, Turner, H A, Ormrod, R and Hamby, S L (2009) Violence, Abuse, and Crime Exposure in a National Sample of Children and Youth. *Pediatrics*, 124: 1411–23.

Frawley-O'Dea, M G (1997) Transference Paradigms at Play in Psychoanalytically Oriented Group Therapy with Female Adult Survivors of Childhood Sexual Abuse. *International Journal of Group Psychotherapy*, 47(4): 427–41.

Hall-Marley, S and Damon, L (1993) Impact of Structured Group Therapy on Young Victims of Sexual Abuse. *Journal of Child and Adolescent Group Therapy*, 3(1): 41–9.

Hawton, K and Harriss, L (2007) Deliberate Self-Harm in Young People: Characteristics and Subsequent Mortality in a 20-Year Cohort of Patients Presenting to Hospital. *Journal of Clinical Psychiatry*, 68: 1574–83.

Hawton, K, Hall, S, Simkin, S, Bale, L, Bond, A, Codd, S and Stewart, A (2003) Deliberate Self-harm in Adolescents: A Study of Characteristics and Trends in Oxford, 1990–2000. *Journal of Child Psychology and Psychiatry*, 44: 1191–8.

Hill, A (2005) Patterns of Non-offending Parental Involvement in Therapy with Sexually Abused Children: A Review of the Literature. *Journal of Social Work*, 5(3): 339–58.

Kelly, L, Lovett, J and Regan, L (2005) *A Gap or a Chasm? Attrition in Reported Rape Cases. Home Office Research Study 293*. London: Home Office.

Khattab, N and Jones, C P (2007) Growing Up Girl: Preparing for Change Through Group Work. *The Journal for Specialists in Group Work*, 32(1): 41–50.

Le, T N and Stockdale, G (2008) Acculturative Dissonance: Ethnic Identity, and Youth Violence. *Cultural Diversity and Ethnic Minority Psychology*, 14: 1–9.

Maier, S L (2008) 'I Have Heard Horrible Stories ...' Rape Victim Advocates' Perceptions of the Revictimization of Rape Victims by the Police and Medical System. *Violence Against Women*, 14: 786–808.

Miller, W R (1983) Motivational Interviewing with Problem Drinkers. *Behavioral Psychotherapy*, 11(2): 147–72.

Miller, W R (1985) Motivation for Treatment: A Review with Special Emphasis on Alcoholism. *Psychological Bulletin*, 98(1): 84–107.

Miller, W R and Rollnick, S (2002) *Motivational Interviewing: Preparing People for Change* (2nd edn). New York: Guilford Press.

Neborsky, R (2003) A Clinical Model for the Comprehensive Treatment of Trauma Using an Affect Experiencing–Attachment Theory Approach, in Solomon, M and Siegel, D (eds) *Healing Trauma, Attachment, Mind, Body, and Brain*. New York: W W Norton and Co.

Ogden, P, Minton, K and Pain, C (2006) *Trauma and the Body: A Sensorimotor Approach to Psychotherapy*. New York and London: W W Norton.

Ogle, C M, Rubin, D C, Berntsen, D and Siegler, I C (2013) The Frequency and Impact of Exposure to Potentially Traumatic Events Over the Life Course. *Clinical Psychological Science*, 1: 426–34.

Porter, L E and Alison, L J (2006) Examining Group Rape: A Descriptive Analysis of Offender and Victim Behaviour. *European Journal of Criminology*, 3: 357–81.

Prochaska, J O and DiClemente, C C (1982) Trans-theoretical Therapy: Toward a More Integrative Model of Change. *Psychotherapy: Theory, Research, and Practice*, 19(3): 276–88.

Shaeffer, P, Leventhal, J M and Asnes, A G (2011) Children's Disclosures of Sexual Abuse: Learning from Direct Inquiry. *Child Abuse & Neglect*, 35: 343–52.

Silverman, M M, Berman, A L, Sanddal, N D, O'Carroll, P W and Joiner, T E (2007) Rebuilding the Tower of Babel: A Revised Nomenclature for the Study of Suicide and Suicidal Behaviors Part 2: Suicide-Related Ideations, Communications, and Behaviors. *Suicide and Life-Threatening Behavior*, 37: 264–77.

Steward, M S, Farquhar, L C, Dicharry, D C, Glick, D R and Martin, P W (1986) Group Therapy: A Treatment of Choice for Young Victims of Child Abuse. *The International Journal of Group Psychotherapy*, 36(2): 261–77.

Sturkie, K (1994) Group Treatment of Sexually Abused Children: Clinical Wisdom and Empirical Findings. *Child and Adolescent Psychiatric Clinics of North America*, 3(4): 813–29.

Sykes Wylie, M (2004) The Limits of Talk: Bessell van der Kolk Wants to Transform the Treatment of Trauma. *Psychotherapy Networker*, 28(1): 30–41.

van der Kolk, B and Pynoos, R S (2009) Proposal to Include a Developmental Trauma Disorder Diagnosis for Children and Adolescents in DSM-V. [online] Available at: www.traumacenter.org/announcements/DTD_papers_Oct_09.pdf (accessed 15 August 2014).

West, M and George, C (1999) Abuse and Violence in Intimate Adult Relationships: New Perspectives from Attachment Theory. *Attachment and Human Development*, 1(2): 137–56.

9 Concluding reflections

Foucault suggests that 'attending to oneself is a privilege; ... as against those who must attend to others to serve them or attend to a trade in order to live' (1994, p 95). However, critical reflection on self and one's own practice is foundational to psychosocial and relationship-based practice.

Indeed, good relationship-based practice requires effective use of self, and effective use of self hinges upon the practitioner's knowledge of self and a good understanding of underlying assumptions we hold about relationships, and the cultural, psychological, emotional and political complexities that shape our identities. As we engage with users of services, we project the condition of our soul onto them, and our way of being together, and onto every aspect of that relationship and practice/intervention. Therefore, the context of practice offers a mirror to the soul of the practitioner's self and professional identity, and if we are willing, and have the containment, to look into that mirror without seeking distraction or running away, then we have a chance to see our personal and professional self and to gain precious knowledge that is foundational for our growth and for the enhancement of our professional identity and practice. This highlights the importance of reflection and reflective practice.

Therefore, in line with the psychosocial and relationship-based tradition and as a reflective practitioner, I wish to take this opportunity to reflect upon some key messages in this book and the experience of completing it, and to share some personal perspectives.

In *The Fear of Freedom* Fromm (1942) describes the idea of automation conformity as the process of becoming the same as others or what we imagine others to be. This means developing and adapting one's self and values based on dominant cultural patterns, and epitomises the notion of a '*cog in a large machine, an automaton ...*' (p 232). This negates individual autonomy and prevents critical thinking and self-directed learning while perpetuating dominant discourses and power imbalances within society. Most importantly, such conformity negates the possibility of moral action and is clearly contrary to emancipatory principles that are the essence and the very heart of social work and its role and mission. Indeed, Fromm posits: '*to the degree to which a person conforms he cannot hear the voice of his conscience, much less act upon it. Conscience exists only when man experiences him-self as a man, not as a thing, as a commodity'* (Fromm, 1955, p 168).

Social work has been subject to increasing demands and continued reforms and restructuring. However, these transformations of the role of social work have led to *deprofessionalisation* and *deskilling* (Dominelli, 1996; Ferguson, 2011; Howe, 2009) of the profession and its practitioners based on a culture of *more for less* focused on cost reduction and economic return. Parton states:

> *Such a culture is not interested in 'meaning' but in 'operationality' and the speed of operation is such that there is hardly any distance between knowledge and action to the point that action becomes more of a 'reflex'. Time and space have become so condensed that the opportunity for using 'theories for practice' seems minimal.*
>
> (2008, p 264)

Historically and from an economic perspective, production and exchange have been driven by scarcity (ie people produce what is lacking or in demand), and exchange that is led by monetary transactions but not confined to them (eg exchange between health or care or well-being vis-à-vis financial or market initiatives focused on cost and monetary return on investment) takes place between parties whose only approach to locating one another is via price. This is dehumanising as it devalues/reduces people's health, care and relationships to nothing but monetary figures instead of well-being. This leads to a culture of deficit that pathologises people, relying on short-term quick-fix solutions to *fix* people and their families. Therefore, it is urgently important to rebalance the purely market-oriented cycle of *production* and *productivity* working in confrontation with nature, with a more committed attitude to research with humane ethics and practice with compassion that can offer a new cycle of hope that prioritises people's needs and human values. Psychosocial and relationship-based practice offers such a possibility and allows social work and social care to reclaim the roots and values engrained in their very names: to do the *social work* that offers *social* and co-productive *care*.

Furthermore, the increasing emphasis on evidence-based approaches based on bio-medicalised models of research and intervention poses an important challenge for the social model of social work practice and research. Therefore, one of the objectives of this book has been to demonstrate that an evidence-informed psychosocial and relationship-based model for practice and research in social work and social care can offer a robust response to the objectifying and reductive models of intervention and *packaged care*.

As mentioned in the introduction, social work has always maintained an applied interdisciplinary approach in its education and practice. Therefore, the recent and increasing demands and recognition for interdisciplinary approaches to research and practice offer unprecedented opportunities for greater appreciation of social work practice and research in general and psychosocial and relationship-based practice and research in particular.

There is an urgent need for a new language of care, and psychosocial and relationship-based practice offers this new language that spells a message of hope and reconnects with people, through empowering relationships and compassionate practice that meet their needs and allow them to achieve their human potential.

Completing this book has been as rewarding as it has been challenging. Writing about a diverse range of theories and approaches with an evidence-informed and critical perspective has involved extensive searching and investigation of relevant research, literature, principles and, most importantly, in-depth reflection upon and searching for meaning and significance.

The telling and retelling and reflecting upon and honouring the hopes, aspirations, pains, distress, despair, challenges and vulnerabilities of human experience and the lived narratives of practitioners and users of services has been an enormous privilege and a profoundly enriching experience both on a personal and professional level.

Gendlin suggests:

> *... actually you affect me and with me you are not just yourself as usual either. You and I happening together makes us immediately different than we usually are ... How you are when you affect me is already affected by me, and not by me as I usually am, but by me as I occur with you.*
>
> (Gendlin, 1998, p 30)

Effective psychosocial and relationship-based approaches generate a relational dialogue that is empowering for users of services '*as a subject who is in dialogical encounter with me and through which encounter inter-relational meaning possibilities unfold themselves to both of us*' (Spinelli, 2005, p 124). Such relationships offer a strong holding foundation that can enable positive change through '*human and humane openness to "being in relation" and all the uncertainty, unpredictability and anxiety that implies*' (Spinelli, 2007, p 14).

References

Dominelli, L (1996) Deprofessionalizing Social Work: Anti-Oppressive Practice, Competencies and Postmodernism. *Journal of Social Work Practice*, 26(2): 153–75.

Ferguson, H (2011) *Child Protection Practice*. UK: Palgrave Macmillan.

Foucault, M (1994) *Ethics, Subjectivity and Truth* (Rabinow, P (ed), Hurley, R et al (Trans)). New York: New Press.

Fromm, E (1942) *The Fear of Freedom*. London: Routledge (work originally published by Routledge & Kegan Paul, 1942).

Fromm, E (1955[2002]) *The Sane Society*. Greenwich, CT: Fawcett Publications.

Gendlin, E T (1998) *A Process Model*. Unpublished manuscript. [online] Available at: www.focusing. org./process.html (accessed 15 August 2014).

Howe, D (2009) *A Brief Introduction to Social Work Theory*. UK: Palgrave Macmillan.

Parton, N (2008) Changes in the Form of Knowledge in Social Work: From the 'Social' to the 'Informational'? *British Journal of Social Work*, 38: 253–69.

Spinelli, E (2005) *The Interpreted World: An Introduction to Phenomenological Psychology*. London: Sage.

Spinelli, E (2007) The Therapeutic Relationship: A View from Existential Psychotherapy. *Therapy Today*, 18(1): 11–14.

Index